BATTLING WITH THE TRUTH

sta

BATTLING WITH THE TRUTH

THE CONTRAST IN THE MEDIA REPORTING OF WORLD WAR II

IAN GARDEN

The
History
Press

This book is dedicated to my ever-supportive parents.

First published 2016

The History Press
The Mill, Brimscombe Port
Stroud, Gloucestershire, GL5 2QG
www.thehistorypress.co.uk

British Library Cataloguing in Publication Data.
A catalogue record for this book is available from the British Library.

ISBN 978 0 7509 5632 1

Typesetting and origination by The History Press
Printed and bound by CPI Group (UK) Ltd

CONTENTS

ACKNOWLEDGEMENTS

This book could not have been completed without the assistance of a large number of individuals and institutions.

In terms of general research, I would like to thank Professor Simon Eliot and Dr Henry Irving for additional information arising from their own research into the history of the Ministry of Information (MOI); Anne Jensen from the Archive and Record Office of *The Times*; the staff at the National Library of Scotland in Edinburgh, the British Library in London and the National Archives at Kew.

There are five other individuals who deserve special mention:

First, Professor Ruth Schröck, who has spent so much of her time over the last few years sharing with me her fascinating experiences of life in Germany during the Second World War. Her insight and knowledge have been irreplaceable sources of inspiration.

Second, Professor William Niven and his colleague, Nick Hayes, of Nottingham Trent University for all their assistance in helping me track down specific research materials. I wish Bill well with his own current project – a book about Hitler's films – which is another subject close to my heart.

Third, Luc Braeuer and his colleagues for providing me with a number of excellent images, which I have been able to include in this book. Luc is a military historian and prolific author who runs a number of excellent war museums in France at Saint-Nazaire (Le Grand Blockhaus), La Rochelle and Quinéville.

Fourth, Steve Sullivan for his willingness to provide me with images featured on his excellent website, Blighty-at-War.net.

Finally, Helen Gillard for all her expert advice and feedback on the content and layout of this book.

There are, of course, many other friends and acquaintances whom I would like to thank for their numerous suggestions and invaluable support during the completion of this project. These include Hanna Awan, Janet Begrie, Campbell Black, Lothar Braun, Clare Brown, Yvonne Burgess, Jo de Vries, Jim Dunnigan, Ed Furgol, Malcolm Hay, Douglas Laws, Michael Leventhal, Ian Lewis, Angus Logan, Sheena McDonald, Bruce McHale, George Milne, Eva Pearson, Hilary

Swanson, Brian Taylor, Mark Taylor and, of course, Chrissy McMorris and her colleagues at The History Press.

It is always difficult with a book of this type, researched and written over a long period of time, to succeed in acknowledging the assistance given by so many different people at various stages in its preparation, so I apologise in advance for anyone whose name has been omitted inadvertently.

Where necessary, every effort has been made to contact the copyright holders of all materials used but, notwithstanding, I express my apologies for any omissions.

INTRODUCTION

In war, truth is the first casualty.

(attributed to Aeschylus, Greek tragic dramatist – 525 BC to 456 BC)

On the afternoon of 16 October 1939, about twelve German bombers arrived over the River Forth on the east coast of Scotland, dropping bombs over the famous rail bridge and almost hitting a train that was crossing the bridge at the time. Fighters were scrambled from local aerodromes, and a couple of bombers were shot down. It was the first raid by the Luftwaffe over Britain, and it was reported as having been a complete failure. Indeed, such was the euphoria surrounding this first downing of German planes by Spitfires that a thrilling documentary was released a few months later. This film recreated the incident with dramatic dogfight footage and gave the distinct impression that the rail bridge had been the main target – hence why the incident came to be known as the Forth Bridge Raid.

The British media coverage of the raid was actually quite wide of the mark. The Forth Bridge had never been the bombers' intended target. The Germans had actually been hoping to attack HMS *Hood* but, as it was not to be found on the river, they had turned their attention to three other naval ships sailing near the Forth Bridge. Press reports not only suggested that damage to these ships was minimal and that naval casualties were light but also indicated that as many as six German planes were shot down that day. This was not entirely accurate.

Damage to one of the ships was actually quite significant and no fewer than sixteen sailors were killed and a further forty-four wounded. Little of this was made public at the time and, in fact, only two German planes were shot down with a third crashing in Holland on its way home.

So, while certainly a significant result for the British, the whole incident was perhaps not quite the complete triumph implied nor as one-sided as was suggested, especially when it is discovered that the only reason the raiders were able to reach their target at all was because of the failure of the nearby radar system at Cockburnspath.

However, if the British gave a somewhat misleading impression of the raid, then the Germans were equally dishonest. They claimed that two British cruisers had been *badly* damaged and that they had shot down two fighters, with two of their own aircraft reported 'missing'. Given that the Germans did not shoot down any British planes whatsoever and that they actually lost three rather than two planes of their own, it just goes to show how the Germans tried to make just as much propaganda out of this confrontation as the British, In fact, the British and the Nazis were both prepared to play rather fast and loose with the truth and, by so doing, both sides were able to claim success.

Now, the false reporting of a single incident may not seem of much significance. However, the misleading coverage of this event was symptomatic of the sort of practices that persisted throughout the war, not just with regard to the reporting of individual incidents but also of whole campaigns.

Take, for example, the Battle of Britain. I have a good German friend who had been resident in Berlin for much of the war and who only moved to Britain in the 1960s. I was quite shocked when she explained to me that she had never even heard of events such as the Battle of Britain until she came to live in this country. She had found it necessary to ask people what was meant by this term since, for her, the whole war was against Britain. It seemed to me totally inconceivable that any ordinary German citizen who lived through the war could have been unaware that there had been a specific 'life or death' air battle between Britain and Germany in 1940, let alone that it was a battle Germany had lost and which, arguably, changed the whole course of the war. And yet, such ignorance of this and similar events was undoubtedly the case.

In effect, history has shown us time and again that the root cause of conflicts between nations often lies in the failure of either side to understand the underlying motivations and perceptions of the other. Add to this the deliberate manipulation, misrepresentation or concealment of the facts by the respective governments of each nation, both prior and subsequent to conflict, and the seeds of a long and bitter dispute can be sown.

A recent example of such a scenario is to be found in the conflict in Eastern Europe with the annexation of the Crimea by Russia and the continuing unrest in eastern Ukraine. For many Ukrainians and many countries in the West, the issue was portrayed as the illegal and belligerent actions of Russia in occupying and seizing the territory of a neighbouring sovereign power. For most Russians, the annexation of the Crimea was seen as the rightful repossession of territory that had been seized wrongfully and reassigned to Ukraine in the 1950s, albeit that the majority of its people are Russian-speaking and feel a greater affiliation towards the East. Many of the people who live in these territories actually share that view, and if there is a perception – true or otherwise – that they are a disadvantaged or even persecuted minority in a foreign land, then it is easy to understand how this could provoke such anger and resentment as to lead to war.

We find stark similarities in the disputes leading up to the outbreak of the Second World War. The loss of much of their territory in Europe, the seizure of their colonies and the dismantling of their armed forces left many Germans feeling persecuted, especially when many held to the mistaken belief that their army had not actually been defeated in the Great War and that surrender had been forced upon them through betrayal by capitalists, communists and Jews. In Central Europe, there is no doubt that there were instances where communities of ethnic Germans, who had been relocated to new countries such as Czechoslovakia or to expanded countries such as Poland, were treated poorly by their new governments and, when the time was right, Hitler was able to exploit such grievances for his own political purposes.

Perception is important, and sometimes it is only with hindsight and when a conflict is sufficiently remote from future generations of survivors that it is possible to analyse objectively the motivations behind each side's actions at a particular moment in the past. What we discover is that the truth is often blurred and never quite as clear-cut as politicians might want us to believe. For the peoples of the Allied countries to contend that they were totally in the right, that only their cause was just and that the Second World War was all Germany's fault, was to fail to recognise that many Germans were just as convinced that they were in the right and that it was they who were threatened by a belligerent Britain and France, who had, after all, declared war on Germany. They would claim Germany was simply recovering territory that had been stolen from it after the Great War and defending the rights of ethnic Germans who, through no fault of their own, now found themselves citizens of a foreign country.

If each side had a different perspective on who was to blame for the very outbreak of war, then it is important to appreciate that once the war had begun, the deliberate manipulation of truth about subsequent events and battles in the war served only to widen the gap in understanding between the two sides – both of whom exploited events for propaganda purposes.

Such was the importance of this propaganda battle that both sides were determined to control exactly what their peoples saw, heard or read about the war and the enemy.

This propaganda war was already partly examined in my earlier book, *The Third Reich's Celluloid War*, which sought to explore the nature of the feature films, documentaries and television programmes the Nazis produced during their period in power and how this compared with what the Allies were screening.

One aspect that book was unable to consider was the role of newsreels and newspapers in influencing public opinion during the Second World War. This book seeks to fill that gap by selecting a number of key events and battles from the war and examining how accurately these were portrayed by both sides. The intention is to try to identify which side was more truthful in its presentation of the war, both to its own people and to the world at large.

The findings are often surprising and quite alarming. There are many instances where both sides massaged the truth for their own audiences – even about the very same event – and frequent examples of the authorities not only concealing vital facts but failing to report bad news altogether. It all helps to explain why, for much of the war, ordinary citizens on both sides were absolutely convinced that their country was fighting a just war and that their side would eventually be victorious.

THE CONTROL OF MEDIA CENSORSHIP DURING THE SECOND WORLD WAR

INTRODUCTION

Hitler had always been jealous of the effectiveness of the British propaganda machine during the First World War and its portrayal of the Germans as a ruthless and dangerous adversary. In his book, *Mein Kampf*, he even went as far as to criticise the German hierarchy and press for having been so conciliatory as to suggest that the German nation shared responsibility for the outbreak of the Great War. Hitler would have laid the blame fairly and squarely on the British and French, and he was determined that once the Nazis assumed power in 1933, there would be no question of the German press reporting anything other than what was permitted by the newly founded Ministry for Public Enlightenment and Propaganda, led by Joseph Goebbels.

As for the British, having grown rather complacent because of the very success of their own propaganda initiatives during the First World War, the first thing they did after that war was to shut down their Ministry of Information. This was in the naïve belief that it was no longer required and, even if such a requirement did arise again in the future, that it would be able to be re-established without any great difficulty.

This introductory chapter explains how, despite their quite different methods of media censorship, both the Germans and the British were able to exercise relatively tight control over the output of their respective media throughout the war – ensuring that the maintenance of the morale of the general public and their armed forces was paramount at all times, even if this often meant the concealment or misreporting of the truth about the conduct of the Second World War.

Hitler was always jealous of Britain's and Ireland's more effective use of propaganda during the Great War – as can be seen in the nature of this Irish recruitment poster.
Library of Congress (LOC) 2003668413

THE BRITISH MINISTRY OF INFORMATION

Structure

Despite the fact that General Ludendorff and Hitler had often complained that Germany's defeat in the Great War was as a result of Britain's superior use of propaganda, Britain actually had no official propaganda agencies in place in 1914. Instead, a hotchpotch of surprisingly successful propaganda organisations emerged which, rather ironically, were established in direct response to Germany's use of propaganda. It was only in March 1918 that Lord Beaverbrook was handed responsibility for establishing a specific Ministry of Information (MOI) which would co-ordinate all Britain's wartime propaganda activities. It was divided into three sections to provide complete control over domestic, military and foreign propaganda. Somewhat appropriately, it would seem, the foreign department was led by John Buchan, the prolific author whose most famous spy thriller, *The Thirty-Nine Steps*, had been published only three years previously.

Typically, however, as soon as peace was declared, the MOI was all but dissolved, and much of its former propaganda work reverted to the control of the Foreign Office.

It was not until 1935 that a government committee was formed for the purpose of preparing guidelines for the establishment of a new MOI in the event of the outbreak of another war. While it was agreed that its primary responsibility would be to issue official news and public announcements, it was also charged with generating propaganda that would not only sustain civilian morale within Britain but would also influence opinion overseas.

While the individual services' departments were allowed to retain their own press officers, the MOI was certainly intended to be regarded as the primary centre for the distribution of all information relating to the war. Its personnel were to be accommodated in the University of London's Senate House on Malet Street. The original plan was to allocate responsibility across five divisions but, by the spring of 1939, this number had increased to sixteen.

Prior to the commencement of war, the British Government had resolved that the press in the United Kingdom would not be required to submit material for censorship approval prior to publication but rather that the press would submit to a policy of voluntary censorship. Indeed, the press would be subject to the same restrictions as all other citizens and organisations in Britain in that its activities would be controlled by Defence Regulations.[1]

---

1 *The French adopted a different policy whereby each newspaper was required to submit its actual printing plates for review. The authorities would simply remove unacceptable comments from these plates, so that the final printed newspaper would be full of deletions. Such obvious and visual censorship was not good for public morale.*

The Ministry of Information was housed in the University of London's Senate House throughout the Second World War. *Wikimedia Commons/An Siarach*

The specific Defence Regulations of most relevance to the media were Regulation Nos. 3 and 39b.

Regulation No. 3 made it an offence for anyone to: obtain, record, communicate or publish [...] any military or other information [...] which would or might be directly or indirectly useful to the enemy.

Regulation No. 39b made it an offence for anyone to: endeavour, whether orally or otherwise, to influence public opinion [...] in a manner likely to be prejudicial to the defence of the realm or the efficient prosecution of the war.

There is no doubt that, at the commencement of war, there were several government and services' department officials who would have been quite happy if the reporting of everything to do with the war could have been banned. However, it was quickly recognised that this would have been a propaganda coup for the Germans and likely to undermine civilian morale. The press had to be allowed to keep the general public informed about the progress of the war and, to assist the press in understanding how this task could be legally fulfilled, a booklet called *Defence Notices and Press Instructions* was circulated to all newspaper editors and censors at the outbreak of war. It contained an extensive list of banned subjects about which it was decreed information should not be published without prior guidance from the appropriate government censorship department.

This booklet was of great benefit to news editors, who were only too willing to submit possibly contentious articles for censorship control since, if approved, they would be stamped as 'Passed for Publication' and, armed with such official authorisation, editors knew that they should be safe from prosecution for breaching any Defence Regulations.

It was not, however, of much help to censors, who were having to make instant decisions as to what information might or might not be of interest to the enemy. Hence, lists of additional banned subjects would be issued on almost a daily basis, in response to the latest developments, to give censors and editors further guidance as to what might or might not be acceptable.

Most of the Defence Notices were quite understandable, such as not reporting the success of, or any mishap to, or any movement of his Majesty's forces, aircraft or ships of war. Other Notices were less clear as to when and how they might apply, such as one under the heading 'Advertisements and Appeals', which decreed: 'special precautions should be taken to prevent the publication of letters or advertisements inviting officers and men to communicate with strangers.'

A couple of noteworthy points arise from the Press Instructions that prefaced the actual Defence Notices.

First, as has been mentioned above, the press was being asked to adhere to a process of self-censorship. However, there was obviously some concern that this voluntary arrangement might not succeed, as could be seen in the thinly disguised threat: 'As in 1914–1918, the censorship of the press, other than of press telegrams, will, for the present, be on a voluntary basis. Power is, however, taken [...] for the imposing by Order, of compulsory censorship either generally or in relation to particular matters.'

Second, it was made quite clear that the censors would only have the right to remove inappropriate material: 'after the deletion of words or sentences which may in themselves be objectionable, additions to or further exclusions from the text are not made by the Ministry except to preserve the sense.'

In other words, there was a clear undertaking from the MOI that its censors would not be altering copy or massaging loss statistics for propaganda purposes. Of course, this still did not guarantee that the initial information, fed to the press from the individual services' departments via the MOI, was accurate.

Likewise, the MOI seemed to find it necessary to protect its own position by declaring that: 'Permission to publish constitutes no guarantee of the accuracy of the news passed. Each item of news is judged entirely from the point of view of its effect on the conduct of the war, irrespective of its truth or falsity.'

That is to say, censors may well have known that an item to be published was untrue or gave a false impression but as long as it did not fall foul of the Defence Regulations, it could still be published.

Day-to-day Operation

In practice, every London newspaper and every provincial newspaper with an office in London had one or more of its representatives based at the MOI in London. Their role was threefold. First, they had to inform their offices of official communiqués issued by Ministry officials. The newsroom was housed on the ground floor of the Senate Building and a large bell would be sounded to signal the release of each new press release.[2] Second, they had to liaise with the censors regarding any copy that their editors had submitted for approval. Two drafts of proposed material would be sent to the censors in the basement via a system of pneumatic tubes. One copy would be returned with any changes marked in blue and bearing an official MOI stamp. The journalists would then phone or cable the amended copy to their head offices. Third, they had to interact with those representatives of other key Government departments who were in the best position to provide the press with additional information on any subject.

All the large news agencies such as the Press Association and Reuters also employed staff at the Ministry of Information. When it came to censorship, all the news agencies with their headquarters in Britain had secured an agreement with the Government whereby their incoming messages were not censored before delivery. This was agreed only in return for a guarantee from these agencies that they would submit for censorship all such incoming news from overseas that had to do with the war before it was circulated to individual newspapers for publication. Newspapers that received information from overseas directly were also spared pre-censorship, but they were left to make their own decisions as to whether such information needed to be submitted for censorship approval prior to publication.

Correspondents of overseas press were required to obtain prior censorship approval for all material going overseas, whether it was being communicated by mail, cable, wireless or telephone. This aroused a certain resentment among foreign correspondents, who were aware that the British newspapers had no such constraints and could export their newspapers overseas without prior censorship approval.

Operational Efficiency

Regrettably, in the early days of its creation, a large degree of tension not only existed between the MOI and the services' departments but often also within the separate divisions of the MOI itself, since there was no clear definition as to where one division's area of responsibility ended and another began.

---

2   *The BBC would generally receive its news content from this same source, although the press was always suspicious that the corporation was given prior warning and had access to additional information.*

The Newsroom in Beveridge Hall at the Ministry of Information. *MOI Digital/Copyright University of London*

Indeed, even after war was declared, there was still a considerable amount of uncertainty as to how the news should be controlled, not least because many of the new officials assigned to work at the MOI were ex-naval men who had little understanding of how media organisations worked.

At the outbreak of war, many censors even felt it was their duty to stop the flow of news about the war altogether. In his book, *Blue Pencil Admiral*, the Chief Press Censor, Rear Admiral George Thomson, was only too ready to admit the confusion that arose when the British Expeditionary Force (BEF) first landed in France, in September 1939. There had been initial landings as early as 4 September, and it was agreed that these should not be reported. However, following the main landing on 10 September, this news blackout seemed unnecessary, since the Germans were obviously already aware of this development, and by 12 September a Paris radio station had already broadcast the news to the wider world. Consequently, the censors agreed at 9 p.m. that evening that the press could report the simple fact that units of the BEF had arrived in France. However, the British general staff soon became alarmed that the press was creating human interest articles out of the news and that there was a real danger that details about the numbers of men involved and equipment they were taking with them would be of real benefit to the enemy.

Consequently, the initial decision to allow publication was withdrawn two and a half hours later. Arrangements were made for any further publication of newspapers that evening to cease and for newspapers already in transit to be seized by the police at railway stations. Chaos ensued and, as it became evident that it would be impossible to prevent all the information being released, the prohibition was lifted once again.

In fact, this issue, together with repeated conflicts between the MOI censors and the individual services' ministries, other public relations disasters and growing complaints about the large number of staff employed by the MOI, led to the transfer of the Ministry's responsibility for censorship and dealings with the media to a separate Press and Censorship Bureau in October 1939.

Nevertheless, neither this change nor a significant reduction in Ministry staff did anything to resolve the underlying problems of continued friction between the new bureau, the Ministry divisions and the services' departments.

Consequently, when Sir John Reith assumed responsibility for the MOI the following year, he concluded that the transfer of censorship responsibility had been a mistake and he initiated a series of changes that would eventually see the reintegration of the Press and Censorship Divisions into the MOI. Nevertheless, following a change of government and Churchill's appointment as Prime Minister in May 1940, Reith was replaced by Duff Cooper. Cooper himself was soon to be condemned for seemingly wishing to introduce a form of compulsory press censorship more akin to the system employed by the Nazis and he was, in turn, replaced by Brendan Bracken, who would remain the Minister in charge of the MOI until the end of the war.

Regardless of the structure, mistakes were inevitable. Censors would have to decide, often at very short notice, if they needed to liaise with the individual services' departments to check whether or not a piece of news could be released. Such was the Admiralty's reluctance to release any information about the location of its ships that apparently there were occasions when, in their haste, the censors even removed mention of the likes of HMS *Pinafore* from articles submitted for appraisal. Particular confusion often arose when a piece of news affected more than one service or government department.

Hence, the press became increasingly frustrated at what it often perceived as unnecessary censorship controls. Take the example of the reporting of German bombing. The Air Ministry would allow the press to mention the names of cities in Britain that had been bombed only once they were absolutely certain that the Germans knew which cities they had actually attacked. When it came to bomb damage, there was often several weeks' delay before the precise areas of a city that had been attacked could be identified and, as for industrial premises, it was even more important that there should not even be any indication of premises that had *not* been damaged.

The press became angry that it often could not report news that was already common knowledge and at a lack of consistency whereby articles about the same story might be approved for one newspaper and declined for another.

In fact, as the war progressed, many editors decided to publish articles that were at the very limits of what was permissible, and some newspapers were even considered to have exceeded these limits on occasions. The *Daily Worker* and *The Week*, both left-wing publications, were banned by the Government in January 1941 – although with little real justification – and the bans were lifted again in August 1942. The *Daily Mirror* was certainly considered a major culprit when it came to breaching Defence Regulation No. 39b and especially for its persistent criticism of the Government and British military leaders; it came very close to being suppressed altogether in March 1942. *The Daily Telegraph* was also accused frequently of disclosing information that might be of military value to the enemy, and it was saved from having formal action taken against it in 1943 only because of the personal intervention of Churchill, who regarded it as a newspaper well disposed towards his Government.

What I find particularly surprising is that, throughout the war, the British press frequently just quoted verbatim what was being reported in the German press or by the German High Command about a particular incident. Not only could the reporting of such information have been regarded as damaging the war effort and being bad for morale, it would seem to have flown directly in the face of Defence Notice No. 6/Gen which stated, 'Great care must be taken in reporting statements which have appeared in the enemy press ...'

It seems that as long as newspaper editors could show – whatever the original source – that the news emanated from publications already appearing in neutral countries, then they felt confident that their reporting of such news was not subject to censorship controls.

It is hard to believe that such an obvious loophole was never closed, especially as the British authorities never sought to deny the content of any German article reproduced in the British press. Instead, they held firmly to the stance, 'We have given our version of events. As a matter of principle we refuse to comment on the veracity or otherwise of any report being printed or released by the enemy.'

Newsreel

Apart from the censorship of the press, the MOI was also responsible for censoring the content of newsreel.

In fact, the authorities were initially rather caught on the hop as to what to do about newsreels. It had been assumed that, at the outbreak of war, the Germans would launch a heavy aerial bombardment, and hence all cinemas and places of entertainment would be closed. Consequently, there would be little newsreel cover- age as there would be nowhere it could be screened. However, when the expected bombardments did not appear, and the cinemas reopened, then the MOI had to re-assess how to respond. At first, its own Films Division tried to produce suitable material, but much of it was too amateurish to be usable, and it was reluctantly accepted that, for information about the war, the British public would have to be served by the various newsreel companies.

There were five major newsreel companies operating in Britain during the war years, namely *Movietone*, *Paramount*, *Pathé*, *Gaumont-British* and *Universal*. None of these was controlled by the British Government.

By 1940, newsreels in the United Kingdom would be watched by more than 20 million viewers weekly – a figure that was to increase to 24 million by 1944. It was little wonder that a Government select committee concluded that of the three principal kinds of film – feature, documentary and newsreel – it was the latter that was the most important for propaganda purposes. Hence, newsreels came to be given priority in terms of film stock.

It was recognised quickly that unlike a newspaper, where it was impossible to control which articles or parts of articles its audience might actually read, a cinema-goer would have to watch a newsreel from start to finish. Therefore, the precise content and the order in which information might be presented was very important, since both these aspects could influence the reaction of the viewer.

Consequently, by the summer of 1941, a clear structure was put in place for the censorship approval of newsreel. First, employees from the Censor's Office would go to the workplaces of each of the newsreel companies and view all pictorial material intended for inclusion in a newsreel. Next, commentaries proposed to accompany each newsreel had to be submitted separately to the Censor's Office.

In fact, the newsreel companies were subject to far more direct censorship than the press since they had to submit their newsreels for approval, both prior to general approval being granted and also after they had made any required changes. Each Monday and Thursday, between 10 a.m. and 11 a.m., completed newsreels were brought to the Censor's Office at Malet Street for a final 'scrutiny' viewing. It was realised that only by viewing the final newsreel for themselves could the censors gain a real understanding of the impression it would make on the general public. It was always every newsreel company's fear that it would be required to make more cuts at that point – something no company could afford to bear because of the further delay in distribution this would entail.

There were strict lists of 'dos' and 'do nots' to which newsreel was subject. For example, the press had been advised that a still photograph of air raid damage could be published only if it also showed at least 50 per cent that was undamaged. Similarly, when it came to newsreel, there was a rule that any scenes of air raid damage must start and end on an undamaged building. The rules were often altered to adapt to changing circumstances. Initially, for example, the newsreel companies had been subject to the general order banning all photographs of military subjects. This meant that, while the Germans could show their forces taking up positions, nothing could be screened about the BEF heading for France. This gave the Germans an unfair propaganda advantage, so the general ban was soon lifted.

Throughout the war, Britain did have one important advantage over Germany in that, through the press, radio and newsreel, it was able to communicate directly with a far larger percentage of its population than the Germans.

GERMAN PRESS AND NEWSREEL CENSORSHIP

It is somewhat ironic that, although Hitler had always thought the Germans had handled propaganda very badly during the Great War, there is little doubt that the determination by the British planners in the pre-Second World War years to establish their own MOI was largely driven by their recognition that the Nazis had already established their own very effective Ministry that was perfectly capable of ramping up its activities in a time of war.

In fact, following their election to power in January 1933, the Nazis had managed to establish their *Reichsministerium für Volksaufklärung und Propaganda* only a couple of months later. This Ministry for Public Enlightenment and Propaganda (RMVP) was headed up by Joseph Goebbels and was initially divided into seven divisions. Goebbels had originally declared that its staff should never exceed 1,000. By comparison, the British MOI originally had a staff of 999 before it suffered sizeable cutbacks following criticism of its performance.

The focus of the RMVP was on propaganda, and this included responsibility for co-ordinating and controlling the content of the press as part of an overall responsibility for ensuring the spiritual direction of the nation. Goebbels believed that the most effective form of propaganda should be simple and at least based on some vestige of truth. In *Mein Kampf*, it is clear that Hitler was certainly not concerned that this should ever necessitate telling the whole truth, 'Propaganda must *not* investigate the truth objectively and, in so far as it is favourable to the other side, present it according to the theoretical rules of justice; yet it must present only that aspect of the truth which is favourable to its own side.'

When it came to control of the media, the three most important divisions of the RMVP were those that handled Broadcasting (Division III), National and Foreign Press (Division IV) and Films and Film Censorship (Division V).

Division IV also incorporated the 'Wireless Service', the news agency of the German radio, which supplied all Germany's radio stations with news and broadcasts. Via its Press Chamber, the RMVP also controlled the guild that regulated entry into journalism. Only those who were 'racially pure' could be expected to attain or retain membership.

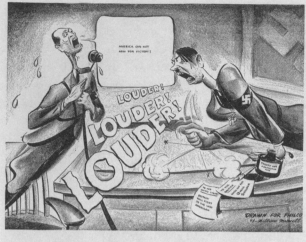

You're Slipping, Doctor Goebbels!

Hitler put Dr Goebbels in charge of the Nazis' own Ministry for Public Enlightenment and Propaganda in 1933. *US National Archives and Records Administration (NARA) 535184*

Unlike Britain, control of what could or could not be communicated to the public was absolute and was achieved by the enforcement of a number of key initiatives that had been set in motion throughout 1933.

First, a number of emergency decrees were issued that had the effect of curtailing general freedom of speech and press liberty. Temporary suspensions could be applied to any publication whose content could endanger security and order, which challenged official regulations or which spread malicious rumours. These decrees were soon employed as a means of justifying a ban on all socialist and communist newspapers.

Second, the Nazis introduced a law whereby a named editor, a *Schriftleiter*, had to be appointed for each newspaper or sub-section of a newspaper, and that person would assume personal responsibility for the content of that section of the newspaper. Furthermore, such editors were required to be of Aryan descent, possess German citizenship and not be married to a Jew. They had to ensure that nothing was published that weakened the strength of Germany or was offensive to German honour and dignity. Indeed, the law required all journalists to 'regulate' their work in accordance with National Socialism as a philosophy of life and as a concept of government. In other words, reporting absolute truth was not the top priority. The penalties for non-adherence could be severe, ranging from simple dismissal to a period of imprisonment in a concentration camp. Suspension from membership of the Press Chamber alone would prohibit further employment in the press industry altogether.

Third, only approved journalists were invited to daily conferences at the RMVP with the Reich's press chief. They would be issued with confidential instructions as to which stories should be reported and how any piece of news should be handled.

The level of detail would include guidance as to the precise headlines to be used and even the content of accompanying editorials supporting the main articles.

Fourth, a new official news agency, the *Deutsches Nachrichtenbüro* (DNB), was created by the merging of Germany's two largest news entities. The DNB accounted for almost 50 per cent of all the news appearing in individual German newspapers, and these would be instructed frequently that such and such a news article issued by the DNB had to be used in its entirety, without any alteration or addition. Just as in Britain, lists of banned subjects were issued and, once again, some of these seemed more relevant than others, such as instructions relating to the mention of the price of margarine or of attacks on women for wearing trousers.

Fifth, when the Nazis came to power in 1933, there were more than 3,500 newspapers being published – of which only around 120 were Nazi-controlled. Something urgent had to be done. So, rules were introduced in 1935 that sought to restrict the ownership of newspapers and the number of competing newspapers in any area. In conjunction with the ban on non-Aryan journalists and editors being involved in the profession, the result was to bring virtually all newspapers, directly or indirectly, under Nazi control. Leading newspapers with Jewish sponsors, such as the *Vossische Zeitung* and the *Berliner Tageblatt*, were soon forced out of business. Other renowned newspapers, such as the *Frankfurter Zeitung* and the *Deutsche Allgemeine Zeitung*, survived only by divesting themselves of any Jewish 'impedimenta'. However, their continued publication gave a rather misleading impression to the wider world of the continuing independence of at least some of the German press. Of course, the Nazis already had their own newspaper, the *Völkischer Beobachter*, the content of which was obviously always favourable to the Nazi regime. Its circulation was to increase from a mere 7,000 in 1923 to 1.7 million by 1945.

When it came to newsreel, the Nazis were soon quick to grasp the importance of this communication medium. Prior to the war, there were four competing newsreel companies operating in Germany, namely *Universum Film*, *Twentieth Century Fox*, *Bavaria Film* and *Tobis*. By September 1939, these had been consolidated into one company led by *Universum Film* and, by June 1940, a single weekly newsreel was released across Germany under the title *Die Deutsche Wochenschau*. Goebbels often personally approved the content and supervised the production of these newsreels, recognising that, in addition to radio, newsreel was one of the most effective means of promoting propaganda. Cinema audiences continued to grow through the early years of the war, as the German people sought to be entertained and distracted from its rigours. The *Wochenschau* newsreels typically ran for around twenty minutes and always preceded the main feature film. To ensure that all German audiences would be inspired and influenced by the propaganda contained in these newsreels, firm rules were introduced that ensured that cinema-goers were in their places prior to the newsreel being shown. Latecomers would be denied access to the main film. The producers of the German newsreels did also have one major advantage over the British in that whole teams of cameramen and war reporters were assigned to each of Germany's fighting units. This provided a ready source of material from across all fronts whose content and tone were obviously always guaranteed to support Nazi ideology and give a positive spin to the progress of the war.

In the light of such censorship controls, this book will examine, in the chapters which follow, just how accurate and complete a picture of the conflict was being reported to the general public in Britain and Germany during the war years.

2

COUNTDOWN TO WAR

INTRODUCTION

The origins of the Second World War were undoubtedly forged in the dying embers of the Great War. For Hitler and, indeed, the majority of the German people, there was complete incredulity as to how a country that had seemingly not been defeated in battle – certainly not on German soil at any rate – should still find itself obliged meekly to accept such an ignominious and draconian peace settlement as the Treaty of Versailles.

Nonetheless, just as a dying fire can be nurtured back to life by careful attention, Hitler and his supporters needed little encouragement to seize the bellows and eventually fan the growing flames of resentment into a blazing inferno. The Nazis exploited the bitterness felt by ordinary Germans and, step by step, won general support for policies that would result in a global war that engulfed three-quarters of the world and cost the lives of more than 60 million people worldwide. How could such an educated and civilised people be manipulated in this way?

If the Nazis had been masters in using propaganda to propel themselves to power, then they were to be just as astute when it came to the use of the German media in the reporting of the key events leading up to 3 September 1939, the date when Britain and France both formally declared war on Germany.

In the mid-thirties, both the British and German media tended to share a common stance with regard to Germany's territorial rumblings in that their significance was largely downplayed. However, as the decade progressed, we began to see a gradual divergence in each side's portrayal of Germany's increasingly forceful geographic expansion, until the focus of each side eventually changed completely, and Germany felt compelled to prohibit the circulation of British newspapers within its borders because of the unpalatable nature of their anti-Nazi sentiments.

There are two clear questions which arise: First, to what extent did Hitler exploit the German media to persuade the German people that the gradual re-expansion of Germany's borders, albeit in breach of the conditions laid down by the Treaty of Versailles, was completely justifiable?

Second, was there any real truth in the claim that the German minorities, who had found themselves redesignated as citizens of Czechoslovakia or Poland after the Great War, were being badly mistreated by their new governments and fellow citizens?

THE ROAD TO PERDITION

The aims of the Treaty of Versailles were threefold. First, to ensure that Germany would never be in a position to threaten world peace ever again; second, that the victorious powers should be reimbursed for the financial costs of the war and third, that Germany should be punished severely for the terrible cost in lives and resources that the Great War had wrought.

In practice, this meant that, in terms of its military forces, Germany saw its army reduced to 100,000 men, the complete loss of its tanks and military aircraft and its navy limited to six battleships. Territorially, Germany forfeited all its overseas colonies; Alsace-Lorraine was passed to France; the Saar Basin was placed under the control of the League of Nations; the so-called Sudetenland in the south became part of the newly created nation of Czechoslovakia; much of West Prussia, Posen and Germany's other eastern territories were eventually to be handed to Poland, and Danzig became designated a Free City. Furthermore, Germany was required to pay the equivalent of more than £6 billion in reparations – a massive obligation that it would never be in a position to fulfil.

The penalties imposed on Germany were certainly severe and for many, even in Britain and France, they went far beyond what might have been considered as just and equitable.

Politically and economically weakened, post-war Germany gradually experienced a complete breakdown of authority, with rival communist and fascist groups vying for power. Frustration with the ruling government continued to grow, and Germans increasingly felt drawn towards the Nazi Party and its charismatic leader. Hitler exuded confidence. He created myths about Germany's historic past and produced a firm 'road map' that would supposedly lead to Germany's future success. He identified a series of scapegoats for Germany's recent ills and intensified resentment against the victorious signatories at Versailles for refusing to reassess the level of Germany's reparations.

Hitler was eventually elected Chancellor on 30 January 1933 and, having eliminated all meaningful opposition, he was able to press ahead with reform programmes that did succeed in reducing unemployment, albeit at the cost of massively increasing Germany's national debt.

Heartened by the strength of support within Germany and conscious of a growing enthusiasm from those areas removed from German control, Hitler sought gradually to regain control over Germany's lost territories.

REPOSSESSION OF THE
SAARLAND AND THE RHINELAND

The small territory of the Saar Basin in western Germany had been confiscated from Germany in 1920 and occupied by Britain and France under a League of Nations agreement that was due to last fifteen years. When this period came to an end in January 1935, a referendum was held in which more than 90 per cent of the voters indicated a desire to be reunited with Germany. Armed only with the moral backing of this ballot, Hitler took the bold step of ordering the reoccupation of the territory, and the League of Nations formally approved the reunification in January 1935.

Buoyed by this success and the lack of any meaningful opposition from Britain and France, Hitler then proceeded to reoccupy the Rhineland in March 1936. Rather surprisingly, quality British press reporting of this significant development was rather placatory. While not denying that this was a breach of the Treaty of Versailles, the general plea in editorials and letters to editors was not to overreact. There was a definite unwillingness to condemn Germany for reoccupying territory that nobody denied was German, and it was felt that the time was right for a new treaty to be agreed between all the key countries.

For the German press, the emphasis was on Hitler's call to the world for peace and his proposal for a new non-aggression pact with France and Belgium. German readers would also have taken heart from the carefully selected headlines quoted from the rest of the world's press. The following was a typical quotation, which appeared in *The Observer*:

There is no longer any reason why this area should be demilitarised and even less that it should be a French, Belgian or British area any more.

The general impression given to the German reader was that, while the rest of the world may have been expressing some disquiet at Hitler's reoccupation, there was also a sizeable sympathy for his actions, and following Hitler's offer to rejoin the League of Nations, there was general agreement that all sides should work together to agree a new treaty.

It is often said that the First World War arose because it was easier for the great powers to go to war to settle their differences than to try to find any other solution. Ironically, it was the very lessons learned from that mistake that led to the British and French being prepared to go to almost any lengths to appease Hitler twenty years later, rather than contemplate another damaging war for which neither they nor their respective populaces had any appetite. This drift to inaction was particularly clear in the case of the Rhineland. Hitler's move to recapture the territory was largely based on bluff, as he simply did not have the necessary forces to retain possession if it had come to blows. Nevertheless, the French were reluctant to provoke another war, and the whole event was generally regarded as nothing more than the return of lands that really did belong to Germany. This laissez-faire attitude was not countered by the British, who were even more sympathetic to the opinion that the Germans did have a rightful claim to the lands.

Annexation of Austria

Austria emerged from the Great War with a large German population, and many within Germany and Austria in the 1920s would have preferred unification, but this was specifically prohibited by the Treaty of Versailles to prevent Germany from re-emerging as a dominant country. It is somewhat ironic that, with the election of the Nazis to power in Germany in 1933 and all that entailed, many Austrians thereafter lost their enthusiasm for such a union, but subsequent political turmoil within Austria actually led to the development of its own unique form of fascist government. With the previous Chancellor having been assassinated by Austrian Nazis in a failed coup attempt, Austria was eventually led by Chancellor Schuschnigg in 1934, and he was determined to retain Austria's independence from Germany.

Nevertheless, attacks against government officials by Austrian Nazis continued to grow until Schuschnigg signed an agreement with Germany in July 1936 that included a requirement to award positions in his cabinet to National Socialists. Hitler was still not satisfied and, eventually, a further agreement was signed in February 1938 in which, in return for an assurance of Austria's continued independence, Schuschnigg undertook to give even more positions of authority to Nazi supporters. One of the key appointments was that of Seyss-Inquart, who assumed the position of Minister of Public Security. However, Schuschnigg's subsequent decision to ask the Austrian people in a referendum whether they wanted to remain independent forced Hitler's hand – especially as he feared that the majority of the Austrian people would support Schuschnigg. When threatened with force, Schuschnigg informed his own people that he had yielded to the demands of Hitler rather than allow any German blood to be spilt. Consequently, and to the cheers of German and Nazi Austrians, German troops entered Austria on 12 March 1938, and Austria was formally annexed into the German Reich.

This time, British press reports, such as those in the *Daily Mirror* of 12 March, were generally far less conciliatory:

Hitler Takes Austria: Stern Warning by Britain

In line with official British Government declarations, the British media roundly condemned the German Government for the ultimata it had presented to the Austrian Government, demanding the cancellation of the referendum and the resignation of the Chancellor. *The Times'* editorial declared Germany's actions:

a blow to the policy of appeasement by leaving it more than doubtful whether appeasement is possible in a continent exposed to the visitations of arbitrary force.

Nevertheless, German press reports gave their readers a completely different impression of the event. In the *Freiburger Zeitung*, much was made of the fact that Schuschnigg had been acting unconstitutionally in declaring such a referendum in the first place without the support of his cabinet, and also in trying to rig the result by restricting votes to those aged over 24. The content of an emotional letter from Seyss-Inquart to the German Government was printed widely, appealing for Germany to send in troops to restore order and save the country from chaos. The whole annexation was depicted by the German press as a mercy mission, in which the century-long dream of unification was finally being realised, and whereby Austrians were now able to go forward hand in hand with their German brothers.

The Sunday 13 March edition of the *Freiburger Zeitung* carried the full speech by Hitler, justifying his actions in respect of Austria. It all sounded so plausible and reasonable. Hitler claimed that more than 6 million Germans in Austria were being oppressed by a small minority who had seized power, and that Schuschnigg had been warned on many occasions that this oppression, the imprisonments and the poverty into which so many of their 'racial brothers' had fallen, had to stop. However, all Hitler's warnings had been to no avail, and the final straw for Hitler was the sudden announcement of an Austrian plebiscite with no guarantee that it would be fair and impartial.

Adolf Hitler announcing the annexation of Austria to members of the Reichstag at the Kroll Opera House, Berlin on 12 March 1938. *NARA 535792*

Given this very different reporting of the event, it is not hard to understand why Germany as a whole could see nothing sinister or unreasonable in Hitler's actions.[3]

REPOSSESSION OF THE SUDETENLAND AND THE INVASION OF CZECHOSLOVAKIA

Encouraged by these developments, and ever conscious of the appeal of the 'new' Germany and the improvement in living conditions and prestige that belonging to the new Reich seemed to bring, it was not surprising that the other ethnic German populations in neighbouring countries also became impatient to be reintegrated into this emerging Greater German Reich.

With the benefit of hindsight, it is difficult to understand why those responsible for redrawing the map of Europe after the First World War could not have envisaged that the minority German populations, who now found themselves citizens of often newly created countries, would always be dissatisfied with their new conditions. Deprived of their German nationality, it was going to be easy for them to claim they were being treated unfairly and for every cause for complaint to be laid at the door of their new host governments.

The 3.3 million Germans of the Sudetenland were just such a case in point. When Germany had its borders trimmed in 1919, one of the first consequences was that the German-speaking people of Bohemia, Silesia and Moravia (together known as Sudetenland) found themselves citizens of the newly established nation of Czechoslovakia. However, they were very much in the minority, with the true nationality of the country being either Czech or Slovak, and they felt isolated and ignored.

Over the years, there were repeated press reports about the discontent being voiced by the Sudeten Germans, but it was fairly low-key and, even as late as February 1938, there were some amusing reports in the British press about such incidents as an Austrian being arrested in Czechoslovakia for wearing boots that left swastika imprints whenever he walked on soft ground.

I will examine later whether there was any truth in the claim that the Sudeten Germans were being oppressed but, whatever the truth, right from the start, Britain was determined to find a way of appeasing Hitler, since, once again, it felt a certain sympathy for these ethnic Germans who now found themselves in a new country. As early as May 1938, Hitler was actually approached by the British and advised that, if Germany spelt out exactly what it wanted in relation to the Sudetenland, then pressure would be brought on the Czech Government to comply with such requests. By 22 September

---

3 Ironically, the plebiscite held in Austria on 10 April 1938 was itself partly rigged by the Nazis in that vast numbers of opponents were disenfranchised, and the election itself was far from secret with completed forms having to be handed to an official rather than placed directly into a ballot box. Some 99.7 per cent of the voters voted in favour of the annexation by Germany.

1938, *The Times* contained the full text of a letter addressed to the Prime Minister from Lord Runciman, Secretary of State for Foreign Affairs, who had been appointed to mediate in the controversy between the Czechoslovakian Government and the Sudeten Germans. Rather undiplomatically, he expressed great sympathy for the Sudeten case:

 It is a hard thing to be ruled by an alien race; and I have been left with the impression that Czechoslovak rule in the Sudeten areas for the last 20 years, though not actively oppressive and certainly not 'terroristic', has been marked by tactlessness, lack of understanding, petty intolerance and discrimination to a point where the resentment of the German population was inevitably moving in the direction of revolt.

Recognising the indifference of its allies, the Czechs eventually reluctantly agreed to everything requested of them by the Sudeten Germans, and it was only when it became apparent that this was still not sufficient for Hitler that British sympathy for the plight of the Sudeten Germans started to evaporate.

Nevertheless, the signing of the Munich Agreement by Britain, Germany, France and Italy on 30 September, which authorised the transfer of the Sudetenland to Germany, was welcomed warmly by all the world's press. British newsreel showed Prime Minister Chamberlain being heartily cheered on his return to Britain for his famous announcement:

 This is the second time that there has come back from Germany to Downing Street peace with honour. I believe it is peace for our time.

The *Daily Express* of the same date went as far as to put its own reputation on the line with its front page headline:

 PEACE! – The Daily Express declares that Britain will not be involved in a European war this year, or next either.

The German press, on the same day, was equally ecstatic with such headlines as:

 The Peace of Europe Saved –
The 4 Great Powers are united

What was perhaps even more revealing were the subsidiary articles in that paper that told of the lies being spread by the Czechs, of Czech soldiers firing on German territory and, above all, of the bestial murder – with their eyes being gorged out – of three German border guards. Right to the very end, there seemed to be a need to justify Germany's annexation of the Sudetenland, even to its own people.

In the meantime, increasingly aware of the implications of their further guarantee to defend the independence of what remained of Czechoslovakia, the British did all they could to wriggle out of this obligation – eventually indicating that they were not prepared to come to the assistance of Czechoslovakia if the aggressor were Germany or Italy *and* if the French declined to fulfil their own guarantee. This betrayal by the British, combined with the Slovaks pressing for their own independence from Czechoslovakia in February 1939, left Hácha, the Prime Minister of Czechoslovakia, with no alternative other than to agree to hand over the rest of his country to Hitler on 15 March 1939, especially when he was threatened that to do otherwise would result in the immediate bombing of Prague.

Until then, the world's press and, indeed, the governments and people of virtually every country, were agreed that Hitler's actions in retaking the Saar Basin, the Rhineland and the Sudetenland were more or less justified, and neither these nor even the annexation of Austria was seen as a threat to world peace.

How then was the world going to react to this 'invasion' of a land where Germany really had no territorial right whatsoever?

At long last, the world's press was finally prepared to condemn Germany's actions. *The Times* of 17 March talked of a broken people and of Prague being under an invader:

 Czech State annexed by Decree

With its grave concern regarding the future fate of Jews in Czechoslovakia and its reporting of the immediate arrest of 5,000 key Czech citizens by Himmler and his secret police, it was perhaps little wonder that this edition of *The Times* was banned from being circulated in Germany.

By the following day, *The Times* also carried reports of President Roosevelt's condemnation of Germany's actions which had resulted in:

 the temporary extinguishment of a free and independent people.

Not surprisingly, the German newspapers of 17 March told a very different story. The key headlines in the *Völkischer Beobachter* were:

 Re-establishment of the basis of a rational Central European Order!
The Führer promises Bohemia and Moravia a long peace!

Much of the subsequent content in this and other newspapers was quoted directly from German High Command. The occupation was seen as a means of German self-preservation, and Germany was portrayed as being the only country fit to re-establish a reasonable order in Central Europe. It was a move that was described as being popular in Czechoslovakia, with great cheering in Prague at the appearance of Hitler. The British were warned not to meddle in a part of the world in which they had no historic influence and were accused of having plotted with the Czechs to re-establish all of Czechoslovakia at some time in the future.

For the German reader, the whole matter was once again presented as Germany simply reintegrating its own territory back into the Reich. It was a logical and legitimate step and no mention was made at all of how Germany was now transgressing beyond its recognisable sphere of influence.

THE INVASION OF POLAND

One final outcome of the Treaty of Versailles was the creation of the so-called 'Polish Corridor'. Some 6,000 square miles of Germany's territory and its associated people in West Prussia were transferred to Poland, thereby splitting off what remained of central Germany from the province of East Prussia on the Baltic coast. At the very right-hand tip of the corridor, Danzig was turned into a Free City whose purpose was to provide Poland with a port with free access to the sea. Further south, vast areas of the German provinces of Posen and Upper Silesia were also to fall under Polish rule.

Given that it was the invasion of Poland that was to result in France and Britain eventually declaring war on Germany on 3 September 1939, and, given that Hitler's ultimate justification for invading Poland was the claim that the German minority who had now found themselves in Poland had been subjected to terrible mistreatment by the Poles, it is surprising that there was relatively little comment in the German media about such tension until the last few months leading up to the war.

The key reason for this silence lay in Hitler's signing of a ten-year non-aggression pact with Poland in January 1934, shortly after the Nazis had assumed power. For Hitler, the purpose of the pact was to allay any concerns that Poland might have had about Germany's new rulers, to settle the damaging customs war that existed between the two countries and, above all, to give Germany time to rearm.

As a consequence, Hitler let it be known clearly that he did not want to hear any more complaints from Poland's German minority and, for their part, the Poles were just as keen to avoid taking any measures that might have raised tension between the two communities. Faced with this lack of support from the respective governments, it is somewhat ironic that, for a few years at least, many local communities did seem to manage to resolve their difficulties and live more easily with each other.

Indeed, it was only as the years passed and political priorities altered that this attitude started to change.

Even after Germany's seizure of Czechoslovakia, the Poles remained largely unperturbed and were more annoyed that they had neither been advised in advance of Germany's intention to invade Czechoslovakia nor had they been offered any share of Slovakia. The Germans were in a weak position and, to muddy the waters, insisted that good terms between Poland and Germany could be maintained *only* if Danzig were handed back to Germany.

Nonetheless, as late as 18 January 1938, there were still bullish British press reports suggesting that a solution to the Polish Corridor problem could be achieved through the building of another corridor across Poland, re-linking central Germany with its East Prussia province.

Indeed, it was only following the Poles' continuing refusal to negotiate over Danzig on 26 March 1939, and his recognition of the value of powerful supporting propaganda, that Hitler finally permitted the German media to make direct reference to the fate of the German minority in Poland. The Poles retaliated by allowing their press to circulate rumours about German soldiers gathering on the borders of Poland – reports that, at that time at least, were completely unfounded.

Raising the tension through the press and newsreel allowed Hitler to seize the moral high ground and to prepare the German people for his eventual cancellation, on 28 April 1939, of the 1934 non-aggression pact with Poland and the 1935 German-British naval agreement. Conscious of their earlier betrayal of Czechoslovakia, the British were now determined to honour their guarantees to safeguard the independence of Poland.

GERMAN MEDIA COVERAGE
PRIOR TO 1 SEPTEMBER 1939

In the German newsreel, in the months leading up to the invasion of Poland, there was little suspicion of the dramatic events that were about to unfold. The *Wochenschau* reel of 21 June contained a wide assortment of reports ranging from the Indianapolis 500 car race in the United States to a German sporting festival. There was no obvious propaganda in the accompanying dialogue and, while a feature on Danzig certainly revealed that there was some dispute over the city, the commentary was purely factual, with no attempt to persuade or condemn.

With the benefit of hindsight, however, it is possible to detect some more disturbing undercurrents. The reel opened with depressing views and commentary on the destruction of the German navy twenty years earlier at Scapa Flow. Interestingly, the film contended that it was the British who sank the ships, whereas we know that the ships were actually scuttled by the Germans themselves and were refloated later by the British to remove some of their precious metal. The film then compared such scenes of destruction with clips of the new German navy in action. Countless battleships and destroyers were shown crashing onwards through the waves – rather surprisingly flying the German war flag, although war had not yet been declared by either side. There was little commentary. Indeed, it was more noticeable by its absence since there was no indication as to why Germany even needed such a navy, but the triumphant accompanying music was certainly designed to evoke Germany's pride in its new navy.

The short feature on the city of Danzig showed it bedecked in swastikas and Nazi banners proclaiming:

 We want to be back in Germany, and Our Motherland is Germany

Goebbels even gave a speech from the town hall, urging the citizens to hold out in the battle for their German culture, and his assertion that 'Germany is every-where where Germans stand' was applauded widely. Nevertheless, throughout the whole reel, there was no threat of war or signs of a rise in political tension.

Even in late August, there was still a certain dichotomy in the news coverage. The newsreel of 23 August began with a rather bizarre item on a Hitler Youth group setting out on a boating trip along the Danube. Only later did it switch to the most significant items in the whole report, namely the poor conditions to which the German populace in Danzig were subject and, almost as a throwaway comment restricted to the last thirty seconds of the report, the signing by Germany of a non-aggression pact with Russia.

What is most revealing is that, unlike the report on Danzig in June, where no real threat towards the safety of German citizens was detected, this report was far more personal and critical.

With depressing scenes of lines of refugees and burning houses, the accompanying commentary was particularly condemnatory:

While those peacefully and loyally living in Danzig wait to be welcomed back into the Reich, those Germans who live within current Polish borders are subjected to the wildest of Polish terror. Many thousands of Germans flee the terror of the Poles and take up residence in temporary refugee camps within the safety of the Reich.

There were many tearful accounts by German citizens of how difficult life had been in Poland and how members of their families had been killed by Poles. They explained how they had been unable to get milk for their children, had been forced to speak Polish and had even been imprisoned for sending their children to German-speaking schools. The whole report was very emotional and was deliberately designed to be so.

In any event, following the signing of the Nazi-Soviet pact on 23 August, there was a noticeable increase in the ferocity of the rhetoric by both the Poles and the Nazis.

In response to Hitler's complaint about the intolerable condition of the German minority in Poland, the Poles claimed that this would be a more accurate description of the Polish minority in Germany, whom they claimed had been tortured and persecuted for many years.

On 28 August, newspapers across Europe published Hitler's letter to Daladier, the French Prime Minister, in which Hitler talked of:

 unbearable terrorism [...] the physical and economic mistreatment of 1.5 million Germans living outside old borders [...] Danzig and the corridor must return to Germany [...] seeing no way of being able to persuade Poland [...] to accept a peaceful solution.

Finally, the combination of the talks over the fate of Danzig failing to make progress and the accounts of attacks on Germany's border posts and territory at Gleiwitz, Pitschel and Hohenlinden by Polish diversionary bands were used as a pretext for Germany's invasion of Poland on 1 September.

MEDIA REPORTING OF THE OUTBREAK OF WAR

On 2 September, both the British and German press carried full details of Hitler's speech to the German Parliament the previous day. In short, he claimed that he had made countless proposals to the Poles for solutions to the intolerable situation in the Polish Corridor but, given that all his proposals had been rejected and that regular Polish soldiers had now been firing on Germany's own territory, he had had no alternative other than to act to secure the safety and rights of the Reich.

It has to be admitted that much of what Hitler said would undoubtedly have sounded very credible and rational to a German audience – especially since, in the weeks preceding the outbreak of war, the likes of the *Völkischer Beobachter* had been full of reports, on an almost daily basis, about some new Polish atrocity or misdemeanour.

On the other side of the Channel, however, and rather prone to the use of emotive and exaggerated headlines, the *Daily Mail* leader of 3 September neatly summed up the attitude of the British:

WAR – we now fight against the blackest tyranny that has ever held men in bondage. We fight to defend, and to restore, freedom and justice on earth.

A 1939 Nazi poster that mockingly compares Hitler, as a soldier who shares the dangers of war with his soldiers on the front line, with the war-mongering Chamberlain, who stays at home and will not walk anywhere without a gas mask. *United States Holocaust Memorial Museum Collection*

By 4 September, the British press was openly blaming Hitler for not wanting to reach an agreement with the Poles,[4] and much was made of Chamberlain's appeals for divine intervention:

 Now may God bless you all. May he defend the right. It is the evil things we shall be fighting against – brute force, bad faith, injustice, oppression and persecution – and against them all, I am certain that the right will prevail.

Nonetheless, if the British thought they were in the right, then – at exactly the same time – the German press was giving its own people a totally different version of the events:

England's Betrayal of Europe

The headlines clearly blamed Britain for the war because of its guarantees to Poland, which had allowed her to carry out all sorts of terrible atrocities towards

4   This is not quite true in that the Poles seemed to have resolved not to give in but undoubtedly even if they had – just as in the case of the Sudetenland – once committed to a course of action, no amount of appeasement would have stopped Germany entering Poland.

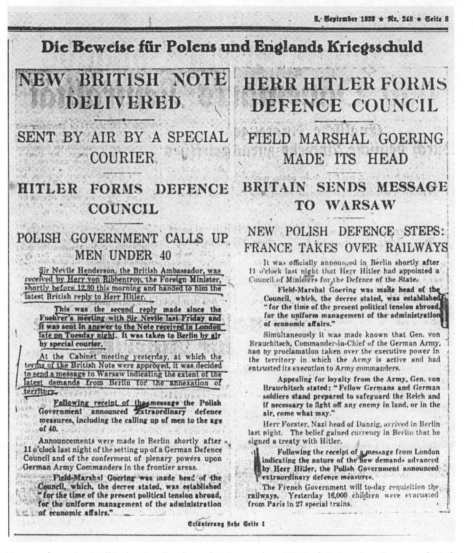

5. September 1939 ★ Nr. 248 ★ Seite 8

Die Beweise für Polens und Englands Kriegsschuld

NEW BRITISH NOTE DELIVERED

SENT BY AIR BY A SPECIAL COURIER

HITLER FORMS DEFENCE COUNCIL

POLISH GOVERNMENT CALLS UP MEN UNDER 40

Sir Neville Henderson, the British Ambassador, was received by Herr von Ribbentrop, the Foreign Minister, shortly before 12.30 this morning and handed to him the latest British reply to Herr Hitler.

This was the second reply made since the Fuehrer's meeting with Sir Nevile last Friday and it was sent in answer to the Note received in London late on Tuesday night. It was taken to Berlin by air by special courier.

At the Cabinet meeting yesterday, at which the terms of the British Note were approved, it was decided to send a message to Warsaw indicating the extent of the latest demands from Berlin for the annexation of territory.

Following receipt of the message the Polish Government announced extraordinary defence measures, including the calling up of men to the age of 40.

Announcements were made in Berlin shortly after 11 o'clock last night of the setting up of a German Defence Council and of the conferment of plenary powers upon German Army Commanders in the frontier areas.

Field-Marshal Goering was made head of the Council, which, the decree stated, was established "for the time of the present political tension abroad, for the uniform management of the administration of economic affairs."

HERR HITLER FORMS DEFENCE COUNCIL

FIELD MARSHAL GOERING MADE ITS HEAD

BRITAIN SENDS MESSAGE TO WARSAW

NEW POLISH DEFENCE STEPS: FRANCE TAKES OVER RAILWAYS

It was officially announced in Berlin shortly after 11 o'clock last night that Herr Hitler had appointed a Council of Ministers for the Defence of the State.

Field-Marshal Goering was made head of the Council, which, the decree stated, was established "for the time of the present political tension abroad, for the uniform management of the administration of economic affairs."

Simultaneously it was made known that Gen. von Brauchitsch, Commander-in-Chief of the German Army, had by proclamation taken over the executive power in the territory in which the Army is active and had entrusted its execution to Army commanders.

Appealing for loyalty from the Army, Gen. von Brauchitsch stated: "Fellow Germans and German soldiers stand prepared to safeguard the Reich and if necessary to fight off any enemy in land, or in the air, come what may."

Herr Forster, Nazi head of Danzig, arrived in Berlin last night. The belief gained currency in Berlin that he signed a treaty with Hitler.

Following the receipt of a message from London indicating the nature of the new demands advanced by Herr Hitler, the Polish Government announced extraordinary defence measures.

The French Government will to-day requisition the railways. Yesterday 16,000 children were evacuated from Paris in 27 special trains.

Erläuterung siehe Seite 1

Feature from the *Völkischer Beobachter* of 5 September 1939 claiming that the reproduced article from *The Daily Telegraph* proved that Britain and Poland were responsible for the war. *The British Library*

Germans in Poland without any fear of retribution. Chamberlain was accused of distorting the facts. German newspapers were full of the success of their armed forces on all fronts and how the people of Danzig were rejoicing:

 The hour of the return into the Greater German fatherland has arrived

As if to support Germany's position, the German press quoted selectively from other European papers to create the impression that the rest of the world was still generally sympathetic towards Hitler's actions. There was a typical quotation from a Spanish newspaper to the effect that responsibility and guilt lay *solely* with England and Poland.

Indeed, by 5 September, the *Völkischer Beobachter* reproduced in English a few columns from *The Daily Telegraph*, with the relevant lines roughly underlined, which it claimed proved that Poland and Britain were responsible for the war:

 'Daily Telegraph' reveals the truth
Documentary proof of responsibility for the war

In summary, the *Völkischer Beobachter* asserted that the British news item confirmed that the Germans had passed a 'peace note' to Warsaw via London, informing Poland of Germany's 'wishes' for settling their dispute peacefully. Poland's immediate response of mobilising its armed forces, and England's support of Poland forced Germany to take its own measures. In other words, the claim was that war was the fault of Poland and Britain rather than Germany.

For once and for all, it was evident that German and Allied media were not going to agree, and it is noticeable that in the news coverage thereafter their focus would be on supporting the war effort and the official positions of their respective governments.

OPPRESSION OF THE ETHNIC GERMANS IN THE SUDETENLAND AND POLAND – FACT OR FICTION?

It emerged at the Nuremberg trials that the final trigger for the invasion (the attack by Poles on Germany's Gleiwitz radio station) was, in reality, a fraud with the bodies of concentration camp prisoners dressed in Polish uniforms being left at the site to incriminate Poland. The revelation that the incident had been staged deliberately by Hitler for propaganda purposes has tended to lead to the world treating everything else that was claimed at that time with a degree of scepticism.

Indeed, as late as August 1939, even the British ambassador to Poland was still describing allegations of persecution of the German minority as being 'a gross distortion and exaggeration of the facts'. But was this fair?

The answer, as you might expect, is not simple and with regard to the position in the Sudetenland, Danzig and Western Poland, each territory needs to be examined in its own right.

THE SUDETENLAND

There is no doubt that, initially at least, the 3.3 million Germans who now found themselves citizens of Czechoslovakia did have some genuine grounds for complaint. There was no German representation in the new Czechoslovakian Government. Wealthy German landowners owned much of the land and, while not a policy designed deliberately to disadvantage the German population, many Germans did lose out financially in the subsequent land reforms. German public servants did account for a much larger proportion of the population than was probably justified, but the dismissal of 50 per cent of these in one fell swoop did seem rather drastic and caused great suffering, as few would find jobs elsewhere. Many Germans were also employed in the glass and textile industries – export businesses that were particularly affected adversely by the recession in the 1920s. By 1932–33, German speakers accounted for more than two-thirds of the country's unemployed.

The SDP played up to the Sudeten Germans' feeling of having a separate national identity while, at the same time, stressing its loyalty to the Czech state and its remoteness from the policies being pursued in Germany under Hitler. The Sudeten Germans were convinced they would benefit from being part of the new Reich and even when Benes, the new Czech Prime Minister, offered them their own state within Czechoslovakia, this was still not sufficient to meet their demands. Finally, Benes was left with no option other than to secede the German-speaking areas to Germany on 19 September 1938.

So, while there may have been some initial grounds for the resentment and dissatisfaction felt by the Sudeten Germans, this was largely due to the world economic crisis. There was no deliberate attempt to disadvantage them and, in the end, they were actually being shown preferential treatment. There was certainly never evidence that Sudeten Germans were being murdered and, while it might have made perfect sense for the Sudetenland to be reintegrated into Germany, this was certainly no justification for Hitler's eventual occupation of the whole of Czechoslovakia.

THE FREE CITY OF DANZIG

The Free City of Danzig was a state created by the Treaty of Versailles which, in addition to the town itself, incorporated its port and a small area of hinterland. Although it was Polish in origin, an increasing number of Germans had settled there from the twelfth century onwards and by 1929 Danzig had a population of more than 400,000 – 95 per cent of whom were German.

In creating a Free City under League of Nations supervision, the Treaty of Versailles had tried to accommodate what were really two irreconcilable provisions. On the one hand, an independent Polish state with free access to the sea (i.e. via Danzig) was to be created but, on the other, this was to be done so that 'all well-defined national aspirations would not be affected in such a way that could lead to discord and antagonism that would be likely to break the peace of Europe and consequently of the world'.

In other words, the city's port, transport links and communication services were to be used for the benefit of Poland, albeit that these facilities would be maintained largely by Germans. The official language of the new state was to be German but, in order to protect the rights of the minority Polish population, it was decreed that the Polish community could retain its own language in its schools and for internal administrative purposes. Undoubtedly, many Germans resident there did resent the fact that in order to continue to live in the Free City and retain the property they owned, they had to renounce their German citizenship and become citizens of this new city state.

From the very beginning, there was tension both between the two internal communities and between Danzig and the rest of Poland, resulting in frequent appeals to the League of Nations about decisions that were being made. Matters came to a head in 1920 when German dock workers refused to unload arms and munitions destined for Poland's war with Russia.

This strike gave the excuse Poland needed to develop the neighbouring town of Gdynia as a major munitions dump and as its main seaport. The impact on Danzig was devastating. In terms of trade, Danzig's tonnage was to fall from 8,615 tons in 1928 to 5,635 tons in 1934, while during the corresponding period Gdynia's trade was to increase from 1,947 to 6,724 tons.

Danzig complained to the League of Nations that Poland was in breach of her obligations to use the facilities of Danzig to the full, and it became increasingly antagonistic toward Poland. Internally, the city was becoming rapidly bankrupt, and a Nazi-led government was elected in Danzig in May 1933, albeit without the two-thirds majority required for any reform of the constitution.

In reality, within Danzig itself, the Germans held such a majority that if any group were to find itself abused as a minority, it was more likely to be the Poles resident there – antagonism towards whom increased as the city fell into increasing financial difficulty because of the recession and the downturn in Danzig's importance as a trading port. Physical attacks on Poles were to increase dramatically in the weeks prior to the outbreak of war.

WESTERN POLAND

It is also important to differentiate between the position in Danzig and the rest of western Poland, which now consisted of much of Germany's former provinces of West Prussia (the Polish Corridor), Posen and Upper Silesia.

Danzig itself was around one eighth the size of the Corridor, which, as a whole, covered 6,290 square miles. The Corridor was between 20 and 70 miles in width and, above all, it separated East Prussia (still German) from the rest of the new smaller Germany. This separation was always going to be an obvious bone of contention. In 1921, there were 175,000 Germans living in the rest of the Corridor area, representing around 20 per cent of the total population, but this was to fall to closer to 105,000 by 1931.

From a peak of approximately 1.4 million, after the First World War, there were actually only 740,000 Germans still living in Poland by 1931, and these were mainly resident in those provinces transferred recently to become part of western Poland. They represented only 2.3 per cent of the total Polish population and, depending on exactly where they were located, they generally did suffer a much harder existence as foreign citizens in Poland.

The official language in western Poland was generally now Polish, and there was little place for educated people such as teachers and lawyers who did not speak it and whose talents were now superfluous. Wages in Poland were also far less attractive than they had been in Germany.

The Border Protection Act of 1927 also made it more difficult for Germans to inherit or even own land in much of western Poland. Requests by Germans to buy land close to the border zone were invariably denied, and this pressure to dispossess the German minority of their land gained pace throughout 1939.

Polish farming methods were often less efficient, and the German minority made itself doubly unpopular by actually still managing to increase milk and butter production, so campaigns were mounted to shut down their co-operative enterprises. In Silesia, the drive to place German-owned enterprises under state control was even more severe, with many German workers being dismissed. Germans who continued to send their children to German schools faced the real threat of imprisonment or of being made redundant. While the overall rate of unemployment in Silesia in 1938 was 16 per cent, this was closer to 60 per cent among the German population. Somewhat ironically, just as the Nazis were forcing their citizens to boycott Jewish shops in Germany, Polish nationalist groups were actively discouraging Poles from using German shops. There were frequent reports of German children having stones thrown at them during their walks to school. Attacks on Germans and their property increased dramatically following the dissolution of the non-aggression pact in April 1939.

Faced with all these obstacles, it is little wonder that so many of the Germans resident in the Corridor and the rest of western Poland had gradually taken the decision to abandon their homes and move back to the Reich. This mass exodus did place increased pressure on Germany's ability to find employment for its former citizens, and it is virtually the only reason that gives any credence to Hitler's repeated claim that Germany needed more *Lebensraum* (living space) for its people.

THE FINAL ANALYSIS

Much of the German and British media's coverage of key events in the years leading up to the war has been shown to be more or less aligned. There may have been differences in emphasis, but there was certainly no really harsh criticism in the British press of Germany's repossession of either the Saar Basin, the Rhineland or even the Sudetenland. Indeed, there was much sympathy for Germany, echoed in both the views of politicians and the general populace that, since all these territories were inhabited by Germans, Germany was really only regaining territory to which it had a legitimate claim. Even the annexation of Austria was never seen as a threat to world peace. Such was the indifference or ambivalence of much of the world that the German press was often able even to provide quotations from major European newspapers that seemed to lend support to Germany's actions.

Indeed, it was only with the formal outbreak of the Second World War that this alignment of German and British media coverage diverged dramatically, and the media on each side loyally supported their respective governments in condemning and blaming each other for having provoked the war.

The claim that the minority German populations in neighbouring countries were being persecuted was probably true only in some parts of western Poland. Nevertheless, the extent of the abuse in that region should not be underestimated, and the moving eyewitness reports contained in the newsreel of 23 August 1939 were probably not falsified, even if their timing was rather fortuitous.

Nonetheless, Hitler was never really interested in the fate of those former citizens. This is evident from the fact that, with the signing of the non-aggression pact with Poland in 1934, he refused to support calls for the reunification of Danzig with Germany or to take any action at that time over complaints raised by Germans in other parts of Poland about their minority status.

In reality, it was only for political expediency and at times of crisis, such as at Munich in September 1938, that he resorted to raising the grievances voiced by the Germany minorities as a major concern. Likewise, it was only after his tearing up of the non-aggression pact with Poland in 1939 that he permitted and even actively encouraged the German media to report at length on the sufferings of fellow Germans trapped in Poland.

Not for the first time, and certainly not for the last, would truth serve as a weapon of timely propaganda for Hitler.

3

THE ROAD TO DUNKIRK

 The vital weapon of our army is its spirit. Ours has been tried and tempered in the furnace. It has not been found wanting. It is this refusal to accept defeat that is the guarantee of final victory.

Anthony Eden, Foreign Secretary, 3 June 1940

Germany's proudest victory – the greatest annihilation in the history of war!

Freiburger Zeitung, 5 June 1940

INTRODUCTION

From the moment at which they crossed into the Low Countries on 10 May 1940, it took only forty-three days for the Germans not merely to complete their invasion of Belgium, the Netherlands and Luxembourg, but also to force the British to evacuate what remained of its Expeditionary Force from Dunkirk and achieve the complete overthrow of France. This new form of *blitzkrieg* (lightning war) was certainly effective and, even more so, when you realise that there was not actually much to choose between the overall sizes of the opposing forces. However, at the very same moment that Germany was announcing to the world 'victory in the west' and celebrating the prowess of its armed forces, Churchill, through his inspiring and motivational speeches, was talking of the 'triumph of a miracle of deliverance'.

To what extent could the withdrawal by the Allies be regarded as a magnificent tactical victory, or were the Germans accurate in their assertion that the Allies had suffered an annihilation in the greatest battle of all times? How far were the facts manipulated by both sides to exaggerate the significance of their respective successes?

THE PHONEY WAR

When Germany invaded Poland on 1 September 1939, the Allies were initially and, rather surprisingly, quite swift to react. They felt duty-bound to honour their undertakings to Poland by declaring war on Germany immediately, and realised that it was important that they proved to Hitler that this time they meant business.

For its part, Germany had certainly not expected Britain and France to go to war over Poland, and Hitler was only too aware of the large number of divisions that the French alone had at its disposition in northern and eastern France. Indeed, some nine divisions of the French Fourth and Fifth armies crossed into Germany on 7 September, seizing a couple of villages and being well positioned to cut off Saarbrücken. Meanwhile, the British immediately dispatched an Expeditionary Force (BEF) of 158,000 soldiers and 25,000 vehicles to France. By 12 September, the French, under General Gamelin, had actually advanced a full 5 miles into the Saarland along a 16-mile front, taking them to within half a mile of the Siegfried Line, behind which the Germans had taken up their defensive positions.

German troops parading through the streets of Warsaw in September 1939. *NARA 559369*

If the Allies had pushed further at that point, we can only speculate as to the future course of the war. The Allies actually had eighty-five divisions ready for action, while Germany had only thirty-four, and twenty of these were really reserves. In addition, most of Germany's tanks and aircraft were still fully occupied in Poland. Given that, in 1944, it was the very threat of the fighting entering German territory that was one of the primary motivations behind Colonel Claus von Stauffenberg and his fellow rebels plotting to assassinate Hitler and bring the war to a close, who can say how the German people would have reacted to a full invasion of German territory in 1939?

However, instead of pressing home their advantage, the French brought their advance to a complete halt on 13 September. Furthermore, with Russia's invasion of eastern Poland, along an 800-mile front on 17 September, and the eventual collapse of Poland on 6 October to this two-pronged assault from Russia and Germany, the opportunity for a swift victory on the part of the Allies had been lost, and the question of what might have been becomes purely academic.

The Allies then became rather uncertain as to how to proceed. The stark facts were that Germany had managed to defeat a much larger Polish Army for the loss of only 15,000 men on its part, largely through their *blitzkrieg* tactics and superiority in terms of modern planes, tanks and mechanised vehicles. The Allies certainly had no appetite for an all-out conflict, and they were certainly still ill-prepared for such a war at that very moment. Even the British troops who had already been dispatched were sadly lacking in terms of the numbers of anti-aircraft guns, aircraft and even basic equipment with which such a force had originally been designed to be equipped. With Poland defeated and its country split between Germany and the Soviets, it was difficult to envisage how this fait accompli could ever be overturned.

While the Allies certainly talked tough, declaring that they were no longer willing to accept any assurances from Hitler regarding the security of the Low Countries, Britain or France, there was little significant action at the front. Western Europe was entering the period which was to be known as the phoney war. By late October, the French had already retreated to the safety of the Maginot Line – offering only token resistance to the subsequent German advance back into the Saarland. They were conscious of the much stronger enemy with which they were now confronted – a German Army reinforced recently with battle-experienced soldiers and mechanised units sent back from Poland.

While the Allies continued to grow their strength very gradually, the Germans used this breathing space to expand their army by another forty divisions.

Nevertheless, everything did not always go according to plan for Hitler. On 10 January 1940, a plane carrying maps and battle orders for the airborne invasion of France by Germany, just four days later, fell into Allied hands when it crashed in fog near the Belgian town of Mechelen-sur-Meuse. This obliged General von Manstein to produce a revised plan for an invasion spearheaded by tanks through the forest of the Ardennes, taking advantage of the fact that the Maginot Line came to an end just south of the Ardennes.

Still trying to agree a way forward, the Allies finally declared on 28 March that they would never agree to any armistice or peace treaty with Germany except by mutual consent between France and Britain. However, while Churchill would have favoured a more forceful pursuit of the war, the French were beset with internal political difficulties and preferred to delay a full-out attack until 1941 or even 1942, as only then did they believe that their forces would be sufficiently robust to achieve outright victory.

By April, the conflict had spread to Scandinavia, and the Allies were beginning to intercept disturbing messages that the Germans were planning an invasion of Western Europe early in May. Even though they expected that any attack would be focused on the Low Countries, they failed completely to predict the scale or strategy of the German attack.

THE INVASION OF THE LOW COUNTRIES

At first sight, it seems almost inconceivable that the Allies, with all the forces available to them in 1940, should have found themselves in danger of being overrun by a German army. After all, Germany had been forbidden under the Treaty of Versailles from having more than a token army and a few planes. How, in such a relatively short period of time, could it not only hold down Czechoslovakia and Poland but also carry on operations in Scandinavia and start a full-scale offensive in the rest of Western Europe? However unlikely, this is exactly what happened on 10 May 1940, with the German invasion of Belgium and the Netherlands.

Actually, in terms of the strength of the opposing forces, there was little to separate the two armies. The Germans launched their attack with 135 divisions against 142 Allied divisions — including twenty-two Belgian, ten Dutch and thirteen British divisions. Although the units of the BEF were heavily motorised, the Allies, as a whole, were short of mechanised transport for their troops and were generally weaker in terms of the quality and manoeuvrability of their armour. When it came to aircraft, with an air force of more than 4,000 planes, the Germans outnumbered the Allies by almost two to one, although this German superiority was generally in the number of bombers they had at their disposal. Nevertheless, the Germans knew exactly where and when their attacks were to be launched and, despite the fact that the Allies were aware an offensive was imminent, 15 per cent of the French forces were on leave on the very day of the invasion.

GERMAN JUSTIFICATION FOR THE INVASION OF THE LOW COUNTRIES

Until this point, and from a German perspective at least, Hitler's justification for his invasion of Czechoslovakia and Poland, based primarily on defensive reasons and the need to protect allegedly abused ethnic Germans in those countries, had seemed perfectly reasonable. So, how could he now persuade his people that it was justifiable to go even further and take the war not only into France but also into neutral Belgian and Dutch territory?

Goebbels was swift to pre-empt any potential criticism from within Germany and the wider world by ensuring that Germany had the first opportunity to seize the moral high ground before the Allies had a chance to respond.

Although the invasion was launched only in the early hours of 10 May, German newspapers such as the *Freiburger Zeitung* obviously had early notice of the attack, because its edition of that very same day carried the following headlines:

Advance on the Ruhr region thwarted!
Belgium was an open deployment zone for the World Powers!

The whole emphasis was placed on the fact that Germany was under threat and that it needed to take pre-emptive action to stop the Allies invading Germany. It was, after all, the Allies who had declared war on Germany, and they were clearly portrayed as being the evil aggressors.

Reports from the German Foreign Ministry and the German Army High Command explained how England and France had, at last, let the mask slip. It was claimed that after the Allies' actions in Scandinavia had failed, France and Britain had then raised the prospect of conflict in the Mediterranean, but the Germans realised this was a deceptive manoeuvre designed to conceal England's real goal – an attack on the German Ruhr region through the Low Countries – according to a plan that had been prepared in secret with Holland and Belgium for some time. In so doing, it was argued that Belgium and Holland had abused their neutral status and had given Germany every right to cross their borders to defend itself. In later editions, further details of apparent Dutch complicity were exposed with the discovery of thousands of maps that the Allies had prepared for their planned attacks on Germany.

For its part, *The Times* of 11 May was completely dismissive of Germany's complaints, describing them as 'lame excuses'. Naturally, the Allies did have their own plans for attacking Germany but, ironically, Belgium and Holland had actually gone to great lengths to avoid openly siding with the Allies so as to deny Germany any opportunity to take such offensive action against them. In any event, two wrongs did not make a right. The whole raison d'être for the Allies to attack Germany was to free Poland and Czechoslovakia, rather than overrunning Germany itself, but such reasoned arguments were never going to appear in the German press.

THE DEVASTATING ONSLAUGHT

Irrespective of the accompanying propaganda war through the media, and not-withstanding a number of heroic short-lived counter-attacks from the Allies especially around Arras, the German Army was soon carrying all before it on the battlefront.

By 30 May, the military authorities in Berlin were talking of:

 a devastating strike against England and [...] the battle of annihilation in Flanders being close to the end.

Accompanying German newsreel reports were keen to emphasise that their fight was against soldiers rather than civilians and blamed much of the destruction on the British and French. For example, they condemned them for not warning the local populace before blowing up their bridges. All the destruction of the war was clearly blamed on the British:

 for wanting to exterminate the German people with this war!

The *Tonwoche* newsreel report for June 1940 devoted considerable footage to the countless lines of trucks and military vehicles abandoned hastily by the Allies on either side of the road in their desperate flight to the coast. Much of the footage was paralleled in the later *Dunkirk* film produced in 1954. The German viewers could not have failed to be impressed by the success of their army and, given the extent of the destruction, the commentator was, rather convincingly, able to mock the Paris and London newspapers which referred to:

 a fully ordered withdrawal [...] one of the most satisfying chapters in England's military history.

Rather surprisingly, there was no mention of the fighting on the beaches at all but simply of a continued determination to convince the viewer that right was on their side:

 The march of our brave troops continues. The aim is the ceaseless extermination of an army which has forced us into war – it is a fight for peace!

British and French
prisoners captured at
Dunkirk, June 1940.
NARA 540152

By 12 June, the German weekly newsreel coverage had been able to catch up with the action around Dunkirk and showed close-ups, with cameras strapped to the front of Stuka bombers, of one ship after another being hit, and of countless warships and transports lying sunk at their moorings, as the Luftwaffe blocked the Allies' attempts to flee back over the Channel.

The commentary was full of rather obvious propaganda when it talked of the English and French plutocracy being prepared to sacrifice the blood of the French population in defending every metre of beach to cover the retreat of the English.

The film coverage was also able to show lines and lines of Allied prisoners. The narrator claimed that 88,000 were captured in the Dunkirk area alone but did not give any sort of breakdown by nationality or say how many had escaped. Somewhat surprisingly, the Germans were prepared to admit that, in the whole campaign since 10 May, 42,350 German soldiers had been wounded, but were just as conspicuous in not reporting just how many had been killed:

The largest battle in world history has come to an end [...] The entire German people thank these men. They spilt their blood to keep the enemy away from Germany's borders and to spare the fatherland immeasurable misery and suffering.

CONFLICTING ALLIED AND GERMAN REPORTING OF THE PROGRESS OF THE WAR

It is notable immediately that there was a dearth of Allied newsreel to document the unfolding drama. The *Movietone* newsreels of 16 and 20 May concentrated on the suffering of the Belgian civilian population, with images of the assistance they were receiving from the BEF, but there was little comment about the progress of the war.

Given the lack of Allied newsreel and its inevitable delay in reaching its viewers, the British public was always going to be dependent on the press and the radio if it wished to follow the progress of the war. It often did not make pleasant reading, as the key headlines in *The Times* made clear:

24 May:
Germans reached Boulogne

28 May:
Brilliant work by Allied Air Forces – 28 German aircraft destroyed or seriously damaged by RAF fighters the previous day.

30 May:
The Defence of Dunkirk – The French and British troops that are fighting in northern France are maintaining with a heroism worthy of their tradition a struggle of exceptional intensity.

When hard facts gave way to a more general patriotic and poetic style, it could mean only that the reader was being prepared for some bad news:

31 May:
A fighting retreat – Skill and Daring of Evacuation – 3 destroyers lost

However, the tone became far more upbeat by June, when it was apparent that thousands of troops were being rescued successfully:

1 June:
Withdrawals far in excess of Expectations

2 June:
Task for small ships

The *Movietone* reel of 2 June was even able to show tenders carrying troops to larger ships and talked patriotically of a magnificent rearguard action:

 They come home in highest spirits [...] our troops know that given a fair chance they can definitely beat the Nazis!

It is hard to see the justification for such blind optimism when the army had just suffered such an ignominious withdrawal and, indeed, this was picked up in the German press of 2 June with headlines that contained supposed quotations from British and Italian newspapers about what the British troops were really saying about the fighting:

 'An Unimaginable Catastrophe' – What English Soldiers are Saying about the Annihilation Battle

DEMORALISING IMPACT OF THE GERMAN BOMBING OF ENGLISH TROOPS

What little remains of some divisions of the former British Expeditionary Force which have made it back to England are recounting how the air attacks by the German bombers far exceeded their expectations, kept them from sleeping – with no resistance against them or way of escaping from them. [...] Thousands are waiting silently on London platforms for what remains of the defeated English Army. The description by the English soldiers of the crushing defeat in Flanders has made a shocking impression on the English people.

Rather effectively, the German press conjured up the image of a ragtag band of soldiers who just made it home, albeit devoid of all of their weapons and completely demoralised. It gave the clear impression that only a very small number made it back, although precise numbers were never given.

Given the lack of relevant newsreel available, the *British Pathé* report of 3 June carried an obvious disparity between the commentary and what appeared on the screen. British soldiers, with their rifles slung over their shoulders, were shown marching proudly through a French or Belgian village, being cheered on by the local populace. However, the accompanying commentary talks of men returning from the hell of Dunkirk and that, although they had been betrayed, an atmosphere of glory hung around these men as they still marched in formation and were grinning:

You might have thought that troops greatly outnumbered by the enemy, less well-equipped and finally treacherously abandoned by a ruler to whose assistance they had marched – you might have thought these boys of ours would have been disheartened to put it mildly!

But, at the joyful sight of troops returning home, the report ended very patriotically with the playing of *Land of Hope and Glory* and the flying of the Union Flag:

 This is the most magnificent sight of a generation [.] While these men live and breathe Britain is safe. The enemy will never pass!

In truth, both sides tried to make propaganda out of the event, since, on the very same day that this inspiring British newsreel was released, the headlines in German newspapers read:

 The Capture of 330,000 English and French soldiers

Aided by dramatic pictorial representations of British rescue ships in flames and of soldiers floating helplessly in the stormy seas, the *Völkischer Beobachter* went as far as to mock the bullish reports being released by the British:

 That's what the 'victorious withdrawal' of the English really looked like!

At sea, the German press was also able to report that two destroyers and a merchant ship had been sunk and that another two destroyers, a warship and a merchant ship had been badly damaged.

The Germans were also keen to show how the rest of the world was now rising up against this weakened Britain, with the Italians, Spanish and Irish all reported as having submitted demands to the British. Italian war aims included the 'liberation' of Tunis, Corsica, Gibraltar and Suez.

By 5 June, the German claims were even more spectacular:

Germany's proudest victory – 1.2 million prisoners, material of 80 Divisions seized, 3500 aircraft destroyed – own losses very small

Even though this phase of the war on mainland Europe would not finish for more than another couple of weeks, Hitler was so certain of victory that he was able to announce that there would be eight days of flag-flying and three days of bell-ringing to celebrate victory:

German press headlines of 5 June 1940 proclaiming 'Germany's proudest victory'.
Freiburg University Library/CC BY-SA

Officially released photograph showing troops rescued from Dunkirk waiting to disembark in the United Kingdom. *World War II Today*

The greatest battle of all times has ended with victory for our soldiers. In a few weeks more than 1.2 million prisoners have been taken, Holland and Belgium have capitulated, most of the British Expeditionary Force has been wiped out and the rest killed or forced off the continent. Three French armies have ceased to exist. The danger of an enemy breakthrough into the Ruhr region has finally been averted.

Nonetheless, for their part, by 6 June, the *British Pathé* newsreel had almost transformed the whole venture into a major victory for the British:

 Evacuation of the BEF – the greatest epic of the War!

Despite revealing that some ships had been sunk, the whole emphasis was on the fact that more than 1,000 ships had transported 350,000 men safely back to Blighty, and there were countless joyful scenes of troops disembarking at ports in Britain:

 Here in pictures is the triumph which turned a major military disaster into a miracle of deliverance.

In that very comment, the British media actually gave quite a fair representation of the facts, and, in the absence of any real victory to celebrate – other than the relief that so many troops made it home – there was a deliberate concentration on the rousing and upbeat speeches by Churchill who talked of:

 a miracle of deliverance achieved by valour, by perseverance, by perfect discipline, by skill and by incomparable vitality [...] all the might of the German air-force failed to stop them. We beat them back. We got our armies away and the enemy paid four-fold for our losses.

It is hard to see how Churchill could ever have justified such an obviously false statistic, but he continued by giving an inspiring vision of the future through one of the most memorable speeches he was ever to make:

 The BEF will be rebuilt. We shall not fail. We shall fight on the seas and on the oceans. We shall fight in the air; we shall fight on the beaches, in the fields, in the streets and on the hills. As we fought in blazing Dunkirk and, like the men who smashed their way out of hellish beaches in Flanders, we shall never surrender.

VICTORY FOR THE GERMANS OR VICTORY FOR THE BRITISH – WHO TOLD THE TRUTH?

On this occasion, the truth lies somewhere in the middle. As early as 30 May, the German press, surprised by the speed of the German advance and inspired by reports from German High Command, was talking of imminent victory. But, in reality, it was just a little too soon to declare absolute victory and, by 3 June, it was admitted that the battle in the north was lasting far longer than envisaged. This was to have significant but unforeseen repercussions.

The Allies did put up stubborn resistance, and the decision taken on 25 May by General Lord Gort (Commander of the BEF) not to pursue a further pointless counter-attack to the south, but rather to use his forces to protect the route to Dunkirk was one of the most important choices of the whole war.

With the help of the French, who at that point did not realise that the British might be looking to evacuate from Dunkirk, a stout perimeter was established around the town. It involved flooding much of the area and creating extremely effective barriers out of existing ditches and canals – all of which slowed down the progress of the German tanks and infantry.

For their part, stunned by the success of their advance – it had taken only four days to break through the French lines at Sédan – the Germans simply did not have any coherent plan for conquering the Allied soldiers caught within the Dunkirk pocket. Each army group had its own objectives, and these – and the very lines of command – were changing frequently. So, there was a certain relief among the generals when Göring took away much of the responsibility from the army by claiming that his Luftwaffe could achieve victory by bombing alone, just as they had done in Poland. While some of his commanders were less bullish that the BEF could be prevented from returning home in this way, Göring's enthusiastic promises held sway. In any event, Hitler and von Rundstedt were concerned that their panzers might literally get bogged down in the fighting around Dunkirk, which would give the French time to regroup or counter-attack elsewhere. On 24 May, the order was given for the tank advance to stop, and they were later to be diverted to continue the attack on France, further south.

What we in Britain tend to forget is that, while we regard Dunkirk, where the last evacuation occurred on 4 June, as the last action of this phase of the war, the reality is that it was only a small part of the overall campaign. The bulk of the rescued French troops were to rejoin the battle elsewhere, with attacks by the Luftwaffe stretching from the Rhone Valley to Marseille. The French were not to concede final victory to Hitler until 22 June.

Returning British soldiers may well have talked of 'an unimaginable catastrophe', but the hard facts were that the failure by the Germans to pursue their advance did allow many more Allied troops to be rescued than might have been expected even a few days earlier. This failure of the Germans to finish off the job was ultimately to prove fatal. Not for the last time, Göring failed to deliver on his boasts.

The British did manage to achieve a remarkable level of fighter cover through large numbers of sorties, which did at least restrict some of Germany's bombing activities in daylight hours, and bad weather restricted German air activity severely on another couple of days.

Bombs dropped on troop-packed beaches had limited impact. Bombs dropped on naval vessels did take a lot of lives, but the sheer volume of the ships and small boats and the numbers of crossings being made each day meant that the Germans were never going to be able to destroy all the ships.

WERE THE GERMANS JUSTIFIED IN CELEBRATING VICTORY?

The Allied armies were certainly comprehensively defeated on the battle front in this phase of the war. Within just six weeks, and with a loss of little more than 30,000 of its own forces, Germany had seized Belgium, the Netherlands, Luxembourg and France, and the BEF had been driven back across the Channel, deprived of the bulk of its armoured vehicles, artillery, machine guns and rifles. It was a truly remarkable success that was achieved through a combination of clever tactics and the effective deployment of bombers and tanks. The Germans had every right to celebrate this victory, but it was not the end of the war.

Against all the odds, four-fifths of the BEF did make it back to Britain. In total, 221,504 British troops were brought home in pre-evacuations and through Operation Dynamo (26 May–4 June). In the following days, a further 144,171 men were to be evacuated from south of the Somme through Operations Aerial and Cycle. This had a tremendously positive impact on British morale. More than 50,000 French troops were also evacuated from Dunkirk on 3 and 4 June, although many of these were to rejoin the fray only to be forced to surrender within another couple of weeks. A further 40,000 French troops defending the Dunkirk perimeter were eventually forced to surrender.

The Allies' achievement in evacuating so many troops was notable but still attained at considerable cost. The Germans made much of the capture or destruction of eighty divisions' worth of equipment and, where possible, captured trucks and lightly armoured vehicles which, while left unserviceable at the time, were later adapted for use by the Germans with machine guns and cannons often replaced by German equivalents. The British Army alone abandoned 2,500 guns, 84,500 vehicles, 77,000 tons of ammunition and 416,000 tons of supplies. Many of France's captured tanks and lorries were to find their way to the Eastern Front in 1941.

The ability of the British to disable much of its equipment successfully is borne out by what happened to the 2nd Anti-Aircraft Brigade. When it moved to Dunkirk, an order was misinterpreted and resulted in the disablement of more than 100 3.7in anti-aircraft guns, which could not be made serviceable again even after the mistake was identified.

The Allies also lost 240 vessels, with a further forty-five badly damaged. This was to include the sinking of six British and three French destroyers, and the crippling of a further twenty-six.

In the air war over Dunkirk itself, the British destroyed forty-two bombers and thirty-six fighters for the loss of eighty-four of its own fighters.

Nevertheless, however sizeable these losses in equipment may have been for the British, it was not a killer blow and, as will be seen later, still left the British with sufficient military strength to fend off any immediate invasion. The campaign in France and the mainland of Western Europe might have been over, but the war was far from won, although there were just too many uncertainties at that time to know how events would play out. Hitler still harboured some remote hope of coming to an accommodation with Britain to avoid further conflict between the two countries. America was not yet in the war, and who could have predicted how effectively the British Isles could still be used as a base for a future counter-attack?

Perhaps the best assessment of the situation was contained in this comment from General Wilhelm Keitel, then chief of the German Army High Command:

 Every war sees missed opportunities and sooner or later one of them proves fatal. This could be the one.

CHANGING ATTITUDES IN BRITISH MEDIA'S ATTITUDE TOWARDS BELGIUM

It is worth noting the changing attitude on the part of the British media towards Belgium and its people as the outlook for victory looked increasingly bleak.

On 11 May, *The Times* was extremely sympathetic towards Belgium, reporting that the Belgian Minister of Foreign Affairs had announced how, for the second time in twenty-six years, Germany had broken her promise to respect Belgium's neutrality. There was loud praise for King Leopold, Commander-in-Chief of the Belgian Army, and for the firm morale of the Belgian people, who:

 like all citizens of free countries, know how to control their nerves in time of danger.

On 23 May there was even praise for the counter-attacks by the Belgian Army, which thrust back German troops across the River Scheldt. But, by 29 May, the press carried a bitter statement from the French Prime Minister regarding Belgium's surrender:

King Leopold III without warning General Blanchard, without one thought, without one word for the British and French soldiers who came to the help of his country on his anguished appeal, King Leopold III of the Belgians laid down his arms. It is a fact without precedent in history …

The Times made its own feelings just as clear:

When every possible allowance has been made for the King's doubtless sincere desire to spare his people suffering, it is impossible not to sympathise with M. Reynaud's bitterness.

British newsreel was even more scathing when it referred to the 'betrayal' by the Belgian king.

In reality, much of this criticism was rather unfair. The Belgians did fight bravely, but simply could not resist the ruthlessness of the Germans' bombing and armoured attacks. Faced with the prospect of the bombing of Brussels, King Leopold telegraphed General Lord Gort at 12.30 p.m , on 27 May, to warn him that the Belgians would not be able to continue the fight for much longer, and similar warnings were passed to French officers. It was not until 4 a.m. the following morning that the Belgians actually agreed to a ceasefire, with their formal surrender document signed later that day. Therefore, it was wrong to say that the Belgians had surrendered 'without any warning', but it probably suited the Allies to have someone else to blame for the catastrophic defeat of their armies.

THE FABRICATION OF ALLIED WAR CRIMES

What is also of considerable interest today is how the Nazis exploited incidents throughout this period for pure propaganda purposes. The weekend edition of the *Freiburger Zeitung* of 11 May contained an article entitled:

 Cowardly Air Attack on Freiburg
No Military Installations Targeted but 24 Civilians Killed

At the very same time, the Air Ministry in London was swift to dismiss the German report of Allied planes bombing the city of Freiburg as pure fabrication. So, who was lying?

It has always seemed rather implausible that on the very day that Germany launched its invasion of Belgium and Holland, the Allies should have nothing better to do than retaliate immediately with a pointless bombing attack on the civilian population of Freiburg in south-west Germany. After all, Freiburg was a city of relatively little immediate strategic importance.

The sad truth is that the sixty-nine bombs which were dropped on Freiburg actually came from a German squadron that had lost its bearings on a mission to bomb Dijon in France. Seeking a secondary target, the German pilots believed that, at least, they were dropping their bombs over a town on the west side of the Rhine. Indeed, the very reason why no air raid siren was sounded over Freiburg prior to the raid was because German observers, having correctly identified these as German planes as they flew towards Freiburg, simply expected them to fly harmlessly past the city.

It was one of those occasions when the German media – both press and news-reel – were cynically manipulated by the Nazi authorities to support what was a downright lie, rather than merely a slight distortion of the facts for propaganda purposes. The true facts only emerged after the war, as the Nazis were never to accept such a loss of face by admitting the truth at the time. Indeed, Goebbels deliberately exploited the tragedy to cast the Allies in a bad light and even used this as justification for the future bombing of Allied civilian targets:

 From now on every planned bombing raid on the German people will be answered by a five-fold number of German planes attacking English or French cities.

Hitler was to repeat the lie in a speech in December 1940, when he accused the Allies of having started the bombing war against civilians with the attack on the undefended city of Freiburg. Other deliberately fabricated lies were soon to follow.

With the resignation of Chamberlain as British Prime Minister and the appointment of Churchill as his successor on 10 May, the Germans were quick to find reasons to denigrate the latter, who was identified immediately as a far more worthy opponent. Hence, we find an article in the *Freiburger Zeitung* of 27 May with the intriguing title:

 Churchill plans a new 'Athenia' crime

Written from Boston, USA, by a supposedly trustworthy source, it was reported that Churchill was planning to sink the passenger ship *President Roosevelt* as it returned from Ireland to New York laden with American citizens and their children. It was described as being all part of a wider plan to blame the evil deed on the Germans so as to drag America into the war against Germany. The carefully worded reference to the sinking of the SS *Athenia* on 3 September 1940 was certainly rather disingenuous:

The incident with the Athenia immediately after the outbreak of war served the same purpose.

This gave the clear impression that the Allies had sunk the *Athenia* themselves and simply blamed it on the Germans to foster sympathy and gain support from the Americans. To be fair, the German media at the time were genuinely convinced that their own navy had not been responsible for the sinking. In reality, it was sunk by *U-30*, but the captain of that U-boat was able to submit a report only when he returned to Wilhelmshaven on 27 September. He always claimed that the steamer was zigzagging across the water, which made it appear to be a military vessel, and that it had been sunk in error. The ship had been sailing from Glasgow to Montreal but, with ninety-eight passengers and nineteen crew killed, the Germans certainly feared it would hasten America's entry into the war.

For that very reason, the Nazis would never admit responsibility for the ship's sinking until after the war and, even though they knew the truth, went so far as to publish an article in the *Völkischer Beobachter* a month later clearly blaming the sinking of the *Athenia* on the British and condemning Churchill for seeking to turn neutral opinion against Germany. It was another total lie.

4

THE BATTLE OF BRITAIN

INTRODUCTION

Never in the field of human conflict was so much owed by so many to so few.

Inspired by the heroics of the fighter pilots of the RAF and, in particular, following the momentous air battle that was fought over Britain and the English Channel on 15 August 1940, Prime Minister Winston Churchill was to utter these memorable words in the famous speech he delivered to Parliament five days later. For the British, the Battle of Britain was one of the key turning points in the Second World War and, if that battle had been lost, then the whole of Europe might have been destined to yield to Nazi suppression. It was, and remains, one of the proudest moments in British military history.

It might, therefore, come as a surprise to many Britons today to discover that this was certainly not how the whole event was evaluated by the German public at the time. Indeed, even after the war, many Germans who lived through that period were often rather confused when they visited Britain as to what exactly was meant by the Battle of Britain. For Germany, the bulk of the war involved conflict with Britain. No indication was ever given to the German public that there was a short, specific period when the fate of Britain hung precariously in the balance, let alone that, during the summer and autumn of 1940, there had ever been a prolonged air battle with the British in which Germany had been defeated.

This is hardly surprising for, while the British media were daily giving upbeat accounts of the vast numbers of enemy planes that were being destroyed, at the very same time the German press was reporting often almost identical numbers of British planes being destroyed by their fighters, and there was a tendency to concentrate instead on the devastating damage inflicted by German bombers on other aspects of the British war machine.

So, just who was telling the truth and were there justifiable reasons for the massively divergent reporting of this campaign by each side?

BRITAIN FIGHTS ON

Historians today generally agree that the Battle of Britain ran for just over three and a half months from 10 July to 31 October 1940, and it is largely perceived as being primarily a battle for air supremacy between the multi-national pilots of the RAF and the skilled fighter and bomber airmen of the Luftwaffe. The term itself derives from an earlier speech by Churchill on 18 June in which he declared:

The Battle of France is over. I expect that the Battle of Britain is about to begin.

Churchill was quite correct. Even before the French had formally surrendered, the Germans were bombing British targets on land and at sea, and the bombing of Britain would continue almost unabated until May 1941.

For the Germans, Dunkirk was only one very small part of war on mainland Europe, and the defeat of France – the country with the biggest land forces in the world at the time – was a colossal victory; the fact that success had been achieved in such a short period of time had even come as a complete surprise to the German military.

Prime Minister Winston Churchill visiting defence fortifications near Hartlepool in July 1940 in preparation for the Battle of Britain. He is pictured trying out an American 1928 Tommy Gun – an image the Nazis seized upon as an excuse to depict Churchill as a murderous gangster.
Rare Historical Photos

Having been forced reluctantly to accept that Britain was not going to be prepared to reach some accommodation with Germany, it was obvious to Hitler that the invasion and defeat of Britain was the next logical step, even if it was one for which Germany was not completely prepared.

For the German civilian, at least, given the speed and ease of victory in France, there was an overwhelming expectation that triumph over Britain could be achieved just as quickly. If you were to believe the reporting of the German media, the war in the West seemed to have already been won. The celebrations were exuberant. Although Britain was described as buzzing around like a rather annoying wasp, it was anticipated widely that it would soon be crushed. After all, had not its small army been wiped out in the first weeks of the war and the miserable remnants of its forces only escaped by abandoning the bulk of their armour, artillery and other weapons in France? Likewise, the RAF had seemingly been largely ineffective in defence of its army in France, so why would it be any different when the battlefield moved to Britain?

Of course, the big difference, and the one that prevented a repetition of the *blitzkrieg* in the Low Countries and France, was the fact that Britain was an island and separated from the rest of Europe by a rather frustrating strip of water. Furthermore, Britain did possess a large and powerful navy.

For the Germans to achieve a successful sea-borne invasion of Britain, they realised they needed to maintain control of both the air and the sea. Göring was rash enough to declare that his Luftwaffe would wipe the RAF from the air in a matter of days, thus paving the way for such an invasion or perhaps even forcing the British to surrender without the need for any invasion at all. Somewhat dubious about these bold assertions, most of the other German generals were only too happy for Göring to bask in the limelight on this occasion.

However, the widespread belief in the complete invincibility of their armed forces was soon reflected in German press coverage. As early as 20 June 1940, and even before France had formally surrendered, the German press was quick to mock Churchill for declaring that England would fight on until victory:

 To victory? Yes, but to German victory!

After all, it had taken not much more than five weeks for France to be comprehensively crushed, and France was now to be made to pay for its guilt in its treatment of Germany after the First World War. This idea that Germany's war was really one of retribution for the excessive punishment to which Germany had been subjected under the Treaty of Versailles was reinforced by the German headlines of 20 June:

 The Revenge on England begins!

The report continued by detailing the success of German raids the previous night on munition works and on a storage depot in Hull, during which the British lost twenty-one planes. This was actually some three weeks prior to what is now regarded as the official commencement of the Battle of Britain, or what really should be called the Battle *for* Britain.

For the British, the fact that the Germans would now turn their attention to Britain was largely expected. Eden's broadcast speech of 27 June talked of tempered optimism:

We are now a fortress [...] we are confident that we could throw a sufficient force against any enemy who attempts to land on our shores, attack him, and defeat him.

Only time would tell whether these bullish claims would be any more than empty rhetoric. When the British Parliament of 18 June had spoken of 'inflexible resolve' and 'confidence in final victory', nobody really had any idea as to whether Britain's Air Force and Navy would be able to fend off an attack by Germany. As far as the Germans were concerned, these were already considered idle boasts and, by 29 June, the German press was reporting enthusiastically how England had been seized by pure panic with everybody asking fearfully when and how the Germans would arrive. The *Daily Express* was even quoted in German newspapers regarding its estimates that between 700,000 and 1,000,000 people had already fled from London out of fear of air raids. The tension increased daily as the German press claimed that a full attack on Britain by air and sea was imminent.

Both sides competed with impressive statistics of enemy losses. As I already mentioned, 10 July 1940 is now considered as the official date of the commencement of the Battle of Britain, and the respective press reports of the events of that day make very interesting reading. The British Air Ministry reported that:

The RAF inflicted the greatest damage on the German Air Force since their bombing raids on Britain began. 14 enemy bombers and fighters were shot down. 2 British fighters lost.

A palpable victory, you might think, which would have given the Germans pause to reconsider their strategy. Nevertheless, this was certainly not the impression you would have obtained from the German newspapers for the same day where the headlines talked of:

Great success for our Luftwaffe
10 fighters shot down – 4 of our own did not come back

So, what actually happened? They cannot both be telling the truth. In fact, it was not a good day for the Germans, whose losses on that day were probably even higher than the British had claimed, and so it was to continue over the next few months, with both sides producing completely divergent loss statistics.

CONFLICTING LOSS STATISTICS

One of the problems in trying to determine who told more truth in their media reporting of these daily events was that often the respective coverage was not comparing like with like. German reports also tended to emphasise the amount of damage inflicted in terms of the tonnage of ships sunk or the number of military installations destroyed rather than to specify losses in the air.

Even where specific statistics regarding both the enemy's and one's own losses were reported, just who was to decide when one air battle commenced and another ended? How can we be sure they were even reporting the same incident? Given that there were several hundreds of sorties taking place each day, how could either side ever keep accurate track of what was happening everywhere, even if there were a desire to report accurately?

Aircraft spotter balanced precariously on the roof of a building near to St Paul's Cathedral in London. *NARA 541899*

Several pilots might even attest to shooting down the same plane only for this 'hit' to be duplicated yet again by a claim from an anti-aircraft battery. In reality, the plane in question may not have been shot down at all and, although badly damaged, might still have managed to limp home. If it was difficult for the British to produce accurate figures for the battles that were raging overhead, then it was even more so for the Germans who had far less chance of independent verification.

What is often more revealing is how both sides tried frequently to downplay their own losses by not releasing the figures at all or, even if they did, through the type of language used to describe such losses. The Germans, in particular, virtually never referred to their own planes as having been 'shot down' but rather reported that 'they did not return' or 'that they were missing'. Thus, the negative message was never quite so emphatic and left hope that they might still return.

The Germans were certainly more loathe to report fully their own losses at the time, especially in terms of airmen. There were very sound motives behind this. Part of the reason lay in the fact that most of the German planes shot down were bombers, typically with a crew of four or five. Most of the British losses were single-piloted fighters. Consequently, it is perhaps not that surprising to discover that the official statistics available today for the whole of the month of August 1940 record the loss of 176 British pilots while the comparable German total was an incredible 993. This latter total was obviously not a figure the Germans would have wished to reveal at the time although, in reality, it was far more difficult for the Germans to report promptly and accurately on their own aircrew losses even if they had wanted to do so. If a plane did not return to its home base, it could often take some time to determine whether it had diverted elsewhere or, if it had been shot down, whether its airmen had been killed or had managed to bail out. If they had bailed out, then had they been taken prisoner in Britain or had they been fortunate enough to land in the sea close to one of the strategically located rescue-shelter buoys from where they could be picked up by a fast patrol boat? It could take weeks for all this information to be collated, and yet there would be a demand for an up-to-date statistical report each and every day.

PENALTIES FOR LISTENING TO FOREIGN BROADCASTS

Given that the official loss statistics reported by each side at the time were either concealed or seemed rather far-fetched, it was little wonder that many civilians sought to determine the true version of the events by listening to foreign news reports, or even the propaganda programmes broadcast by the enemy.

In Germany, listening to such foreign broadcasts was a crime and, almost as soon as the Germans had started their invasion of France and the Low Countries, front page reports appeared in German newspapers warning readers of the harsh penalties that were being imposed on anyone caught listening to foreign stations.

In fact, when Goebbels had arranged for the distribution of the first of his cheap 'people's receivers' in August 1933, the Nazis had already been very careful to ensure that this type of radio could only pick up German radio stations. Listeners would have required far more sophisticated models to listen to foreign broadcasts. A German woman who lived in Berlin during the war years told me that her father, who worked for Siemens at the time, had brought home a prototype model that could pick up foreign transmissions. However, their family had to be most careful that the children realised they could never tell anyone else they listened to such broadcasts. This specific model was so sophisticated that by pressing one button it would immediately switch to the previous station, so, whenever there was a knock at the door, the family would quickly press this button to switch the radio to an acceptable German station. Such precautions were essential when the penalties for transgression were very severe, even at the start of the war.

The *Freiburger Zeitung* of 29 June 1940 went to great lengths to vilify the numerous citizens across Germany who had been sentenced to up to five years in prison for listening to foreign news reports and for disseminating such lies to others, thereby endangering the resistance of the German people. By 1944, the penalty for such illicit activity could easily have been death!

Nonetheless, as if to justify the severity of the penalties for such transgressions within Germany, it is somewhat ironic that the German press was just as willing to report on the sentences being imposed on citizens in Britain for any 'non-patriotic' behaviour:

 London reacts with prison!

The *Freiburger Zeitung* of 11 July 1940 reported that:

Such is the nervousness in England over the fear of spies – that foreigners are getting heavily penalised for the smallest of crimes – such as a Swedish citizen who got three months in prison for not informing the police on time of his change of address, or a nurse in Bristol who received a five year sentence because she mentioned on a postcard that she listened to German radio. A porter earned a similar sentence for the same crime and another woman received two years for having a map which could have been of use to the enemy. Another man was punished for lighting a cigarette during an air raid and another was given fourteen days for making fascist-friendly crosses.

What, of course, it does not mention is that Germany had been transmitting its own *Germany Calling* propaganda broadcasts to Britain in English via Lord Haw-Haw from as early as September 1939. For a while, they even ran a *Radio Caledonia – The Voice of Scotland* service that promoted the case for Scotland's independence from the rest of the United Kingdom, and which continued broadcasting until August 1942.

The German press also failed to mention that it was not, in fact, a crime for British citizens to listen to such broadcasts. It was only a crime to spread malicious rumours or to report defeatist talk.

VILIFICATION OF THE ENEMY

The air battles and bombings continued almost ceaselessly throughout July, August and September 1940. It was a war of attrition – a battle of wills between two stubborn opponents – and, in this competition at least, pure geography and, in particular, the distance the Germans had to fly to reach their targets, meant that the rivals were a little more equally matched.

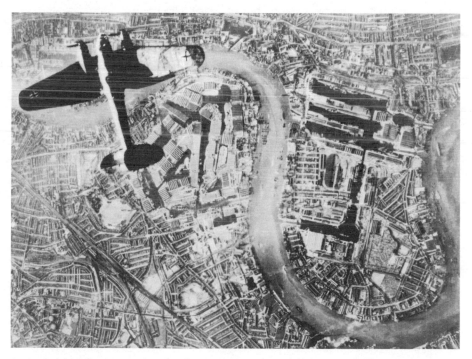

A Heinkel 111 flying over the Isle of Dogs in the East End of London on 7 September 1940.

Having for months repeatedly talked of annihilating battles in the air and of massive bombing raids across the whole of Britain, the German media showed a growing frustration that echoed the very views of the German High Command and the thoughts of the German people. How could the British possibly continue to resist when they had reportedly already suffered so much damage and destruction? The German media often quoted liberally from other apparently neutral newspapers, as if to convince everyone that Britain's determination to fight on was sheer madness.

Such was the intensity of the air raids on Britain and the reported scale of British losses in terms of ruined factories, munition works, docks, ships and aircraft that there was a real danger that the ordinary German might actually have started to feel some sympathy for the plucky British for continuing to resist when the odds were stacked so heavily against them. There was a growing respect for a worthy enemy, an enemy who, after all, had never been quite as insistent on the full satisfaction of the terms of the infamous Treaty of Versailles as were the French who, throughout history, had been Germany's more natural enemy.

The German leaders simply could not allow any such feelings of empathy to develop, so every opportunity was taken to remind German readers and newsreel viewers that these were simply retribution attacks for British 'outrages'. After all, it was Britain that had started the war. Britain was out to bring Germany to its knees and, by enforcing a naval blockade around northern Europe, was causing starvation and despair to millions of innocent people. The whole reason for the Germans being in France at all was to provide Germany with the necessary security to carry out a war forced upon it by England. British pilots were portrayed as little better than air pirates who, at the behest of Churchill, were committing repeated war crimes such as the deliberate bombing of civilian homes, schools and hospitals:

3 hospital buildings destroyed – 9 children killed

German headlines such as these certainly hit the mark, and the seeming validity of the German claims was even more effective when supporting newsreel reports showed hard evidence of the extent of damage to civilian property in Germany. All of this was compared constantly to the German assertion that German planes only ever bombed military targets in Britain.

The *Wochenschau* report of 25 September went to great lengths to give the impression that the British were attacking civilian targets deliberately. This film revealed the destruction caused by the British to the Bethel Hospital near Bielefeld on the night of 18 September, during which twelve handicapped children were killed. The film showed a huge Red Cross on the main hospital building, implying that there should have been no grounds for confusion. The incident was undoubtedly an accident in which one bomb had gone astray, but this did not prevent Goebbels from denouncing the bombing as a particularly gruesome act of terror by 'murderous British fire-raisers'.

Naturally, the report failed to mention that the damage took place at night when the Red Cross markings would have been almost impossible to detect, but telling only half the truth is one of the secrets of successful propaganda.

Generally, the German newsreel reports throughout this period were very effective. They frequently contained some action footage of a bombing raid on harbours, industrial plants or airports and invariably concluded with the stirring war song, 'Bombs on England'.

Nevertheless, it would be wrong to conclude that any propagandistic disparagement of the enemy – whether or not the claims were valid – was confined solely to the German media. As early as 24 June, *Movietone News* was describing in graphic detail an air raid on England, and the film contained harrowing shots of a ruined school near Southend and a row of damaged houses in a Cambridgeshire town. On 30 July, there was a report from the British Air Ministry condemning the Germans for using seaplanes bearing the Red Cross emblem to fly reconnaissance missions over British convoys.

The *British Pathé* newsreel of 5 September showed British fighters successfully shooting down a German plane, and the accompanying commentary used very evocative language to describe the enemy. The German pilots were described as:

Göring's young rats who now seem to favour the machine-gunning of any British airman bailing out by parachute as an added experience to the bombing and gunning of women and children.

The same newsreel contained a further item entitled 'Nazis' war on children', which contained footage of the survivors of a torpedoed evacuee ship and referred to a 'bestial U-boat commander' and Hitler's attempts to drown innocent children.

Somewhat ironically, just as the German press was swift to praise the accuracy of their bombers over London, the British newsreel reports were equally keen to emphasise that the British were successfully bombing Berlin and that, unlike the Germans, the British were not dropping their bombs at random but were ensuring that they hit the right targets.

This was pure propaganda. In reality, we now know that neither side was able to guarantee precision bombing and that civilian targets were frequently hit by both sides, even if they had not been deliberately sought out. In fact, post-war studies have confirmed the accuracy of censored reports produced at the time, which concluded that between May 1940 and May 1941, only around 5 per cent of British bombers setting out on a night raid dropped their bombs within 5 miles of their actual target. Therefore, to boast of the accuracy of British bombers in August

1940 was rather ridiculous. Indeed, initial German night bombing was actually far more accurate because of their *Knickebein* and subsequent beam systems that guided their pilots directly to the target, albeit the British were soon able to employ very effective countermeasures that reduced the capability of such devices.

PROGRESS OF THE AIR BATTLE OVER BRITAIN

Modern historians tend to divide the Battle of Britain into four principal phases. First, there were the battles over the English Channel, which lasted from approximately 10 July to 11 August 1940; second, the attacks on the coastal airfields from 12 to 23 August; then the specific focus on all military airfields from 24 to 6 September and finally, the bombing of suburban areas across Britain from 7 September. Although there were numerous key actions within that period, there are two dates that merit particular attention, namely 15 August and 15 September.

On 15 August, the Germans launched more than 2,000 sorties, with bombers and fighters being scrambled from bases extending from Norway to the north-west of France, and with targets ranging from Scotland to the south-west of England. The attacks were to stretch the British defences to the full and would result in some of the heaviest air battles in the whole war. So, just how was this event reported by the press?

For the Germans, there had been growing excitement in the days leading up to 15 August that the raids on Britain were about to move up a gear. There was a general expectation that Britain would soon capitulate, and the overriding question was whether the surrender of Britain would bring peace or whether the successful German armed forces would then turn their attention elsewhere.

Nevertheless, the statistics displayed proudly in the *Völkischer Beobachter* headlines of 17 August were truly astounding:

 The Most Successful Day in the Air War Against England!
143 planes and 21 Barrage Balloons Destroyed

And all of this was achieved with only thirty-two German planes 'not making it back' and nine German airmen and one British pilot rescued by their sea patrols. If this sounded like a major victory for the Germans, then their readers would have been somewhat perplexed if they had read the headlines in the *Daily Express* for the very same day:

 UP, UP, UP! 144 DOWN
They came in hundreds – this morning their wreckage litters our coasts

In their small print, British readers would discover that they had lost only twenty-seven fighters in the process. Such was the divergence between the two sets of press reports that *The Times* was to claim in its editorial of 17 August that the German authorities were now waiting half an hour or so after the release of British statistics before giving their own figures and then, more or less, reversing them. This seems a reasonable assertion until you discover that virtually the same headlines had appeared in the afternoon editions of German newspapers the previous day so, while not impossible, the Germans would have had to be very swift to have waited until they heard the British statistics before concocting and publishing their own figures. Nevertheless, the same *Times* article concluded that no credence should be given to the German reporting since the Germans had already been so far wide of the mark in other areas, such as their claims for ships sunk. To illustrate this point, *The Times* asserted further that, since the start of war, the Germans had claimed to have sunk or seriously damaged seventeen more battleships, three more aircraft carriers and twenty-one more cruisers than Britain had actually possessed the previous September!

So, what was the truth about the air battle on 15 August? While both sides were fairly wide of the mark in terms of actual numbers, it now transpires that the raids on that day did, indeed, culminate in one of the heaviest defeats for the Germans in the whole campaign, with the loss of seventy-six aircraft and 128 men, compared with thirty-five aircraft and eleven men lost by the RAF. Damage to military targets caused by the bombing was minimal.

Such was the euphoria in Britain about German losses on this and subsequent days that there was already talk of Britain having 'won the first round'. However, the air battle was far from over and, with the Germans' change of tactics to the bombing of towns and cities by early September, the next major assault was to take place on 15 September. Göring was still convinced that a sustained massive attack – and more than 1,000 German sorties took place that day – would overwhelm British Fighter Command completely.

Once again, his attack failed. While there was widespread bombing of London and some damage to local utilities and railway lines, little of real military significance was destroyed – and all at the cost of another sixty-one German planes and ninety-three airmen. British losses were thirty-one aircraft and sixteen airmen.

Once again, press reporting by both sides of the size of their respective hits and losses was somewhat detached from reality. *The Times* reported:

 175 Raiders Shot Down – 30 British Fighters Lost
The RAF inflicted on the German Air Force one of the most Severe Defeats it has yet suffered!

In subsequent days, the British press eventually increased German losses to 185 and British losses were reduced to twenty-five. For once, even the German press was obliged to curtail its normally extravagant claims regarding British losses:

 In Spite of Bad Weather: Uninterrupted Air Raids
79 Enemy Planes Wiped Out – 43 of our own Planes Missing

From the reporting of these two days alone, we can see a general trend emerging. On many occasions, both sides massively overestimated the size of enemy losses while, at the same time, they under-reported their own losses – although, to be fair, the British were usually a lot more accurate in the recording of their own losses.

Nonetheless, if, for the reasons previously given, there might well have been good justification for both sides finding it difficult to give an accurate assessment of successes and failures on any specific day, surely it would have been harder to conceal the truth over a longer period? Sadly, this was simply not the case, and the same trends were equally apparent in British reporting of even monthly events.

So, looking at the statistics for the whole of August 1940, *The Times* declared proudly:

The number of enemy aircraft destroyed in air attacks on this country during this month now exceeds 1,000!

Was this correct? No. In fact, the Germans lost only 694 planes, but, admittedly, this still compared very positively with the number of British planes destroyed, namely, 382, and even more so in terms of the total of pilots and aircrew killed – 993 versus 176.

Likewise, for the month of September, *The Times* claimed on 2 October that the Germans had lost 1,000 planes and probably 3,000 airmen during the preceding month. In reality, the Germans had lost 629 aircraft and 829 airmen.

There is no doubt that during this campaign, there were occasions when the British newsreel gave completely misleading information. Take, for example, the *British Movietone* newsreel report of 19 August. Under the title of 'Britain's air toll of Nazi Blitzkrieg', the presenter talked of 169 German planes having been shot down and continued by raising the specific question:

How long can the Nazi Air Force stand such losses which on August 15 were in the ratio of 5:1? The Germans need to strike now before Britain's output of aircraft becomes overwhelming.

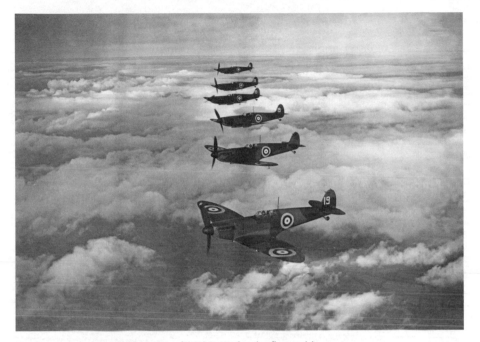

Spitfire patrol over Britain in October 1940. *battleofbritainblog.com*

As we have seen already, the claims by the British for German losses on 15 August were greatly exaggerated and, while still a significant victory for the British, the actual ratio of aircraft losses on that day was closer to 2:1. Likewise, while some doubt was raised as to whether Germany could continue to endure such losses, it is somewhat ironic that for the week ending 17 August, Britain had actually lost seventy-eight more fighters than it had produced that week. This shortfall in production was to be repeated in the fortnight up to 7 September – a point at which the British were also desperately running short of pilots. The Germans were actually able to replace their lost aircraft fairly comfortably, but their far greater loss of airmen was disturbing, and the urgent question that was eventually posed by the officers of the German High Command themselves was whether there was any point in continuing to sustain such losses of men and material if no military advantage was being gained.

In Guy Hamilton's epic 1969 film, *Battle of Britain*, there is a very moving sequence close to the end of the film when Air Chief Marshal Dowding, played by Sir Laurence Olivier, receives a phone call from the Air Minister, asking whether he has any evidence to support the amazing numbers of destroyed German planes being reported by the British. The problem was that the Americans were seriously questioning the validity of the claims. Dowding hesitates and then responds, 'I'm not very interested in propaganda. If we are right they'll give up and if we're wrong they'll be in London in a week.'

This comment was absolutely correct for, whatever the reality behind the actual statistics and the propaganda to be gained by giving inflated accounts of their respective successes, the plain truth was that the German losses were very high and, while they could have been sustained for some time, the bombing raids were simply not having the desired effect. Hindsight suggests that if the Germans had continued their attacks on the airfields, rather than switching to the bombing of cities, then they might well have gained an upper hand in the air, but they were not to realise this at the time. After an air campaign of more than three months, the British were no closer to surrender, and the prospect of a sea-borne invasion was more remote than ever.

For the British, 15 September 1940 was generally regarded as signifying the defeat of the Luftwaffe and a key turning point in the war, and Churchill was later to declare this as Battle of Britain Day. Rather defensively, and perhaps with some degree of foresight, the *Völkischer Beobachter* of 10 September had already declared:

 It is a mistake to call the present action the Battle of Great Britain [...] it is merely the Battle of London from which the Battle of Great Britain will develop.

It was as if the authorities were trying to make excuses as to why final victory had not yet been achieved, especially since such high expectations of a short war had been raised following the speed of the defeat of Poland, Belgium, Holland and France.

However, any talk of a swift victory could only ever have been wishful thinking because, after the action of 15 September, even Hitler was finally forced to accept that all was not going according to plan, and this culminated in his formal announcement to his generals on 17 September that the invasion of Britain was to be postponed indefinitely.

Of course, this was not a decision that was reported to the German nation as a whole, and the German populace remained ignorant of the fact there had ever been a specific Battle of Britain, let alone that the German Air Force had lost such a battle.

To compensate for the lack of substantive military success against Britain, the German press thereafter was forced to concentrate on subjective reports of how discontent in London was growing and how the morale of Londoners had reached a low point. England was described as being lost and waiting in vain for some miracle to come to its rescue.

Nor would many British civilians have felt that the war in the air had been won. For the British, it was a constant struggle for survival against the incessant bombing. The Italian Air Force was brought in to assist the hard-pressed German Luftwaffe, and relentless night-time bombing raids were to continue until May 1941.

However, in reality, the immediate danger of invasion had passed by the autumn of 1940, the focus of the war had moved elsewhere and the Luftwaffe would soon be faced with a far greater priority following the German invasion of the Soviet Union in June 1941.

5

SAINT-NAZAIRE – 'THE GREATEST RAID EVER MADE'

INTRODUCTION

Throughout the early months of 1942, the British press reported a whole series of ambitious raids made by British forces on Nazi-held locations across occupied Europe.

First, in January, there was confirmation of earlier attacks on a number of occupied Norwegian ports by British commandos and Norwegian troops. This resulted in the capture of a number of prisoners and the destruction of an enemy plane and vessel – all with minimal casualties on the Allies' side. Then, in February, there was a parachute landing at Bruneval in the north of France and the successful capture of German radar equipment.

Whatever the underlying objective of such raids, and regardless of their actual success, there is no doubt that even the declaration that such attacks were taking place at all helped raise morale on the home front and forced the Germans to continue to hold back men and resources that might otherwise have been committed to the Eastern Front.

However, in the spring of 1942, one of the most daring and possibly one of the most bizarre and perilous raids was made on the docks at Saint-Nazaire, at the estuary of the River Loire, on the west coast of France. Against all odds, the raid was undoubtedly successful in terms of the achievement of its primary objectives, and the bravery of the men involved in the attack resulted in the awarding of five Victoria Crosses, which was more than would be earned in any other single operation in the whole war. Nevertheless, neither side released the full facts about the raid, either at that time or in the weeks and months which followed – even though by then the truth was most certainly known.

So, what were the real facts about Operation Chariot – which came to be regarded in British military circles as 'the greatest raid ever made' – and were there good reasons why even the British press gave rather contradictory and inaccurate accounts about it?

OPERATION CHARIOT

By March 1942, Britain had been at war with Germany for some thirty months and, although the imminent threat of the invasion of Britain had passed and the entry of America into the war did provide some solace, Britain was still involved in a desperate bid for survival. The convoys carrying much-needed food and supplies to Britain were being decimated by U-boat attacks in the Atlantic. Furthermore, Germany still possessed the largest and most heavily armed battleship in Europe in the form of the *Tirpitz*. While the *Tirpitz* was lurking in a fjord in Norway, the British were only too aware of the havoc and destruction it could wreak if it were to take to the open sea. In one engagement in May of the previous year, its sister ship, *Bismarck*, had not only managed to sink the British battlecruiser, HMS *Hood*, but had also damaged the battleship, HMS *Prince of Wales*, severely. Nevertheless, *Bismarck* had suffered some damage in the engagement and was obliged to head for the port of Saint-Nazaire to effect repairs, as this was the only convenient port outside Germany that had a dry dock large enough to handle such a vessel. Ultimately, through a subsequent hit on its steering gear by a torpedo fired from a Fairey Swordfish biplane, *Bismarck* was so incapacitated as to be unable to flee, was subjected to relentless shell fire from the Royal Navy and was eventually scuttled by its crew when its sinking was already all but inevitable.

Notwithstanding this achievement, the British military recognised that they had been extremely unfortunate and were determined to do all that they could to dissuade *Tirpitz* from putting to the open sea. It was believed that if the dry dock at Saint-Nazaire, the so-called Normandie Dock, could be destroyed, then the lack of any suitable repair facility on the west coast of France would dissuade *Tirpitz* from taking any part in the war in the Atlantic.

Churchill asked for the destruction of the dock to be given top priority. The only problem was that the dry dock at Saint-Nazaire was very close to the city itself and, given the inaccuracy of Allied bombing, it was almost inevitable that any major bombing raid would result in the deaths of hundreds of innocent French civilians, which would have been a propaganda fiasco. Likewise, the port itself was heavily defended against attack from the sea, and torpedo nets had been installed to prevent any attack from submarines or motor launches.

Eventually, Lord Mountbatten, the Chief of Combined Operations, aided by information provided by the French Resistance, produced a draft plan that involved a small naval force entering the port, led by a destroyer that would ram the caisson or lock gate. The bow of the destroyer would be crammed full of almost 5 tons of explosives, which would be set to detonate several hours after it had struck the gate. At the same time, the naval force would be supported by a team of commandos that would set about demolishing other key port installations. Immediately prior to the raid, the RAF was to bomb the surrounding area with the intention of distracting the German defenders from what was happening at sea.

It was recognised immediately that the mission had only a very small chance of success, and that the safe recovery of many of the commandos and naval personnel involved in the raid would be unlikely. For this reason, the Royal Navy refused initially to provide any destroyer for the raid – as it could not afford to lose a single ship, let alone for such a speculative venture – and the RAF indicated that it would be able to provide only around thirty-five aircraft rather than the 100 initially requested.

Nevertheless, the Royal Navy eventually relented and agreed that the obsolete First World War American destroyer, USS *Buchanan*, which had been given to the British under the Lend-Lease Agreement and renamed HMS *Campbeltown*, could be used to ram the dock gates and carry the necessary explosives concealed in concrete in its hold. By removing two of her four smoke stacks and altering the shape and size of the remaining funnels, it was hoped that the German defenders would be misled into believing that it was, in fact, a German destroyer.

By destroying the dry dock at Saint-Nazaire, it was hoped that the Germans would be reluctant to let battleships including the *Tirpitz* take any part in the war in the Atlantic.
Washington Navy Museum

The naval force eventually set to sea on the afternoon of Thursday 26 March 1942. Apart from HMS *Campbeltown*, it consisted of two Hunt Class Destroyers, HMS *Tynedale* and HMS *Atherstone*, the submarine HMS *Sturgeon*, Motor Gun Boat *314*, Motor Torpedo Boat (MTB) *74*, twelve wooden motor launches to assist with transporting the 241 commandos and four additional motor launches, each armed with two torpedoes. One of the motor launches was to break down with engine trouble before it reached the Loire Estuary.

The additional destroyers eventually broke away from the main flotilla off the coast of Saint-Nazaire, while the submarine acted as a directional beacon to guide the remaining force towards its target.

The bombing raid began around midnight on 27 March but was hampered by fog and low cloud, and it is now believed that, rather than distracting the German ground forces, it actually alerted them to the fact that something was amiss. Nevertheless, the naval force made good progress. When they were eventually challenged by shore parties, through a combination of bluff, the use of captured naval codes and the disguised appearance of HMS *Campbeltown* (now flying a German war ensign), the flotilla was able to get within 2,000yd of its final target, before it came under heavy fire from German shore batteries.

Hoisting the White Ensign, HMS *Campbeltown* and supporting vessels were then forced to return fire. Under a hail of bullets and explosions all along its deck, HMS *Campbeltown* pressed on regardless, bursting through the protective torpedo net and eventually slamming into the steel caisson of the dry dock, with its prow coming to an abrupt halt over the dock gate at exactly 1.34 a.m. Meanwhile, the accompanying motor launches, which were attempting to disembark their commandos at pre-arranged landing points, came under sustained fire. Many boats were unable to reach their target points before being set alight by enemy gunfire. Their chances of success were not assisted by the fact that each launch carried two exposed 500-gallon auxiliary tanks of fuel on its upper deck.

As planned, the commandos alighting from HMS *Campbeltown* did manage to destroy the pumping house and winding huts beside the dry dock, and the surviving commandos who managed to land from the remaining motor launches set about fixing explosives to other gates and bridges around the port. However, by 2.30 a.m., and with their tasks completed, it soon became obvious that, with so many motor launches permanently crippled and the escape routes of many of the others blocked, most of the shore parties were going to have to find another way home. Indeed, only three of the motor launches were to make it back to Britain.

In the ensuing hours, fierce running battles raged in the streets around the port, with the commandos having to take refuge in local houses. With the approach of daylight and their ammunition expended, most of the survivors were forced to surrender, although five commandos did manage to escape the town and eventually returned to Britain via Spain.

Of the 611 sailors and commandos who had entered the Loire Estuary, 169 were killed – mainly in the river battles – 215 were taken prisoner and only 227 made it back home. The losses were truly staggering.

Had it all been worth it? Had the objectives been achieved?

HMS *Campbeltown* had certainly hit the caisson, but the lock gates had been only slightly damaged. As a consequence, the German defenders genuinely believed that the British had underestimated the amount of force needed to destroy the gates and thought that the concrete-filled bow had been there only to add extra punch to the ramming action. Likewise, while MTB *74* had also fired two torpedoes at the lock gate of the old entrance leading to the Saint-Nazaire basin and submarine pens, these had not exploded on impact but had simply sunk to lie at the foot of the gates awaiting delayed detonation. With the main force having withdrawn by 3 a.m. and the bulk of on-shore fighting having ceased by daylight, the Germans were convinced the attack had failed.

Over the next few hours, hundreds of German soldiers, officers, military experts and civilians were to descend on the port and clamber over the ship to inspect the damage, take photographs and collect souvenirs. Eventually, and to the complete surprise of the Germans, whose experts had declared the ship safe and who had failed to discover the deadly cargo hidden in the bow, the explosives in HMS *Campbeltown* detonated at 11.35 a.m. (local time) – many hours later than expected. This time, the outer lock gate was completely destroyed, but hundreds of people in the immediate vicinity of the explosion were also killed. Against all odds, the raid had, nevertheless, been a military success.

HMS *Campbeltown* photographed lying across the lock gates of the Saint-Nazaire dry dock prior to the detonation of the explosives hidden in its bow. *Le Grand Blockhaus Museum, Batz-sur-Mer/BABild 101II-MW-3724-02/Schaaf*

MEDIA COVERAGE OF THE RAID

When it came to press coverage of the event, the Germans were the first to react. Given that the raid began only late on Friday 27 March and that fighting in the port did not cease until the early hours of 28 March, it is quite astonishing that a regional paper such as the *Freiburger Zeitung* was still able to carry the following headlines in its weekend edition:

 Unsuccessful British Landing Attempt

Troop Units Landed at the Mouth of the Loire Surrounded and Wiped Out

Enemy Suffers Heavy Ship Losses

No Damage inflicted on the U-Boat Base at St Nazaire

The accompanying short article reported how, during the night of 27–28 March, English forces had attempted to land troops at the mouth of the Loire to attack the U-boat base at Saint-Nazaire and destroy the port's lock gates. This report claimed that, under heavy fire from German shore batteries, an old American destroyer, laden with explosives and which was supposed to ram one of the lock gates, was blown into the air before it could reach its target.

It also asserted that, apart from the destroyer, nine motorboats and four enemy torpedo boats were destroyed in the action; that the enemy left behind more than 100 prisoners in addition to a number of dead and that not a single naval vessel was destroyed on the German side, nor was any damage inflicted on the U-boat base.

All of this information was, of course, provided by German High Command, and the only reason it was able to appear so early was because the weekend edition was not printed until 28 March. Given that this first report must have been prepared at very short notice – possibly even before dawn – some aspects of it were remarkably accurate and especially the statistics referring to British losses in terms of naval vessels destroyed. In the darkness, it was also just possible that the Germans genuinely mistook the various explosions they heard – mainly from the British motorboats that had exposed fuel tanks on their decks – as emanating from the main ship.

Nevertheless, the Germans were seemingly still unaware of just how many British servicemen were killed, and their estimate of prisoners taken was less than half the actual figure.

In any event, this early German report gave the clear impression of a comprehensive and humiliating defeat for the British and gave no indication that the dry dock gates had been completely destroyed.

However, in this particular case, the report was probably not designed to be a piece of pure propaganda but was based on the sketchy facts available at the time. As we have already seen in the chapter on the Battle of Britain, there is no doubt that, in the fog of war, due to poor communications and a delay in accurate information being collated and sent back to base, it was often difficult to appreciate exactly what had taken place at any one location immediately after the event and, if we are to be generous, it could be argued that this was exactly what happened here.

At the time that this newspaper was going to press, it was likely that it was still late on the Saturday morning. As we know, the dry dock gate was actually rammed at around 1.30 a.m. It would now appear that some of the explosions heard around 4 a.m. were either the delayed detonation explosives used to scuttle HMS *Campbeltown* or exploding fuel tanks, so it is quite possible that a) the Germans did consider the U-boat pens to have been the main target, b) that they did believe, at that point, the destroyer that had smashed into the lock gates had not done much damage and c) the Germans genuinely had not sustained much loss of life, at that point. Indeed, to be accurate, virtually no damage was inflicted on the U-boat pens themselves, but this had never been the primary target.

However, no such leeway or excuse can be extended to the further German press coverage that would appear by the Monday. By that time, the German High Command would certainly have known of the delayed explosion of the destroyer at 11.35 a.m. on Saturday. The destruction caused by that explosion was so severe that the dry dock was to remain out of commission until two years after the end of the war and more than 360 Germans were to be killed in the explosion, including sixty high-ranking officers, who were inspecting the ship at the very moment of the explosion. So, it was pure propaganda and entirely misleading for the German press to persevere with such defiant headlines as:

 The Defeat at the Mouth of the Loire
Military operation ordered by Stalin completely thwarted

This article continued by giving a much more detailed account of the raid as presented by the German High Command; this can be summarised as follows:

- Enemy planes dropped bombs over area shortly after midnight but did not cause any damage (fundamentally true)
- Idea was to distract defenders' attention from the sea (true)
- Meanwhile, British naval forces were discovered in the Loire basin (true)
- Destroyer headed for lock gates but was destroyed in a huge explosion before it could reach its target (completely untrue)
- Those who did land were soon shot or captured (partly true)

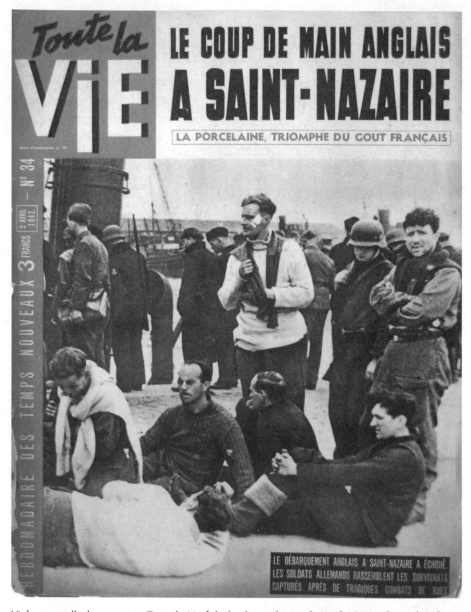

Vichy-controlled magazine *Toute la Vie* falsely claimed in its 2 April 1942 edition that the British attack at Saint-Nazaire had failed and that HMS *Campbeltown* had exploded at sea before it could reach the lock gates. *Le Grand Blockhaus Museum*

There was no mention of the subsequent late-morning explosion that did completely destroy the lock gates, killed hundreds of Germans and caused the damaged shell of the destroyer to be swept into the dry dock itself. Of course, having initially downplayed the effectiveness of the raid to such a great degree, there would have been a complete loss of face if the German authorities had been forced to admit that the attack had, after all, been successful.

Instead, in another report, the British were mocked for allowing themselves to be dictated to by Stalin, and Churchill was accused of being a poor commander and even poorer at propaganda. The headline in the *Völkischer Beobachter* certainly did not mince its words:

Churchill's amazing Pack of Lies about his St Nazaire Fiasco

He was blamed for allegedly lying about the success of this mission and initially playing down losses in terms of men and ships, before finally having to admit that the operation 'had not been without losses' and expressing only the hope that the mission had been successful.

Throughout, the German press firmly placed the emphasis on the fact that the U-boat base had not been damaged and that the destroyer blew up before it could reach the lock gates. Nevertheless, if it is believed that even these later German newspaper articles might still have been subject to timing delays, there was absolutely no excuse for the content of a short newsreel created by the *Wochenschau* team and initially screened to the world's journalists on 10 April – a full thirteen days after the event.

This newsreel was probably shot largely in the late-morning of 28 March. It showed British commandos being flushed out of a block of flats – presumably a post-event scene specially staged for the camera, as all reports suggest that those soldiers and sailors forced to surrender had done so before 8 a.m., whereas this film was clearly shot in bright daylight. There were poignant images of British dead lying scattered on the streets and of the smouldering wrecks of British motor launches in the water. Most notably, there were several images of HMS *Campbeltown* clearly displayed as having rammed the docks but with its bow having been forced up into the air and its steering house now in line with the dock gate. The ship was clearly intact, so the earlier reports in the German press that the destroyer had blown up before it reached its target were plainly untrue. The very fact that Germans were shown clambering over the ship, and two sailors were proudly displaying the fake German ensign, which the British had used to disguise their destroyer, proves once again that the claim that HMS *Campbeltown* had exploded into smithereens before it reached its target was clearly untrue.

Two German sailors proudly displaying the fake German ensign that HMS *Campbeltown* had been flying. *Le Grand Blockhaus Museum*

It has to be asked what the Germans hoped to achieve with such misleading reports at this time, since the world's press had already seen aerial photographs of the docks after the raid, and they clearly showed that the lock gate at one end had completely disappeared.

What is perhaps even more surprising is that the Germans did not make more propaganda out of the tactics adopted by the British in the raid. Several German feature films at the time condemned the British for sailing their ships under a false flag and then raising the British ensign only after they had opened fire on an unsuspecting target. So, the fact that the British had tried to disguise their destroyer as a German vessel and had flown a German naval flag until they had virtually reached their target could easily have been portrayed as another example of the 'unsporting' actions of the British. Likewise, the death of 360 people when the explosives in the ship detonated could have been seen as cold-blooded murder – especially since the captured British officers could have warned the Germans that this was likely to happen, and many innocent French civilians were also killed in the explosion. However, there was certainly never any mention of this in the German press, and the only reason must have been that the German authorities did not wish to highlight the fact that the British mission had actually been a success.

BRITISH REPORTS

Were the British press any more accurate in their reporting of the raid? On 30 March, *The Times* carried the dramatic headlines:

Daring Combined Attack on St. Nazaire
Dock Gates and Harbour Works Wrecked

It continued by saying it had now received a graphic account from a press correspondent, who had accompanied the raid, which supported the earlier official statement that the main lock gates of the dry dock had been destroyed and that damage was also done to the entrance to the U-boat basin and to harbour installations – thus refuting German claims that the raid had failed to achieve its objective.

The accompanying editorial was rather confusing. On the one hand, it drew comparisons with a British raid on Zeebrugge on 23 April 1918 that attempted to block the exit of German U-boats to the Channel by sinking block ships in the Bruges Canal. On the other hand, it surmised that the intention of the raid had only been to put the base partly out of action for some months. Actually, the German press also made reference to this incident and, unlike the British report, correctly reminded its readers that the British attack in 1918 had been a complete failure. In fact, on that occasion the ships had been scuttled in the wrong place and more than 500 British servicemen were killed in the process.

However, what is perhaps most baffling in *The Times* of 30 March is the content of an accompanying article that contained full details of the communiqué issued by Combined Operations Headquarters the previous night.

This item appeared under the rather uninspiring sub-headlines:

Lock Gate Rammed
Cargo of Explosive

While this report confirmed that the dry dock was the primary objective of the raid and described how HMS *Campbeltown*, laden with 5 tons of delayed-action high explosive, had rammed the centre of the lock gate, there was absolutely no indication as to whether the explosives had actually detonated. It did talk of the successful demolition of the pumping station and dock-operating gear, and of two delayed-action torpedoes fired at the entrance to the U-boat basin. It even referred to the returning forces hearing a couple of explosions at 4 a.m., but it did not specify to what these explosives related.

Given that we now know that the explosives in the hold of the destroyer did not, in fact, detonate until late morning on 28 March, it is evident that even more than a day later, the military authorities in London were still uncertain whether the dry dock gates had been completely destroyed. They were waiting for photographic corroboration. In fact, this aerial confirmation was reported in the British press only on 31 March, with reproduced photographs actually appearing in newspapers on 1 April.

What this means is that at the point when the first reports appeared in the British press, while it was certainly known that the dock gates had been damaged, nobody could be sure of the extent of the damage. It was only the subsequent detonation of the explosives that completely destroyed the gates and caused what was left of the destroyer to be swept into the dock itself.

Therefore, it is fair to conclude that the bullish headlines appearing in the British newspapers on 30 March were rather misleading, since if the explosives had not actually detonated, then it was unlikely that the ramming damage to the gates would alone have put the dry dock itself out of commission for more than a matter of a few weeks or months.

Indeed, it was only in the later reports on 31 March and 1 April that reference was made to the photographic evidence that proved that the large lock gate had been completely destroyed.

However, what the British failed to do in this or, indeed, in any subsequent reports was to mention, in any detail at all, the frightful statistics in terms of British men and vessels lost in the completion of this operation. There was a far greater emphasis on panic-stricken Germans firing on friend and foe alike. The official report simply stated that:

Their task accomplished, our troops commenced to withdraw in motor-launches detailed for the purpose to re-join the covering force of destroyers. Enemy machine guns appear to have prevented the full withdrawal of some of our forces.

The report clearly gave the impression that most of the force did make it back, and there was no mention at all that fourteen out of seventeen MGBs and motor launches were lost in the process. *The Scotsman* of 30 March certainly admitted that while the raid had been successful, 'the cost has not been light', but this was the only passing reference to any casualties and, after 1 April, there was virtually no further mention of the raid in any British press reports.

Given the secrecy of the raid and the fact it took place in darkness, it is perhaps unsurprising that there was no Allied newsreel of the raid at the time, although there was a short *British Movietone* newsreel on 20 July 1942 that showed Commander Robert Ryder RN being awarded the Victoria Cross for the valour and devotion he had displayed during the raid on Saint-Nazaire.

CONCLUSION

The truth is that the raid itself was successful and was good for British morale; indeed, for those in military circles, the worldwide significance of the raid was clearly understood. The cost of success, however, was very high, and the whole story could not be made known to the British public.

It is doubtful whether, for the ordinary man-in-the-street at the time, the destruction of an empty dry dock in France would ever have appeared to be much of a victory over the Germans – even if there were some vague notion that this might stop the *Tirpitz* putting to sea. It might have been different if it could have been shown that the U-boat pens and even a few submarines had been destroyed, but this was simply not the case. Whatever the reality about the threat of the *Tirpitz* having been nullified, this would never be known for certain until the end of the war, and it would have appeared even more of a pyrrhic victory if the British press had been allowed to report that almost two-thirds of the attacking force had been killed or captured in the process.

To make matters worse, many innocent French civilians in the dock area and several French female partners of the German soldiers exploring HMS *Campbeltown* were killed outright when the ship exploded. There was further bloodshed when the delayed-detonation torpedoes that had lodged at the foot of the main basin lock gate exploded two days later, at 4.30 p.m., on 30 March. Such was the resulting anger and confusion among the German defenders and the belief that there were still British troops in the port that several Organisation Todt workers and civilians were shot by mistake by trigger-happy German soldiers. In the weeks that followed, the civilian population would be forced to move from their homes in the Old Town, before the whole area was systematically razed to the ground by the Germans.

Nonetheless, if some aspects of the raid were discomforting for the British, the raid was even more of a humiliation for the Germans. Having at first reported the raid was a failure, they simply could not afford to admit two days later that the dry dock had indeed been put out of action and that hundreds of German officers and soldiers had been killed in the process. It would have looked like complete incompetence on the part of the Germans, who actually had a force of more than 5,000 guarding the port. Hitler was furious, and the success of this raid was one of the driving forces behind the decree issued in October 1942 that, thereafter, any captured commandos from other missions were to be shot as spies.

Once again, the German public would be deceived as to the true course of the war. From the reports they were reading, it would have been easy for them to have believed that virtually all Allied attacks were resulting in glorious failures but, as will be seen in the following chapter, in one further major raid in 1942, the German press reports were, for once, to prove to be entirely accurate.

6

THE DIEPPE RAID

 It is not in the scheme of things to sit back with satisfaction at the results.

Allied newsreel

 In spite of the massive amount of men and materials, the landing on the coast turned into a complete catastrophe!

German newsreel

INTRODUCTION

Wednesday 19 August 1942. For the soldiers of the German 302nd Infantry Division this was likely to be just another ordinary day. However, by noon, they would be completely exhausted, and the date would remain forever etched on the memory as one of the greatest military disasters to beset the Allies, and in particular, the Canadians – in the whole of the Second World War. Out of an available landing force of more than 6,000 British, Canadian and other Allied troops, not many more than a third were to return to Britain, and more than 1,000 were to be killed outright. Notwithstanding the bravery shown by so many Allied soldiers, sailors and airmen that day, this raid was, to all intents and purposes a complete catastrophe. And yet, the British press was filled with stirring comments from the Canadian Prime Minister, heralding the operation as 'an opportunity to strike a telling blow at a Nazi stronghold'. So, what really happened that day and how was it reported by the respective news media at the time?

BACKGROUND TO THE DIEPPE RAID

While Japan's attack on Pearl Harbour on 7 December 1941 could be regarded as beneficial to the British in that it then gave the United States an excuse to enter the war, it was still going to be some time before America's involvement would help turn the tide against the success of the Axis Powers. Rommel continued to inflict defeats on the British Army in the desert war in North Africa; Singapore was soon to fall to the Japanese and, above all, the Germans were making rapid progress towards Moscow.

Morale on the Home Front was faltering, and the Allies badly needed some token victory to raise their spirits. Churchill was also coming under increasing pressure from Stalin to undertake some major operation in Europe that would provide tangible assistance to the Soviets by deterring the Germans from diverting more resources to the Eastern Front.

While a number of 'hit-and-run' commando raids were constantly taking place all along the coast of occupied Europe, in practice, these were often nothing more than 'bee stings' – certainly annoying but with no long-lasting effect on the Germans. Something far more dramatic was required and, through the spring of 1942, numerous proposals were submitted for consideration by Lord Louis Mountbatten and his staff.

Eventually, the decision was taken to authorise an amphibious attack on the port of Dieppe. The scale of the operation was truly breathtaking when considered against anything that had preceded it and would require close liaison and co-operation between the army, navy and air force. The raid was designated a 'reconnaissance in force'. The aim of the operation was to test the ability of the services to work together effectively and to inflict as much damage and chaos on the enemy as possible. There were a number of specific objectives, which included stealing some of the Germans' invasion barges for closer examination, capturing secret radar equipment and inspecting the beach defences.

OPERATION JUBILEE

The original raid was planned to take place in July 1942 but, because of bad weather, it was delayed until 19 August under the new code name Operation Jubilee.

The sheer size of the raid made it a logistical nightmare. It was going to involve the landing of more than 6,000 men, mainly Canadians from the 4th and 6th Infantry Brigades, but also supported by British Commandos, American Rangers and some Free French. The naval force required to effect these landings included eight destroyers, nine landing ships, forty-three escort ships and close to 200 landing craft of all types, including those designed to transport thirty Churchill tanks. Above all, the operation was to be supported by a number of British and American bomber squadrons and more than sixty squadrons of fighters, mainly consisting of Spitfires and Hurricanes. The aim was to force the German Luftwaffe to join in the fray, and the clash that ensued was to become the largest air battle since the Battle of Britain.

Outcome

Given the elaborate plan and its key objectives, what actually happened? Arguably, this turned out to be one of the saddest catastrophes suffered by the Allies in the whole of the Second World War. Just about everything that could go wrong did go wrong.

Failure to Damage Enemy Positions Prior to Landings

First, there was meant to be a pre-shelling of enemy positions by Allied naval destroyers, but as these ships had only 4in guns, they inflicted virtually no damage on the Germans' defensive emplacements. While this shortcoming had already been identified, the navy was simply not prepared to risk losing a capital ship armed with bigger guns to enemy submarines or bombers. Furthermore, as the RAF was due to bomb the German defences prior to the raid, it was considered that this aspect was already fully covered. Totally unaware of this issue, however, in the interim, the RAF had decided to cancel its planned bombing raid so as not to alert the Germans to the forthcoming attack. There was a complete lack of communication between the services.

Partial Failure to Land Intact, on Time and at the Right Place

Second, apart from the main frontal attack on the port of Dieppe itself, it was planned to disembark Allied troops on a number of beaches on either side of Dieppe, in advance of the main beach landings, to destroy the various heavy gun batteries protecting the town and to support the main attack. In practice, due to a combination of mishaps – including the left flank of the naval force being intercepted by German vessels while at sea; delays in disembarkation meaning that some groups arrived at their targets in broad daylight rather than in the dark; and the fact that one landing party arrived initially on the wrong side of a river estuary – only one group, the 4th Commando unit, led by Lord Lovat, actually managed to land successfully and blow up the Hess Gun Battery that it had been assigned to destroy. To a greater or lesser extent, all the other groups failed to achieve their objectives.

Underestimation of Strength of Enemy Positions

The port itself was far better protected than the Allies expected. In addition to the large coastal gun batteries, the beaches were heavily mined and wired. Machine guns – many well hidden from view – covered the whole shoreline. There were large numbers of anti-tank guns, and all exits from the beaches were blocked very effectively.

Delay in the Landing of Tanks and Failure to Move them off the Beaches

When it came to the attack on the main beach, one of the biggest obstacles confronting the landing troops was that they had to traverse two thick lines of barbed wire. Thirty of the new Churchill tanks were supposed to be landed from special tank-landing craft to give protective fire to the soldiers as they crossed the wire, but the tanks arrived far too late – long after the troops had actually landed – and so many lives were lost because of this delay. Because of their weight, many of the tanks themselves got bogged down on the pebbles and shingle and only fifteen tanks managed to leave the beach. To make matters worse, only one of these tanks managed to pass beyond the promenade, because the explosives and men designated to unblock the exits to the town beyond the beach had all been lost in the landings.

It was a complete disaster and, by late morning, the decision was taken to withdraw, but even that went badly with many escape routes blocked and further timing delays that resulted in even more casualties. In the end many troops had little option other than to surrender or face the certainty of being either wounded or killed.

The final tally was truly horrific. Of the 6,000 troops due to land, only 2,067 men returned to Britain. More than 1,000 men lay dead and between the Canadians and commandos, 3,637 men were either killed, wounded or captured. The Royal Navy was to lose 550 men and the RAF a further sixty-seven pilots. By comparison, the total German losses among soldiers, sailors and the Luftwaffe (including ground crew) were 712 men killed or wounded.

Legacy

It is often claimed that, despite the carnage, valuable lessons were learned from this disaster that were put to good use at the time of the D-Day landings but, as will be shown in Chapter 11, this is only partly true. While the raid did confirm that a full frontal attack on a French port would be suicidal, and thus the Allies would need to build their own Mulberry harbours, the services were still dogged by poor cross-communication, and attempts to find alternative ways of landing tanks on the beaches were still largely unsuccessful.

MEDIA COVERAGE OF THE RAID

While both sides reported the raid in detail in their press and newsreels it would often be difficult to guess that they were describing the same event.

British Newsreel Coverage

To the accompaniment of lively triumphant music, the nine-minute *British Movietone* newsreel of 27 August 1942 began with a caption that, while giving an overall upbeat assessment of the whole raid, also alerted the viewer to the lack of film footage of the main action:

Dieppe – In presenting this dramatic record of a Memorable Raid let us pay tribute to the gallant men who laid down their lives in furthering the Fight for Freedom of the United Nations. Cameras ashore were restricted because of the intensity of the action, but these pictures fully portray the brilliant co-operation of all services in this 'Reconnaissance in Force'.

The film coverage itself was indeed rather limited. While there were initial scenes of planes and ships preparing for the raid, and shots of landing craft of all types waiting to re-embark the soldiers they had landed, true action shots were restricted to bombers operating over Dieppe or the sight of distant planes crashing into the English Channel. Quite a lot of footage was devoted to a Canadian pilot being rescued from the sea who, despite the exhaustion of his ordeal, 'kept a cheery smile in reserve'. The film concluded with interviews with a variety of wounded soldiers of different nationalities back in Britain, all of whom made light of their injuries and were looking forward to getting back to the fight again.

Despite the dearth of images of the actual battle, the tone of the whole film was very upbeat and was full of inspiring commentary. There was repeated emphasis on the marvellous co-operation displayed between the army, navy and air force and, in particular, on the support provided to the army and navy by the RAF in what was such a significant air battle. Praise was lavished on the Canadians and commandos who 'fought like lions' and who 'by patient training, by careful planning and by sheer guts cracked open the Germans' supposed impregnable defences staying ashore and destroying and killing for 9 hours'.

Regardless of the lack of solid facts, the commentator was always keen to give the impression the raid was a great success with such lines as:

 We can certainly take heart from this attack [...] We can be sure the force which landed struck a very hard blow [...] The German (air) losses were certainly as great – probably greater than our own.

Allied losses were consistently played down and were often included in a throwaway comment or attached to a more positive observation:

 Many gallant men lost their lives and others were captured of course, but, as for the rest, the ships which had waited all day brought them safely back.

Throughout, the triumphant exciting background music helped reinforce this positive impression of the whole action. *British Pathé News* also produced a shorter seven-and-a-half-minute newsreel of the action that contained much of the same footage but concentrated even more on the air war and was prepared to give some actual

Wrecked landing craft abandoned at Dieppe. *The Dover Historian/Ron Akines*

figures for Allied and German losses. Once again, the tone was upbeat, giving the impression that the raid was a great success, stressing the indefatigable courage of the armed forces and playing down any danger with the typical British humour of understatement. There was one clip of a soldier returning with a huge hole in his helmet, where the accompanying comment was 'Gosh – who did that? Mice?'

The other addition to this report was praise for the restraint shown by the people of Dieppe in heeding advice not to assist the Allies so that the Germans would have no excuse for any blood-letting in reprisal. We will discover in later newspaper reports that the Germans actually set aside money to help pay for the repairs of civilian property damaged by the Allies during their attack on Dieppe. The final postscript was in some ways even more inspiring than the *Movietone* newsreel:

When we hit out again we need no finer soldiers than these, we ask for no better seamen than the sailors who for centuries have ruled the seas and we seek no nobler airmen – Europe awaits them.

British Press Reports

Whereas newsreel reports were not released until more than a week after the raid, press reports appeared the very next day. The content of these was often dependent on official communiqués from Combined Operations Headquarters or censored articles submitted by local journalists, and it meant that details of the raid were altered or clarified in later days as more information became available.

With the exception of the reporting of aircraft losses on both sides, what is apparent throughout was the complete lack of factual information concerning the number of men or amount of equipment involved or of losses incurred by either side. The key headlines of *The Times* of 20 August 1942 were simply:

 Nine-Hour Raid on Dieppe Area
Tanks And Troops in Heavy Fighting
Time Schedule Kept – Many Objectives Destroyed

Despite an admission of heavy casualties and that some tanks had been lost, the editorial was still keen to give an upbeat assessment describing the story of the raid as 'heartening news'. Equally surprising is the fact that by 21 August, and, despite a continued lack of hard facts from the Allied side, *The Times* was prepared to print the German version of the raid, which was full of distressing statistics for its readers:

 Enemy landing troops wiped out; all 28 tanks landed being destroyed; initial estimates of 1,500 prisoners taken; 112 Allied planes shot down against a total of 35 German planes; only 400 German losses.

German soldiers were happy to pose on one of the many wrecked British tanks left abandoned on the beach at Dieppe. *Wikimedia Commons/S. Pallad*

There was no attempt to insert a quotation from any British Government spokesman refuting the German version, and we can only assume that it had been included in the hope that its content would be considered so far-fetched as to lose all credibility. In order to add further doubt as to the validity of the German reports, items were included from Vichy sources in Paris, confirming that the Germans had suffered heavy losses and that the British estimate of ninety-one German aircraft being destroyed was correct. In fact, the earlier British report had actually claimed that eighty-two planes were shot down and a further 100 German planes had *probably* been destroyed, whereas we now know that the total number of German planes destroyed and damaged was only seventy-two.

In subsequent days, there was a recognition in comments from the Commander-in-Chief of the 1st Canadian Army that a heavy price had been paid by their troops, although still no concrete figures were given. But the sacrifices were still considered worthwhile because 'a powerful and resounding blow has been struck in the just cause for which we fight'. There was an increasing emphasis on the fact that even heavier losses had been suffered by the Germans, and an accompanying item from a Free French Commander claimed that the Germans had actually lost 4,000 men – a figure which we now know was ridiculously inaccurate.

German Newsreel Coverage

The *Wochenschau* newsreel of 27 August 1942 began by building up a graphical representation of the large numbers of Allied ships, landing craft and fighters involved in this operation.

Unlike the Allied newsreels, it was seemingly able to show more of the actual action, with guns firing on the invasion craft and German soldiers rushing from their shelters to take up defensive positions. Claims that British planes were driven back time and again by German anti-aircraft fire were reinforced with images of a British plane crashing into the sea and another burning on the ground – its distinctive red, white and blue roundel (albeit in black and white) clearly visible. There was the humiliating sight of lines of dishevelled Allied soldiers surrendering, many with torn uniforms and walking in their bare feet.

The streets of Dieppe were shown to lie in ruins, and there were countless shots of burnt-out boats, corpses floating in the water and destroyed landing craft and tanks stranded on the beaches. It was a scene of complete devastation, reminiscent of an area that had been hit by a typhoon.

Much was made of the obvious contradiction between these scenes of total desolation and the triumphant reports on London radio and in British newspapers of a great aerial victory and a boost to the morale of men thirsting for a fight.

The report ended with the confident assertion that the German coastal defence forces were prepared to repel every landing attempt by the British and Americans with the assured confidence of an army with hundreds of victories behind it. The final frames concluded with typical triumphant images of German soldiers marching to their positions, the Luftwaffe victorious in the air and the bow of one of their destroyers crashing forwards through the waves.

Compared with the Allied newsreel, the commentary was far more formal and the content far more factual. In the initial graphical representation, the report went out of its way to fill the screen completely with images showing the massive scale of the Allied attack. This was all for the very good reason of being able to claim that – despite the size of the raid that they report as a long-planned, full-scale invasion attempt – the Allies had either been wiped out or forced back into the sea after intensive close quarters fighting.

It accurately reported there was a mix of English (they rarely distinguished English from British), Canadian, American and De Gaulle forces involved in the action and that the naval task force had lost some units to the German Navy. It even mentioned that 300–400 landing craft were protected by thirteen to fifteen cruisers and destroyers.

Without reporting their own losses, they asserted that the Allies lost a total of 172 fighters and bombers together with twenty-eight of the most modern tanks. The horror of the complete picture of destruction was broken by triumphant music, as a sweep along the beach revealed the full extent of the carnage and the large number of tanks and boats abandoned on the beaches. Concentrating on such scenes of destruction gave full credence to their sarcastic criticism of Allied news reports, which claimed 'the success of the landings produced a smile of satisfaction on the face of every Englishman'.

The German newsreel was far more direct with close-ups of bodies floating in the water and of the Canadian badges on their uniforms, the reporting of the actual names of destroyed landing craft and the image of piles and piles of Allied rifles. The sad spectacle of empty Allied helmets being washed over by the waves was especially effective.

The sight of the dead bodies also gave the commentator an excuse to add some blatant propaganda to the report by mocking Churchill's allegedly amateurish strategic planning and for allowing himself to be blackmailed by Stalin into embarking on such a disastrous adventure.

German Press Reports

While expressing incredulity that the Allies should have been able to land any equipment at all on the well-protected beaches in France and amazement at the speed with which the tanks were unloaded, the German press was quick to downplay the effectiveness of the raid. Over the following days, the *Völkischer Beobachter* was able to capitalise on the failure of the raid with a whole series of damning headlines and articles:

Nazi-orchestrated poster in French mocking the Allied defeats with the French phrase 'never two without three' or more idiomatically in English 'bad luck always comes in threes'. This perpetuated the myth that the Saint-Nazaire raid had been a failure. *Le Grand Blockhaus Museum*

German Victory in the English Channel

Scarcely Born, the Second Front Dies in Dieppe

Cheap Excuses from the Defeated: only a 'Dress Rehearsal' for the Second Front!

Such was the extent of the apparent Allied failure that the German press was even able to carry a headline from the Japanese press claiming that:

 Germany's Coastal Defence Impregnable!

The whole event was perceived as being more for political rather than military reasons – the outcome of Stalin's demand on Churchill for a second front. The *Börsenzeitung* mockingly declared it to be a '10 hour second front'.

Keen to portray the raid as the repulsion by the Germans of a full-scale invasion attempt, Goebbels was soon quick to add his own particular propaganda 'spin' in the Nazi newspaper:

 Since Mr Churchill cannot attempt the Second Front when he considers it opportune and practicable, but only when the Kremlin commands him to do so, he is a prisoner of the Kremlin. Since June, 1941, he has become the tool of Moscow. But one day Nemesis will take her revenge.

WHICH SIDE REPORTED THE FACTS ABOUT THE DIEPPE RAID MORE ACCURATELY?

Misleading Reporting by the Allies

While much of the Allied reporting, either in the press or in newsreel, rarely told outright lies, there is no doubt that the commentary was often very misleading. There are three newsreel comments in particular that stand out and deserve closer scrutiny.

Concealing Tank Losses

The first of these concerns the scene featuring the new tank-landing craft. The accompanying comment in the *Movietone* clip was:

Tank-landing craft were making their first appearance in a show of this kind. They took our tanks across and if some of them came home light – well you'd hardly expect to evacuate all the tanks.

This statement gave the clear impression that most of the tanks were recovered and that perhaps only one or two were lost. In reality, out of the twenty-eight tanks that were landed not a single tank was recovered. So, this statement was quite deceptive.

Misreporting Air Losses

Likewise, the reporting of Allied and German air losses was quite wide of the mark. It was claimed that:

 Ninety-one German fighters were accounted for and about twice that number probably destroyed – while ninety-eight of our aircraft of all commands were lost.

In reality, the Allies had 120 aircraft lost or damaged beyond repair, and the Germans had only seventy-two aircraft lost or destroyed. Proportionately, the German losses in terms of aircraft and pilots were probably more significant to the Germans than the losses suffered by the Allies, but this did not excuse the inaccurate figures reported.

Giving the Impression of Mission Completed According to Plan

As early as 20 August, a report in the *Daily Express* was claiming that 'the Dieppe Raid is considered a complete success'. Even with the benefit of hindsight, a much later *Pathé News* report declared that six minutes after the time when scheduled re-embarkation began and with their tasks completed, the landing parties started

The scene of complete destruction following the Allied attack that the Germans were keen to share with the world. *Le Grand Blockhaus Museum*

on their homeward journey, and that behind them much of Dieppe lay in flames. It is obvious that these comments were simply included because the narrator wanted to give the impression that the action was well thought out and went according to plan, but this was simply not true. Given that communication between the shore and ships was unreliable and the decision to evacuate the beaches was taken at short notice, it would be hard to claim that any of the groups re-embarked according to the timetable that had been agreed before the raid began.

When you consider all these facts, you start to appreciate just how the Allied news media completely distorted the truth about the raid. As the following overall newsreel comment clearly displayed, either through the complete lack of hard facts or the misleading reporting of others, the impression was given that the raid had been a great success when, in fact, it was a tragic failure:

It is not in the scheme of things to sit back with satisfaction at the results. Dieppe is a dress rehearsal for more and bigger raids. The Nazis have it coming to them and men like these are eager for another blow.

Misleading Reporting by the Germans

Rather surprisingly, the Germans actually did tell quite a lot of the truth about the raid – at least when it came to reporting the scale of the attack and many of the Allied losses. There were more than 300 ships and boats involved in the attack and all twenty-eight tanks that landed were captured or destroyed.

In the air battle, 120 Allied planes were destroyed, whereas the Germans claimed 172. However, just as they over-assessed the number of Allied planes shot down, the Germans under-assessed their own aircraft losses, actually reducing the initially reported total of thirty-seven to thirty-five. The true figure was seventy-two. While they made no mention of their own losses in terms of men, the Germans also underestimated the number of prisoners taken, ultimately claiming 2,095 when, including the wounded, the figure was probably closer to 2,900.

There were, nevertheless, also some other factual inaccuracies. The assertion that nowhere did the Allies succeed in penetrating the German positions was simply not true. We know that Lord Lovat's commandos did destroy the Hess Battery and that German air losses in planes and pilots, while fewer in numerical terms, were far more significant than Allied losses.

Conclusion

The following table summarises the conflicting factual information conveyed to their respective viewers by the Allied and German newsreels and how far this deviated from the truth.

Captured Allied prisoners being paraded through the streets of Dieppe. *Le Grand Blockhaus Museum*

	ALLIED CLAIMS	GERMAN CLAIMS	TRUTH
Allied Tanks Lost	No comment (impression loss minimal)	28	28
Allied Planes Lost	98	172	120
German Planes Lost (includes probable)	182	No comment	72
Allied POWs	No comment	2,000+	2,900

It is evident that both sides tried to underplay their own losses by either not reporting any figures at all or by giving figures that substantially underestimated their own losses. Likewise, the Allies consistently overestimated the losses suffered by the enemy.

Overall, the Germans did report the proceedings more accurately, but then they could afford to do so, as it was a great propaganda coup that was not even of their own making.

For the Allies, the landings were not the success which they would have desired, and it is quite understandable why they just could not afford to tell the truth to their own people at that moment. There had already been so many setbacks. Hence, they could only try to obtain some positive propaganda from the raid by praising the audacious nature of this well-planned attack on the enemy and concentrating on the splendid co-ordination of the three armed services and the courage displayed by all military personnel. Their only hope was that the raid would at least make the Germans think twice about depleting their resources further on the Atlantic coast to support their advance on the Eastern Front.

7

OPERATION CHASTISE – THE DAMBUSTERS RAID

INTRODUCTION

Arguably, if there were one single event during the whole of the Second World War in which the British would take most pride, even up to this very day, then it has to be the audacious attack on German dams carried out on the night of 16–17 May 1943 by the RAF's 617 Squadron.

There is no doubt that Paul Brickhill's famous 1951 book, *The Dam Busters*, aided by the thrilling 1954 feature film of the same name, did much to generate the British public's post-war enthusiasm for that raid. There were countless reprints, and it was still being claimed as Britain's biggest-selling war book in the 1970s.

In terms both of the ingenuity of the method employed to breach the dams and also of the undoubted courage and skill of the bomber pilots involved in the mission, the raid is quite justifiably rated very highly in the annals of war history. The positive impact on British morale cannot be overestimated. The sheer audacity of the raid and resultant enthusiastic media response engendered a wave of euphoria that swept not just across Britain but also across all those countries of the Empire whose pilots had participated in the raid. The impossible seemed to have been achieved. Much of the supply of water and power to the great industrial factories of the Ruhr Valley had been stopped, and it was widely believed that this was a hammer blow for the German war machine.

However, for their part, the German media hardly reported the incident at all and, rather than being a catastrophe for the German war machine, the raid was simply portrayed as yet another barbaric extension to Britain's terror bombing of civilian Germany, but at the expense of a high number of Allied aircraft and their crews.

It is only now, with the benefit of hindsight and constantly updated statistics, that we can try to ascertain whether the mission was a success and the extent to which either side told the truth.

CONCEPTION AND DELIVERY

At the outbreak of war, it was Barnes Wallis, the renowned British aircraft designer and inventor, who came forward with the idea of a heavy bomb that, if delivered correctly, would produce a shock wave sufficient to destroy the largest of dams. It was his understanding that three Ruhr dams – the Möhne, the Eder and the Sorpe – accounted for virtually all of the water supply required to produce Germany's munitions and machines of war. It took 8 tons of water to produce 1 ton of steel, so if the water supply could be severed, then this would undoubtedly hamper German war production.

Having eventually persuaded the British authorities to support his plan for bombing the dams, 617 Squadron was created with twenty-one crews from No. 5 Group RAF who had already shown a special aptitude for low-level bombing. They were to be led by the experienced 24-year-old Wing Commander Guy Gibson. A number of difficulties had to be resolved. Primarily, a means had to be found to drop a large bomb in such a way that it would not detonate on impact but rather sink to the bottom of the dam wall and explode only when the full weight of water was behind it, so as to achieve maximum destructive force from the shock wave created in the process.

Sir Barnes Wallis conceived the idea of the 'bouncing bomb', or water-skimming mine. *Borough of Hillingdon*

The solution was found in the form of a rotating, bouncing bomb delivered from a sufficiently low height to prevent it from disintegrating on hitting the water, but also at just the right speed and distance from the dam wall.

So it was that, on the evening of 16 May 1943, after several weeks of intensive low-level training, nineteen Lancaster bombers set out to attack the Ruhr dams in what was known as Operation Chastise. The attacking force was divided into three groups. The first group consisted of nine planes, and its mission was to attack the Möhne dam before proceeding to the dam on Lake Eder further east. The second group was composed of five aircraft, and its primary target was the Sorpe. The third group was a flying reserve, composed of five aircraft, which took off two hours after the main force, with the intention of either supporting the main attacks or bombing three smaller dams.

Given that the planes had to fly very close to the ground to avoid radar detection, it is not surprising that the squadron suffered heavy losses from crashes and enemy flak long before the planes even reached their targets. The second group was particularly unlucky, with two aircraft having to turn back and two others crashing en route. Nevertheless, eight of the first group did reach their targets, eventually managing to breach both the Möhne and Eder dams.

The Sorpe dam was actually situated only 10 miles south west of the Möhne dam but was very different in construction from the others, with a wide earthen barrier behind the dam wall. Because of the topography of the valley, any bombing attack also had to be made parallel to the dam wall. For both these reasons, it was always unlikely that the wall would be breached. As it was, only three aircraft reached the Sorpe and, although the dam wall was hit, the damage and resultant water loss was relatively insignificant. It was later reported that the Ennepe dam also had a minor breach, although commentators today tend to believe that it was the Bever dam rather than the Ennepe dam that was actually attacked.

At the time, any disappointment over the failure to breach the Sorpe dam seemed to be more than compensated for by the damage inflicted on the other two dams. The successful bombing of the Möhne dam released 116 million cubic metres of water from its reservoir. The resultant flood waters swept away all buildings and bridges on the valley floor for at least 50 miles from the dam. In terms of physical destruction, several power stations, 125 factories, forty-six road and railway bridges and more than 1,000 dwelling houses were damaged or destroyed. At the Eder dam, 155 million cubic metres of water escaped and, because the valley was broader, the resultant floods affected areas as far as 250 miles from the dam. However, apart from some damage to a few power stations, the immediate physical damage here was comparatively light. The tidal waves produced at both dams were to take many hours to reach the towns and cities on the lower reaches of the rivers. The bombings certainly created major havoc in the surrounding areas.

Photograph of the breached Möhne dam taken by Flying Officer Jerry Frey from a Spitfire on 17 May 1943.

More than 600 German civilians were killed or reported missing and, as will be explained later, an even greater number of non-Germans were to lose their lives in the floods. Parts of major towns such as Dortmund and Kassel were flooded, and there was a complete or partial loss of power and water supplies in several areas for a number of weeks.

However, in addition to all the physical damage and loss of life on the ground, the cost to 617 Squadron was equally horrific. Of the nineteen aircraft that set off on the raid, two were forced to return early, five were shot down or crashed on the way to the target, one was shot down over the target and a further two were shot down on the homeward journey. The loss of eight aircraft, and the deaths of fifty-three out of a total of 133 crew in one operation, made this one of the most costly missions of the whole war.

The British Media Response

Given the enormity of the task and the seeming mayhem caused by the breaching of the dams, it was actually quite surprising that the first headlines about the attack that appeared in quality newspapers such as *The Times*, on 18 May 1943, showed a typical British penchant for understatement:

 Ruhr Dams Breached
Daring Low-Level Attack by Lancasters
Walls blasted out with 1,500lb mines
Vast Damage By Floods

It was left to the main article to include a quotation from Sir Archibald Sinclair, the Secretary of State for Air, proudly stating that the RAF attacks were 'a trenchant blow for victory'. The *Daily Express* and *Daily Mirror* were certainly far more upbeat, and there were exciting reports in all the papers from airmen who actually took part in the mission, describing how their aircraft flew as low as 100ft through heavy enemy fire, as they lined up to drop their special bombs on the dams. It was claimed that at the Möhne and Sorpe reservoirs, which controlled two thirds of the water storage of the Ruhr basin, they had blasted a gap 100yd wide, and that the Eder dam, the largest in Europe, was also breached.

The reports gave the clear impression that all three dams were ruptured – an impression supported by the lead headline in *The Daily Telegraph*:

 R.A.F. Blow Up Three Key Dams In Germany

We now know that the Sorpe dam was almost untouched but, given the lack of solid information at that time, the press was forced to indulge in wild speculation. Much was made of the fact that if all the dams had been drained, not only would there have been substantial flooding to the industrial areas of cities such as Kassel but that, if water levels could not be maintained, then the River Ruhr itself might have become unnavigable. There was also a before-and-after aerial photograph of the Möhne dam, revealing the wide breach in the dam wall and how the power station below the dam had been swept away by the force of the water pouring out of the reservoir.

Wing Commander Gibson was quoted as having declared on his return:

 We had high hopes, but the immediate results of breaching the dams were far beyond our expectations.

Air Chief Marshal Sir Arthur Harris was obviously delighted at the success of the mission, concluding a special congratulatory message to the head of the bomber group involved in the mission with the words:

In this memorable operation, they have won a major victory in the battle of the Ruhr, the effects of which will last until the Boche is swept away in the flood of final disaster.

Nonetheless, what undoubtedly stands out to any reader today is that there was absolutely no indication of how many planes took part in the raid nor of how many returned home safely. These were basic facts that were almost always detailed, albeit often erroneously, for virtually every other bombing raid in the war, but not on this occasion. Nor was there any specific mention of the ingenious design and method of delivery of the special bouncing bombs used in the raid. Indeed, despite the fact that they captured one intact, the Germans were unaware that these were bouncing bombs at all, and it took them more than a year to make that discovery.

By 19 and 20 May, a clearer picture did start to emerge in the press, with new photographs showing the area flooded below the Eder dam and reports that the floods were still spreading over an ever-increasing area:

A practice 10,000lb bouncing bomb attached to the bomb bay of Wing Commander Guy Gibson's Lancaster at Manston, Kent, while conducting dropping trials off Reculver. *The National Archives*

Ruhr Riot as Havoc Spreads

The Scotsman was swift to include facts provided by Reuters and neutral sources that told of fifty-four towns having been flooded, 4,000 Germans killed and 120,000 people having been driven from their homes. A German underground radio station was reported as having even admitted that it was Germany's biggest catastrophe since the beginning of the war.

Apart from mentioning the initial destruction caused by the flooding, *The Times* assessed at great length how the loss of water in the dams would not only reduce hydroelectric power production but would disrupt coal mining and lead to a short age of fuel to drive German armament production. It was also claimed that the destruction of so many roads and bridges would reduce the flow of supplies to the Eastern Front.

However, in all of these almost daily updates on the damage inflicted on the Ruhr Valley, and in spite of stirring speeches from the likes of Sir Archibald Sinclair about the magnificent achievements of the raid and how it was Bomber Command that would eventually paralyse German war power, there was still no mention in the British press of the number of aircraft shot down in the mission. Ironically, *The New York Times* of 18 May did mention that eight planes were lost, but as the same article failed to specify how few aircraft were involved in the mission overall, the reader still remained blissfully ignorant of the frightening loss rate.

The *Daily Express* was one of the first newspapers to reveal the truth on 20 May, but the emphasis was on how such a small force had wreaked such destruction:

 Dams were burst open by only 19 Lancasters

Thus, for the loss of eight machines and possibly 64 gallant airmen, a blow has been struck at the enemy which would have required the services of many divisions of land forces.

Indeed, it was not until 28 May, with the announcement of the award of a Victoria Cross to Wing Commander Gibson for leading the force that attacked the dams, that many other papers finally revealed this truth. The 42 per cent loss rate was exceptionally high, and it is little wonder that Barnes Wallis was later reported as saying that if he had known how many aircrew were to be killed in the raid, then he would never have contemplated carrying out the mission in the first place.

Newsreel coverage of the event was in equally short supply. The *British Movietone* film of 24 May admitted that no actual film had been received of the raid but that it had been reconstructed using stills and other film footage. In fact, many of the scenes showing a 'devastating orgy of flooding' were actually plucked from the 1939 feature film, *The Rains Came*. Triumphant music preceded a speech by the

Air Secretary, explaining to a hushed audience that Bomber Command had struck a heavy blow of a new kind at the sources of German war power. The commentator did also mention early in his report that eight aircraft did not return but still omitted to add how many planes had actually participated. *British Pathé News* also released a film on 3 June that featured Gibson introducing the King to other members of the team who had taken part in the mission:

> Gibson's brilliant achievement was accomplished with the gallant support of a band of brother airmen. [...] the breaching of the dams was superbly executed and resulted in enormous damage and dislocation to Germany's war industry. [...] one of the most devastating attacks of the war. The floods created a serious situation in the Ruhr Valley.

The film also concluded with a moving, if rather contrived, interview with Gibson's wife in which she admits she feared for his life at all times and then added:

> If my husband's efforts and all the boys of the services with him can bring the war to an end quickly then so much the better – then we can enjoy ourselves.

Her thoughts and words are particularly poignant when you discover that her husband was to die in action over Norway within a mere fifteen months of that interview.

The German Media Response

If the British authorities had hoped that the triumphant reports of the mission appearing in the British and much of the world's media would be matched by equally depressing reports in the German media, then they were to be sadly disappointed.

There were very good reasons why the British were short of relevant film footage of the raid, but the Germans, usually so quick to show footage of their own triumphs, also failed to provide any film coverage whatsoever of either the damaged dams or the flooded areas. It is somewhat ironic that the weekly *Wochenschau* report of 26 May should contain images of flooding near Volkhov on the Eastern Front but absolutely nothing about the flooding within Germany itself.

Likewise, given that time and again during the war we discover that the German press was able to carry full details of a particular raid only a few hours after the actual event occurred, we might well have expected that the German afternoon press on Monday 17 May would have carried at least a passing reference to this major event. In fact, while there was a radio announcement from the German High Command on 17 May that two dams had been damaged by British bombing during the night of 16–17 May and that a lot of civilians had been killed in the ensuing flood waters, there was virtually no mention in the German press that day.

While the *Deutsche Allgemeine Zeitung* on 18 May admitted that a combination of recent RAF attacks had turned the districts between the Rhine and the Ruhr into a theatre of war, there was no specific mention of the attacks on the dams. The purpose of the article was to criticise the British destruction of civilian areas rather than to highlight that war production had also been affected by such raids. For its part, the *Völkischer Beobachter* of the same day did carry a fuller report but only hidden away in a general report from the German High Command, and it certainly did not merit any special headline. What it did report was that:

 There had been heavy losses to the civilian population caused by the torrent of water released from two dams damaged [...] by a small force of British planes. Eight of the attacking planes were shot down and a further nine planes were shot down over occupied Western Europe.

By the time the *Neue Vetschauer Zeitung* (NVZ) came round to reporting the specific dams raid on 19 May – as the newspaper was published only every other day – the emphasis of its report had been completely distorted. Instead of detailing the extent of the destruction, the lead headline in that day's paper was:

 Jewish Man behind the Dam Attacks
A former Jewish specialist suggested the bombing of German Dams!

The article itself referred to a Reuters' item appearing in the foreign press that cast far more light on the background to this so-called 'criminal terror attack':

 Writing for the Daily Mail on 18 May, Guy Bettany, a Reuters correspondent formerly based in Berlin, claimed that some time previously, a well known Jewish doctor from Berlin but now practising in London, had asked him why the RAF had never bombed the German dams. Bettany had passed on the information to the Air Ministry, and a reply was received, thanking him for the suggestion which was being carefully investigated.

As far as the *NVZ* was concerned, this foreign report left no room for doubt that Jews had been the inspiration behind the attack. This then gave the paper the chance to insert a forty-line rant, blaming the Jews for all of Germany's woes:

 It was Jews who stirred up Germany to go to war when Germany was at pains to find a peaceful compromise. It was Jews who were responsible for the war spreading to one country after another. It was Jews who were responsible in the war for crimes like the bombing of civilians and the massacre of the Polish officers in the woods of Katyn.

Thus, the hatred in the article intensified, line after line, with no further mention of the actual raid on the dams whatsoever. What is interesting is that even *The Scotsman* was reporting on this same claim by Bettany in its edition of 19 May, but as a little aside hidden away in an inside article that simply stated:

 A famous German Jewish specialist exiled from Berlin suggested the great dams raid to the RAF. [...] He is now practising in Britain.

However, by 20 May, obviously concerned by all these anti-Jewish claims that were now circulating around Germany, the British Air Ministry felt obliged to issue a lengthy denial:

Misleading statements have appeared about the origin of the recent air operations against the Möhne, Eder and Sorpe dams. The Air Ministry frequently receives advice from many sources on possible objectives for attack. Suggestions are always welcome, though for obvious reasons it is seldom possible to state whether a particular project is feasible, let alone in contemplation.

It is true that the attack on the dams was suggested on several occasions by members of the public, but the operation did not, in fact, originate with any such suggestion.

All objectives of importance to German war production, including the dams, have long been methodically examined by the intelligence and planning authorities, with a view to attack at the most favourable moment.

It is perhaps understandable that such a clear rebuttal did not find its way to being reported by the German press. What is perhaps more revealing is that German radio claimed on 19 May that, apart from 370 Germans killed and thirty-six missing, no fewer than 341 prisoners-of-war of various nationalities were also killed as a result of the bombing. While *The Times* was prepared to quote this report verbatim the following day, no horror was expressed at this unexpected outcome – nor was there any attempt to comment on the potential veracity of this claim.

Even more notably, the British authorities never refuted these German claims – and with good reason. In fact, according to the most up-to-date assessments, the final number of Germans killed exceeded 600 – mainly civilians and mostly from the flooding in the Möhne and Ruhr valleys. However, even more tragically, more than 1,000 French and Belgium prisoners-of-war and Dutch, Polish and Soviet forced labourers, housed in a number of camps close to the breached dams, also died in the floods. These included close to 500 female labourers from the Ukraine who had been sent to Germany to assist with land production. None of this was ever reported as a separate article in the British press.

By 21 May, while the German press was still making oblique reference to the raid on the dams, it was only so as to give it more ammunition for a further onslaught on the Jews:

 Jews inspire the air gangsters

The *NVZ* claimed that the very fact the British press was prepared to mention the role of a Jewish expert in the attack proved that the Jews were proud to be associated with this 'infamous terror raid'. With an obvious allusion to the number of civilians killed in the floods, the alleged air gangsters were accused of using new methods that were an affront to every true soldier.

Instead of bemoaning the impact on the war effort that the damage to the dams would have caused, the emphasis was on stressing that the war would continue until final victory – progress to that victory amply illustrated by the added report that the Germans had already shot down 10,000 enemy aircraft since the start of the war.

Reality Versus Fiction

As early as 18 May, the official German News Agency was claiming:

The damage done to the dams caused appreciable casualties among the civilian population, but the damage to important industrial objectives is relatively minor. It can be repaired within a short time.

However, at the very same time and in the immediate aftermath of the raid, even the American media was to hail the operation 'the most devastating single blow yet dealt from the air [...] well-planned, audacious, spectacular and extremely destructive.'

As in the British media, the clear impression was given that Operation Chastise had dealt a major, if not fatal, setback to the Germans and would hasten an end to the war. Even Harris was to contend, in an official letter written five days after the mission, that he felt that a blow had been struck at Germany from which she could not recover for several years. Both sides could not be correct.

In truth, it was probably just too early for either side to predict the lasting impact of the raid. The positives for the Allies were that two out of the three dams were breached, water levels did fall significantly, and the floods did cause great confusion, distress and loss of life to the local civilian population. However, even if the non-German deaths are included, the total death toll was never as high as the so-called neutral figure of 4,000 that was reported widely in the press outside Germany at the time.

Nobody was ever going to be able to judge the true extent of casualties until several months after the event, and the long-term impact on German war production would become known only after the war.

When Albert Speer, the minister responsible for Armament and War Production, came to inspect the destruction caused by the bombings, he was pleased to be able to report to Goebbels that the damage was not as bad as first feared, and that he hoped to have the armaments industry back to full production before the end of May. His top priority was to restore water and power supplies to the factories in the Ruhr area as quickly as possible – even if this meant confiscating equipment from other factories in Germany and diverting human resources from elsewhere. To this end, he arranged for 50,000 Organisation Todt workers and 20,000 armament workers to be transferred from other vital tasks, including work on the Atlantic Wall, to assist in the urgent rebuilding of the dams and flooded factories and other plants. A further 5,000 troops were brought in to assist with repairs and the clearing up of damage in the Eder Valley.

The transfer of all of this extra manpower did achieve remarkable results. The total water production in the Ruhr was to return to normal levels by 27 June, and alternative electricity supplies were soon provided by diverting water from the Alps. In fact, there were few factories or households in the region that were without electrical power for more than a fortnight. The breaches in the Möhne and Eder dams themselves had been repaired by the end of September.

Nevertheless, coal extraction levels in May did fall by more than 800,000 tons, and 30 per cent of this was directly due to the breaching of the Möhne dam. A further knock-on effect was that there was some disruption to the total industrial production in Germany as a whole in June, but this was not all due to Operation Chastise and, from July onwards, previous production levels were being equalled or exceeded.

There was also some direct, if often only temporary, disruption to the German war effort. The damage to the Ruhr waterways delayed the shipment of vital war equipment, including tank turrets, and aircraft production stalled. Flak guns were immediately relocated to protect other major dams, and this made a deep impression on Hitler, who was genuinely concerned at the shortage of self-propelled guns now available for fighting elsewhere. The additional manning of anti-aircraft positions around all the major dams would also be a lasting obligation.

However, one of the most serious, if rather unexpected consequences, was the long-term adverse effect on agricultural production caused by the flooding of so much arable and dairy land. About 3,000 hectares of arable land were ruined, and 6,500 cattle and pigs killed. Goebbels was to note in his diary that the resultant 100g reduction in the meat ration had a very serious psychological effect on a civilian population that had been taught to believe that Germany was still winning the war.

In his 1969 book, *Inside the Third Reich*, Speer was to claim that if the British had destroyed three other key reservoirs in addition to the Möhne dam, then the Ruhr Valley would have been completely deprived of water in the coming summer months. Furthermore, he admitted if the bomb that hit the Sorpe Valley dam had been only a few inches lower, then it could well have resulted in the trickle of water that escaped from the reservoir being transformed into a raging torrent, which would have had a significant effect on war production. Nevertheless, he also claimed that the attack on the Eder dam was a complete waste of time, as it had nothing to do with the supply of water to the Ruhr.

The other mistake he highlighted, and with which Barnes Wallis was in complete agreement, was that the Allies did not continue to harass and bomb the repair parties on both dams. For some odd reason, this was not done, with the result that sufficient repairs were effected to both dams by September to allow them to capture the rainfall in the late autumn and winter of 1943 and thus satisfy all their supply needs for the following summer.

CONCLUSION

Neither side told its people the whole truth about the Dambusters Raid at the time. Much of the mis-reporting on the British side was through ignorance and wishful thinking. Everyone wanted to believe that all three dams had been breached and that all the damage caused by the flooding would constitute a decisive turning point in the war. We now know that this was not the case.

However, there was also a great deal of non-reporting – which was presumably deemed necessary to conceal the less glorious aspects of the mission. Any indication that more than 40 per cent of the airmen and their aircraft involved in the raid had been lost would have been truly heart-rending and would have detracted from the achievements of the mission. Likewise, to have to admit that there had been a vast number of innocent deaths, especially among prisoners-of-war and forced labourers, would have been extremely embarrassing for all concerned. While *The Times* was prepared to print that the German press was claiming that hundreds of prisoners-of-war had been drowned, the British press failed to express any horror at such claims or even to question whether they might be true. Nowadays, it would be almost inconceivable for a foreign power to make such a seemingly outrageous statement without the press hounding its own politicians for a denial or confirmation of such external reports.

It is perhaps worth noting that, since 1977, any such raids on dams would be considered war crimes under the Geneva Convention if it were known that such an attack would be likely to cause 'the release of dangerous forces from the works or installations and consequent severe losses among the civilian population'.

However, at the time, for the British and, indeed, for much of occupied Europe, the greatest value of the raid lay undoubtedly in its propaganda impact. The photographs of the broken dams that were circulated around the world proved to be a major morale boost for the Allies. Rightly or wrongly, the British people truly believed that a major blow had been struck and that the Germans were getting a taste of their own medicine. Within a matter of days, the RAF was to drop leaflets over several occupied countries, including France and Holland, showing before-and-after photographs of the Möhne dam and explaining in great detail the nature of the raid and the damage that had been inflicted.

For Churchill, it was a much-needed shot in the arm. His American and Russian allies had started to fear that he was only good at spouting inspiring rhetoric. This operation seemed to show that Britain was, at last, doing something positive to win the war.

For their part, the Germans were keen to downplay the significance of the raid. There was very little direct press coverage, and formal announcements from German High Command stressed the ineffectiveness of the raid in hampering Germany's war effort, and condemned the inhumanity of the British for having such scant regard for the lives of so many civilians and prisoners-of-war killed in the floods. It also provided a further excuse to castigate the Jews.

While the results of the raid were a failure in that it had only minimal impact on Germany's arms production, it certainly did have a demoralising effect on the German public. It was yet another sign that, despite what they were being told, it was hard to see how they were winning the war. They already knew they had suffered great losses on the Eastern Front, and the further cut in their rations did little to inspire confidence.

The fact that the British were now able to bomb precisely and with such force was a major blow for the German High Command. Speer was to admit that the German steel industry would have all but collapsed if the British had systematically destroyed all the dams in the region. Hitler was deeply worried by the attacks and had been furious with the Luftwaffe for being so ill-prepared. It meant that, for the rest of the war, the Germans had to divert manpower and put additional defences in place to protect key installations and infrastructure.

They were right to be worried: 617 Squadron was to go on to conduct a whole series of successful missions against important targets such as the battleship *Tirpitz*, the U-boat pens at Brest and the V-1 and V-2 weapon sites – all of which would hasten Allied victory.

8

THE BOMBING OF CITIES

INTRODUCTION

On 14 May 1940, the *Freiburger Zeitung* was to carry a heart-rending report on the funeral service held for fifty-two civilians killed by the deliberate Allied bombing of the historic Black Forest town of Freiburg on 10 May – the very day that Germany launched its invasion of Belgium. The article employed very emotive language:

 These innocent children and helpless men and women were the victims of a cowardly, murderous bombing.

In later weeks, harrowing film footage of the funerals and the pointless destruction of ordinary dwelling houses would be screened in cinemas throughout Germany and distributed to friendly and neutral countries across the world. There was universal condemnation of this apparent act of barbarism. After all, on 30 September 1938, the League of Nations had unanimously approved a resolution declaring that the intentional bombing of civilian populations was illegal and that any attacks on legitimate military objectives had to be effected in such a way that the civilian population in the neighbourhood could not be bombed through negligence. Consequently, no side wanted to be accused of breaching this resolution and going beyond what might be considered morally acceptable in a time of war.

But, the claim that the Allies had bombed Freiburg was a complete lie. The deaths and destruction had certainly occurred but, as we learnt in Chapter 3, the bombs had actually been dropped by German pilots who, having missed their primary target and having lost their bearings, mistakenly believed that their planes were still over French territory.

Not only could the German High Command never admit to this catastrophic blunder, but Goebbels was even prepared to go so far as to employ the incident for propaganda purposes by making extravagant threats that the Luftwaffe would respond five-fold if the Allies were to persist with such inhumane practices in the future.

Unquestionably, the bombing of civilians did pose a serious moral dilemma for everyone involved in the conflict but, as we will see, as the war progressed, attitudes toward this issue were to change on both sides, not only in the decisions taken by the respective military and political leaders but also in the reporting of such events by the media.

THE BOMBING OF ROTTERDAM

Given Goebbels' feigned outrage at the supposed Allied bombing of Freiburg, one might be forgiven for thinking that the deliberate aerial bombing of civilians had simply not taken place previously.

In fact, during the First World War, more than 500 civilians had been killed in night-time raids on British cities by German Zeppelins, and 167 Londoners were slain in a single daytime raid by German bombers on 13 June 1917. No fewer than 1,500 people were killed by the Luftwaffe in the Basque city of Guernica in 1937, and several tens of thousands were lost in Germany's ruthless bombing of Warsaw in September 1939.

Photograph taken on 14 May 1940 showing aftermath of the bombing of Rotterdam. *NARA 535916*

Nonetheless, it was only really as a result of the massive devastation caused by German planes to the Dutch city of Rotterdam a few days after the Freiburg incident that the British hierarchy started to take seriously the prospect of Germany bombing British cities in the Second World War.

Units of the German Army first arrived in Rotterdam on Friday 10 May 1940. Having initially made good progress, the Dutch Army gradually regained the upper hand, and by the Monday the Germans had been pinned back to the left bank of the river. Frustrated by their lack of success, the officer commanding the German forces gave an ultimatum to the Dutch defenders that if they did not surrender, the Luftwatte would be instructed to bomb the city. Nevertheless, by the time a message was relayed via the Dutch government that a delegation would be sent to enter into negotiations, the first wave of Heinkel 111 bombers had already been dispatched. Observing radio silence and failing to notice red flares fired to abort the mission, more than 100 tons of explosives were dropped on the centre of the city, resulting in more than 900 civilian deaths.

British media coverage of the bombing of Rotterdam was actually rather sparse. On 15 May, *The Times* carried a communiqué from the Netherlands Legation explaining that the Dutch troops had been forced to surrender to avoid further blood-shed – especially since Rotterdam had been retaken by the Germans. Likewise, *The Scotsman* of the same date squarely placed the emphasis on the role of fifth columnists for the Dutch defeat:

 The Battle for Rotterdam
How the Nazis and Traitors Worked from Within

Indeed, this report admitted that the German bombing during the first three days had been primarily against targets of military importance on the edge of the town and on the railway station. Later, the bombing was said to be aimed at Dutch gun positions. There was absolutely no indication of any great loss of civilian life in the bombings.

In fact, it is only on 20 May that *The Scotsman* carried a small item from the Dutch legation in Paris supposedly detailing the true extent of the devastation caused, albeit that the number of deaths was far from accurate:

100,000 Killed in Bombing of Rotterdam
A Third of the City Destroyed

For its part, the German High Command was just as reticent to report to its own people the extent of the damage and any loss of civilian life caused by the bombing of Rotterdam. Its focus was on:

The Capitulation of the Dutch Army
[...] in the face of superior German force on the land and in the air.

Nevertheless, it was this incident rather than any other that was to change the attitude of British politicians towards the bombing war. It seemed irrelevant that the Germans might not have intended to bomb Rotterdam that evening. The point was that their pilots had always been prepared for such a mission and, whether or not it had been that particular night, if the Dutch had not surrendered, the Luftwaffe would eventually have indiscriminately bombed the city with the full blessing of its leaders.

The British might well have wished to hold the moral high ground. After all, even after war was declared, Chamberlain was determined to stay faithful to an undertaking he had given to President Roosevelt not to bomb civilian populations or unfortified cities. However, this was a moral stance that it was always going to prove impossible to sustain.

THE TIT-FOR-TAT BOMBING OF LONDON AND BERLIN

Around 11 p.m. on the evening of 24 August 1940, the Luftwaffe dropped a number of bombs on Oxford Street and the financial district of London, during which nine civilians were killed. What is claimed today to make this different from any other previous bombing of London or, indeed, other British cities, is that this was the first occasion during the Second World War when it was believed that civilian areas in the United Kingdom were targeted deliberately. Until then, it was generally assumed that any civilian deaths were purely accidental, albeit the inevitable consequence of the bombing of legitimate military targets.

If this were true then, given the frightening significance of that evening's bombings, it is somewhat surprising that the event did not provoke a much greater furore from the authorities. The sub-headlines in *The Times* of Monday 26 August, actually made very little fuss about the bombing:

 Bombs and Flares dropped on London
Few Casualties and Little Damage

The emphasis was far more on the fact that eighty-nine German planes had been shot down over the weekend and that a city centre church had been hit. There are numerous explanations for the lack of outrage at this bombing raid. First, it was certainly not the first time that civilian areas of London had been bombed. Indeed, even on 23 August, two cinemas, a bank branch and a number of houses had been bombed in the Metropolitan area although, by some miracle, nobody was killed.

Second, to prevent any panic arising among the general public, it was essential to convince the populace that damage was minimal and that the Germans had suffered heavily in the process.

History now records that the bombing on 24 August was probably a mistake in that the German pilots lost their bearings and dropped their bombs over what they thought was open ground rather than carry them back home. In any event, Göring was so incensed by their actions that he immediately ordered those responsible to be transferred to the infantry.

Whatever the truth, nobody in London realised it was a mistake, and the incident so upset Churchill that he ordered that Berlin should be bombed the following night in reprisal. A total of eighty-one bombers set out on the raid but, such was the ferocity of the German defences that only a third of the aircraft ever claimed to have reached the city, and even these were forced to drop their bombs on the outskirts of Berlin, causing little or no damage.

Even though this was quite plainly a retaliatory attack, the British press was keen to stress that this was not a tit-for-tat bombing since, unlike the Germans,[5] the British were not bombing indiscriminately but aiming for military targets. This may well have been the intention of the British planes but, given the great difficulty in bombing accurately, numerous residential buildings were certainly destroyed.

Rather surprisingly, however, just as the British press passed little comment about the bombing of civilians in London, the Germans said little about the bombing of Berlin:

The First Enemy Raid over Berlin
Fire-Bombs on the Edge of the City

While it was certainly admitted that there had been a first bombing of the German capital, it was suggested that this was an indiscriminate attack on non-military targets and that, in any event, no damage was inflicted. Göring had always promised that Berlin would not be bombed and hence, even if there had been significant damage, reporting of this was always going to be kept to a minimum. Instead, the sole emphasis was on the fact that seventy-two enemy planes had been shot down in a number of different actions that evening. The incident did, however, provide Hitler with the opportunity to utter one of his most famous rants at the Sportpalast a few days later:

5   Rather ironically, the Völkischer Beobachter was to make the exact opposite assertion on
    28 August, claiming that the Luftwaffe had taken care to direct its bombing purely on ports,
    munitions factories, strategic transportation links and military airports, while the RAF – driven
    by a dangerous desire for vengeance – was bombing completely indiscriminately.

If the British Air Force drops two, three or four thousand kilos of bombs, then we will drop 150,000, 180,000, 230,000, 300,000 or 400,000 kilos, or more, in one night. If they declare that they will attack our cities on a large scale, we will erase theirs!

Even if little real damage had been inflicted by either side on the evenings of 24 and 25 August, the real significance of these dates was that 'the gloves were now officially off', and neither side was going to be so cautious about civilian casualties in the future. Bombing raids on London were to intensify and, indeed, by the end of August, more than 1,000 civilians had been killed across Britain.

Such attacks now meant that Germany had to take the threat of the future bombing of Berlin seriously and, by 20 November 1940, the *Wochenschau* Newsreel 533 showed children between the ages of 3 and 17 being evacuated out of Berlin to country areas. The whole exercise was portrayed as an exciting adventure for the children, who would enjoy better meals than they might have had at home and would still have regular school classes each day.

THE BOMBING OF COVENTRY

For the British, if there is one bombing event of the war in the United Kingdom that was seen as more shocking than any other, then it was the bombing of Coventry on the night of Thursday 14 November 1940.

Coventry had actually already been bombed as early as 18 August but the scale of the November raid was unparalleled because it was as destructive as any raid on London until that point. More than 500 German bombers were involved and, while their primary targets were undoubtedly the city's many industrial factories and its utilities, it was always evident that a great deal of damage was likely to be done to the city itself. Four churches, including the cathedral, four schools and half the city's rest centres were badly damaged. More than 4,500 houses were destroyed, 568 people were killed and close to 1,300 were injured in the raid and the fires that followed. In terms of the number of civilian deaths from one raid, this attack had certainly reached a new peak, and it was considered to be the first deliberate attempt to wipe a city off the map. Ironically, the overall impact on war production was minimal, as much of the essential work had already been moved to units on the outskirts of the city, and many of the factories were quickly repaired. The reporting of *The Times* on the event on 16 November was remarkably forthright:

 Big Attack on Coventry
1,000 Casualties
The Cathedral Destroyed

The editorial referred to Coventry as being 'a martyred city' and suggested that it was right that the Government should not conceal the gravity of the damage which had been caused by the Germans' policy of indiscriminate bombing. However, even this item concluded with a patriotic rallying cry:

 It is certain that Coventry will not flinch any more than London and other cities that bear the honourable scars of resistance to barbarism.

Prime Minister Winston Churchill walking through the ruins of Coventry Cathedral on 28 September 1941, with members of the Anglican clergy.

The *Daily Express* headlines cried out for retaliation:

A VERY GALLANT CITY – It is time for our deepest, most inspired anger.
Coventry cries: Bomb back and bomb hard

Nevertheless, even as late as 18 November, the press was still reporting the number of dead as 250, whereas the true toll was more than double that figure. In reality, the raid did have a very negative impact on the morale of the local people. Despite reports released by the press and authorities, which talked of 'the people of Coventry bearing their ordeal with great courage,' Mass Observation analysts reported that many inhabitants felt the city was finished, and large numbers did indeed leave the city for ever.

For its part, the German press was euphoric about the success of its bombers:

How Coventry was annihilated
Over 500,000 kg of bombs and 30,000 kg of incendiaries
Nothing remains of Coventry but a pile of ruins

As might be expected, the reports went to great lengths to emphasise that this was an attack on one of the most important of Britain's munition centres, and they proudly listed the names of famous engine and aircraft manufacturers whose factories had been destroyed including *Armstrong*, *Standard-Motor*, *Daimler* and *Hillman*. It was only a reference to an item in a Dutch paper that suggested that thousands of people might have been killed in the process. However, given that the report also stated that the raid was favoured with good weather and the pilots could clearly see their targets, then, for once, the German authorities were not able to claim that the civilians had been killed by mistake.

Likewise, German newsreel that showed action footage of the raid claimed that Coventry had been levelled to the ground and mocked Churchill for talking of the invincibility of his own air force – presumably a rather unsubtle attempt to make Göring's vain promise that Berlin would never be bombed sound less ridiculous.

The German High Command actually claimed the attack was in reprisal for the Allied bombing of Munich on 8 November – a raid often considered to be a deliberate attempt to kill Hitler, as he had been due to speak at an annual rally there that day.

THE BOMBING OF COLOGNE

Whereas the heaviest bombing of British cities was to take place between September 1940 and May 1941, as the war progressed and the Americans entered the fray,

Cologne Cathedral was to be hit fourteen times by Allied bombs in the course of the war but was still standing tall against a devastated city centre in this photograph from April 1945. *NARA 531287*

the size and intensity of the Allied bombing raids on German cities would continue to grow. There was now an acceptance by the British that, even if they still intended to avoid civilian targets, it would at least be acceptable to inflict damage that would cause maximum inconvenience to the general public.

Sir Arthur Harris, who was later to become Commander-in-Chief of Bomber Command, was convinced that if the RAF lacked the technology to bomb military targets accurately, then they should concentrate on the bombing of the centres and industrial areas of Germany's cities. He firmly believed this would not only cripple German war production but also break the morale of the German public. The first 1,000 bomber raid was to take place against Cologne on the night of 30–31 May 1942. The planes mainly carried incendiaries, interspersed with a number of delayed-fuse bombs designed to kill or maim anyone fighting the fires on the ground.

The Scotsman of 1 June carried the headlines:

R.A.F. Makes World's Greatest Raid
Over 1250 Planes attack Cologne and Rhineland

The Air Ministry was quick to describe the raid as an outstanding success, and the British press was only too ready to stress that it was targets in the *industrial* Ruhr that were attacked, and that fires had sprung up all over the *industrial* areas of the city.

There was absolutely no mention of the potential destruction of residential areas or the numbers of civilians who might have been killed in the process. Notwithstanding the fact that during the whole operation over Germany that night, forty-four planes were lost, British losses were still described as low compared with the number of planes involved in the raid. The general tone of the British press was summed up in a couple of key headlines:

 Herald of what Germany will receive
Reaping the Whirlwind

The number of planes employed in this raid was described as being twice as many as the Germans had ever used in a single raid over Britain. There was a feeling that, just as the Germans had bombed Warsaw and Rotterdam ruthlessly into surrender, it was quite justifiable that the British should now do the same to Germany.

There was no attempt nor, indeed, any need to justify the morality of such raids, since the reports simply failed to provide any material facts regarding the scale of destruction in residential areas. In fact, we now know that more than 13,000 buildings were destroyed, 45,000 people were made homeless and 469 people were killed. The latter was a remarkably low figure given the scale of the physical destruction.

It rapidly became a simple point-scoring exercise where the apparent revenge bombing of Canterbury by the Germans the following night was almost gleefully described in *The Scotsman* as:

A Poor Revenge for Mass Raid on Cologne

The German press, for its part, was quick to condemn the attack on Cologne as another terror raid and admitted that great damage was done to the inner city of Cologne, including the destruction of three churches and two hospitals. Particular anger was reserved for Churchill, who was mocked for congratulating the 'victors' of Cologne, albeit they had bombed only innocent civilian areas and had lost forty-four planes in the process. The initial German reports had talked of having downed only thirty-six planes but were quick to seize on the forty-four figure that appeared in the British press the following day. This figure was certainly greater than had been lost in any single raid on Germany in the past.

At this point, it is difficult to judge just who was winning the propaganda war, when both sides were able to make some capital out of the same event. The scale of the raid was certainly said to have boosted morale among the British public, while the Germans were determined to fight on against what they regarded as such brutal bombing and would certainly have taken comfort from the large number of British planes shot down in one night.

THE BOMBING OF HAMBURG

During the final week of July 1943, the bombing of a single city, in this case the port of Hamburg, was to reach an even higher degree of intensity. Over a ten-day period from Saturday 24 July, no fewer than 10,000 tons of bombs were dropped on the city by RAF and USAAF bombers. It was a greater weight of bombs than had been discharged on any other target until that point in the war.

A prolonged period of good weather permitted almost constant bombing, and such was the heat generated from the vast fires that ensued, a firestorm was created with winds of up to 150 miles per hour that sucked people and buildings into the inferno. Almost three-quarters of the city was destroyed and a million people left homeless.

From the very start of the raids, the Air Ministry issued reports justifying the attacks on the basis of Hamburg's importance as a port, where more submarines were built than in any other German-controlled city in Europe. Day by day, more information was provided. By the following Saturday, graphic details were given of the individual districts in Hamburg that had been destroyed, and further justification for the concentrated pummelling on the basis that:

This persistence has been necessary because Hamburg is such a sprawling target, with more than 100 miles of docks, landing stages and quays, and with its industrial and war factories dispersed all over the town.

Daylight photography was said to show the 'neutralisation' of Hamburg as a port and production centre. All the reports gave the impression of clinical attacks that had merely wiped out buildings and infrastructure employed by the enemy for war production. There was absolutely no attempt to detail the human cost in terms of the number of civilians killed or houses destroyed. In the small print, you would find reference to the number of British planes shot down each day – '28 missing after Thursday night' – but it was hard to keep an accurate tally as such losses were intermingled with details of raids on other German cities.

By 2 August, reports were appearing in the Stockholm press of the panic in the city, of 5,000 Danes fleeing Hamburg for Denmark and of a general evacuation with thousands of refugees streaming eastwards. And yet, despite all of this, there was still no mention of how many people had been killed or wounded during the bombings. The true horror of what was being suffered by the citizens of Hamburg was just not reported in the British press.

In fact, a greater tonnage of bombs was to be dropped on Hamburg during that ten-day period than during the whole of the Blitz on London from the summer of 1940 to May 1941. During the whole war, the total number of civilians killed in the United Kingdom by bombs or V weapons was around 65,000. We now know that the ten-day bombing of Hamburg resulted in the death of almost 43,000 civilians with another 37,000 badly wounded and injured. Perhaps it was felt that this was just too hard a truth to tell the British people.

However, if the British press remained silent, surely the German press would be far more outspoken? Absolutely not. Rather surprisingly, given the scale of the catastrophe, the German High Command actually said very little about the raids on Hamburg. The headlines in the *Neue Vetschauer Zeitung* of Monday 26 July 1943 were:

 Futile attempts (by the Soviets) to break through in the area of Belgorod
New sea battles off the Dutch coast – English Terror Attack on Hamburg

The main focus of the lead article in the paper was on the failure of the Soviets to break through on the Eastern Front. The report on the Hamburg bombing was, in fact, restricted to a mere seven lines, accusing the British of a terror attack on Hamburg causing heavy civilian deaths and the destruction of residential areas and cultural public buildings. Other papers stressed that the spirit of the citizens of Hamburg remained unbroken.

By 28 July, the bombing was relegated to page three of the newspaper and, even then, all it did was to condemn Britain for bombing Hamburg's churches, showing an old photo of the St Nikolai church that had apparently now been completely burnt to the ground. There was no indication of the number of casualties. By 31 July, there was absolutely no mention of the bombing at all, although by then the sad truth must have been known to everyone. Train-loads of fleeing refugees were arriving in every other major German city, and German civilians knew from their own experience that flattened cities entailed the deaths of thousands of people. By 2 August, there was more focus on victories over the Soviets and a mere photograph of a downed Stirling bomber after one of its attacks. The authorities were keen to stress that the Germans did not formally record any 'reported kills' unless verified by an independent source.

THE BATTLE OF BERLIN

As if the bombing of Hamburg had not been sufficiently horrific, it was not long before the Allies' attention was fully focused on Berlin, and the British press seemed to revel in the almost daily reporting of some new record either in terms of the number of bombers involved in a mission or in the number of bombs dropped within a certain period of time.

Over three nights from 18 November 1943, the biggest force of RAF heavy bombers ever sent to Germany dropped a total of 12,000 tons of bombs on the German capital. The British press was keen to give the impression that the sheer scale of the bombing raids would soon force Germany to surrender. *The Scotsman* of 20 November 1943 showed images of the huge 4,000lb blockbuster bombs that were being used in the mission and illustrated how no fewer than four people could stand inside the casing of a single bomb:

 350 'Block Busters' on Berlin
Record Attack by R.A.F
May be Start of Final Air Assault
Bombing Germany out of the War

Further heavy attacks were to continue the following week, demolishing the Kroll Opera House and setting fire to the homes of Goebbels and Hitler. While there was no attempt to conceal the fact that vast residential areas were being bombed, once again, there was no mention of the numbers of civilian casualties, and the focus was on the fact that the loss of twenty-six or more bombers on each of these raids was very small compared with the numbers of planes employed – a figure we are never told – and certainly far fewer than the 5 per cent average losses being sustained overall.

But while the Allies considered the bombing raids on Berlin of 17, 18 and 19 November as some of the most significant in the whole war, you would have been hard-pressed to recognise this from the reading of typical German newspapers. The *Neue Vetschauer Zeitung* of 19 November concentrated on victories in the fighting on the Eastern Front and mentioned only that some British planes had bombed western Germany the previous evening. The German High Command report was relegated to one of the inner pages the following day and simply mentioned that some bombs had fallen on Berlin, but that few lives were lost and that the Germans had successfully shot down forty-six British and American bombers. Even this heavy bombing of Berlin was portrayed as a bit of a sideshow to the main action.

By 22 November, the Germans were still playing down the significance of the raids on Berlin, and the continuing emphasis was on the effectiveness of their own air defences:

 Success of the German anti-aircraft defence force
Another black day for the English/American air-force

While the article continued by admitting that substantial damage had been inflicted on Mannheim, it also claimed there had been very small loss of life and that, in that one raid, the Allies had lost at least forty-six heavy bombers and 350 aircraft personnel. As might be expected, the truth about the Battle of Berlin lay somewhere in the middle.

This aerial campaign lasted officially from November 1943 to March 1944 and, although Berlin was always the primary target, many other large German cities were also bombed as part of this operation. The Allies certainly caused much physical destruction, disrupted the German war effort and forced the Germans to divert precious men and machines away from the land war, but the Allies were suffering an equally heavy toll in aircraft and personnel losses. Almost 3,000 aircraft were lost or damaged and a further 7,000 aircrew killed or captured. While such losses were still theoretically sustainable, just as the Germans had found in their bombing of London, there was no point in persevering with such tactics if it was not forcing Germany to beg to surrender.

Allied losses on individual missions continued to mount as the Germans became more efficient at predicting likely targets and harassing RAF bombers on their route all the way back and forth across Europe. The final straw was when the Allies lost ninety-five bombers (almost 12 per cent of their attacking force) on a raid on Nuremberg on the night of 30 March. The German press actually claimed that 134 aircraft were shot down and made huge counter-propaganda out of the success of their air defences.

The Battle of Berlin was brought to an abrupt end and is generally considered to have been a defeat for the Allies, as it simply did not achieve its main objective of bringing the war to a swift conclusion.

THE BOMBING OF DRESDEN

It would be almost inconceivable to write a chapter on the bombing of cities without including mention of the infamous raid on Dresden, on 13 and 14 February 1945. While virtually every German city and many small towns were to be bombed by the Allies before the end of the war, the attack on Dresden is still regarded by many Germans as just as great a crime as the bombing of Coventry was for the British so much earlier in the war.

By February 1945, the German Army was in full retreat, being squeezed between the Soviets in the east and the Americans and British advancing from the west. The air bombardments continued to grow in size, with British aircraft usually attacking by night and American bombers operating during the day. With an ever-decreasing amount of anti-aircraft fire and little German fighter opposition, given that the Germans were running short of fuel, planes and pilots, the Allied aircraft losses were now averaging less than 2 per cent per raid.

As the headlines in *The Times* of 15 and 16 November made clear, the fearful scale of the attack on Dresden was truly horrific:

 Smashing Blows at Dresden
650,000 incendiaries
14,000 tons on Germany
Dresden Again

In addition to the incendiaries, not only were hundreds of 4,000lb bombs being dropped but also a number of 8,000lb bombs. With Germany so close to defeat and so much of its military infrastructure already eliminated, the largely unanswered question is: why Dresden was chosen for such punishment at that time? *The Scotsman* claimed that the attacks were made to help the advancing Russian armies since, according to the Air Ministry, Dresden was still an important centre of communications and a base for the defence of eastern Germany.

In reality, Dresden was full of refugees fleeing from the advancing Russian Army and, since the main railway lines ran to the north of the city centre, it is difficult to understand why the sports stadium close to the very centre of the city was used by many aircraft as their primary target.

Once again, while the British press did not conceal the scale of the attack and admitted that the resultant fires were concentrated in the centre of the city, there was no mention of the number of civilian casualties, and the rumoured destruction of the opera house was simply regarded as 'another of those regrettable, but seemingly inevitable, sacrifices of historic buildings'.

There was never any attempt to question the morality or even the real purpose of the raid and the commentator of the *British Pathé* newsreel of 22 February even tried to make a joke out of the images of the battered city:

Before this, Dresden had been planned as a substitute capital for Berlin. After this, Hitler will have to look for a substitute for the substitute.

The *Völkischer Beobachter* of 15 February carried little comment from the German High Command about the raid – other than to report there had been a terror attack on the city of Dresden, and that thirty-seven Allied planes had been shot down in the process. Indeed, it was left to the likes of the Berlin correspondents of Swedish newspapers to report the city had been turned into one huge inferno, in which tens of thousands of refugees from eastern Germany had been killed. A Swiss paper claimed there were up to 34,000 casualties in the first two days of the raids.

Later, the German authorities would attempt to make more propaganda out of the raid by falsely claiming that more than 200,000 people had been killed in the bombings.

The true figure was probably closer to 25,000. Nevertheless, such was the outcry across the wider world, and especially in the United States, at a claim by an RAF officer (which was censored in Britain) that 'the Allied strategy of the deliberate terror bombing of German population centres was a ruthless expedient to hasten Hitler's doom', that Churchill was forced to think again.

Even if there were many who thought that the 'war-loving' Germans deserved such treatment when the true horrors of the concentration camps were revealed, Churchill eventually conceded on 28 March that the Allied bombing campaign and, in particular the bombing of Dresden, had been a mistake.

The time had come to bring the civilian suffering to an end, and the last heavy bombing raid by the RAF took place on the night of 25 April 1945.

CONCLUSION

There is no doubt that both sides were only too well aware of both the positive and negative propaganda the bombing of cities could generate. At the beginning of the war, the bombing of civilians was definitely considered taboo, and this is the reason why both sides went to great lengths to stress they bombed only targets with a military function, be it aircraft or munition factories, marshalling yards or railway stations.

The Germans, in particular, constantly insisted that Allied bombs hardly ever hit military targets because of the effectiveness of the Luftwaffe fighters and the devastating defensive fire from their flak guns. British pilots were accused of being air pirates for deliberately attacking workers' homes, hospitals, schools, churches and the residential areas of German cities.

In fact, both sides were reluctant to mention the destruction done to their own military installations and, except for the final months of the war, generally only made reference to civilian casualties when these were few in number. The focus was always on how many enemy bombers had been shot down.

Initially, it is fair to say that most civilians were killed by chance – the inevitable consequence of living close to factories, docks and military establishments. Nonetheless, from the start of the 1,000 bomber raids on German cities, it was obvious that the destruction of civilian property and the mass killing of civilians was a deliberate policy being pursued by the Allies. The indiscriminate area bombing of whole cities probably was a crime against humanity, for which military leaders today would be called to account. Harris genuinely believed that the Germans could be bombed into submission. He was wrong – just as the Germans had been wrong in believing that bombing British cities would have such a devastating impact on the civilian population that the British Government would be forced to sue for peace. Instead, such bombing simply generated in the German people a stubborn stoicism and determination to fight on against what they considered to be a cruel and barbaric enemy intent on wiping their country off the map.

As the scale of the Allied bombing increased, it is somewhat ironic that, while the media on both sides provided vivid descriptions and even occasional photographs of vast areas of cities laid waste by bombing raids and fires, there was virtually no corresponding detail of the toll in human life.

Devoid of hard facts, the British public was genuinely pleased to hear that the Germans were starting to get a taste of their own medicine. Just as many Germans had a sneaking suspicion as to what might be happening in the concentration camps, most Britons who had experienced aerial bombing had a pretty good idea as to the huge cost in human life that the Allied bombing must have been inflicting on German cities. Few were prepared to speak out openly about their misgivings.

Likewise, ignorant of the same hard facts, the German public did not generally feel any particular animosity towards the British, as they believed the British were suffering the same fate at the hands of German bombers. In fact, it was only with the bombing of Dresden that the true anger and hatred of the German public was roused. The war was lost. Dresden was not a particularly important city. It simply reeked of spiteful vengeance.

Opposite: Photograph of a bombed London street during the Blitz. NARA 195566

We can only surmise what would have happened if the British public had known the true extent of the German death rate. Or, if the German public had known the extent of their civilian losses, would there have been sufficient opposition to Hitler to effect a successful coup? We will never know. While the Allied bombing of German cities certainly helped divert valuable military resources from the front and may even have shortened the war, it did not in itself end the war. After all, even in Japan, it was to take something far more horrific – the dropping of two atomic bombs and the eventual deaths of almost 250,000 people in those bombings – to force the Japanese to surrender.

9

EL ALAMEIN AND THE DESERT WAR

INTRODUCTION

Even today, most Britons have heard of El Alamein and, without knowing any of the precise details, have some understanding that it was a very important battle in the desert of North Africa between Montgomery and Rommel, and that the Allies came out on top. Many will also be able to quote the famous lines Prime Minister Winston Churchill uttered about the Battle of El Alamein during his Mansion House speech of 10 November 1942: 'Now this is not the end. It is not even the beginning of the end. But it is, perhaps, the end of the beginning.'

What few people realise is that, between June and November 1942, there were actually three battles at El Alamein, and it was really only the last of these which would eventually lead to a decisive victory for the Allies in North Africa.

The significance of that third battle is indisputable but, as we will see, contrary to the many myths that have arisen in the interim, it was always a battle the British and their allies should have won, and that victory in itself was not the end of the Afrika Korps in North Africa, although it would hasten their eventual annihilation and Rommel's flight back to Germany.

Nevertheless, the prolonged nature of the campaign, the constant change in fortune and the failure of Montgomery to execute a final coup de grâce made it comparatively easy for the warring nations' respective media to give their audiences a completely different perspective on the course of the desert war.

BACKGROUND TO THE WAR IN NORTH AFRICA

Fighting in North Africa actually began in June 1940, immediately following Italy's declaration of war on Britain on 10 June. British forces carried out a series of raids on Italian positions in Libya and, in response, Mussolini ordered his Tenth Army to invade Egypt. However, the Italians encountered a number of problems and

General Erwin Rommel with the 15th Panzer Division in Libya in 1941. *NARA 540148*

were soon forced to retreat. By January 1941, the British had not only captured the port of Tobruk, but the Tenth Army had also been destroyed – with 170,000 of its men having been taken prisoner. Mussolini appealed to his German ally for assistance, and Erwin Rommel duly arrived in Tripoli in February with lead units of what would become known as the Afrika Korps. The British and Commonwealth forces having been weakened by the transfer of experienced troops elsewhere, Rommel soon forced the Allies to retreat, and he laid siege to Tobruk. For the next eighteen months the action moved rapidly back and forwards. The siege of Tobruk was lifted initially in January 1942 but, armed with fresh men and equipment, Rommel counter-attacked in June, recapturing Tobruk and driving the Allied forces out of Libya and back into Egypt.

The defeats in June 1942 represented the nadir of Allied fortunes in North Africa, and this was fairly accurately reflected in the British media coverage at the time. The headlines of *The Times* of 22 June simply read:

 Fall of Tobruk
Perimeter Breached by Air and Tank Attack

There was no attempt to conceal the significance of the capture of Tobruk:

The capture of Tobruk is not only a victory of prestige for the enemy, of which the most will be made, but it will also give him clear lines of communication along the coastal road.

It was reported that the Axis Powers were claiming that 25,000 prisoners had been captured together with immeasurable quantities of booty. The only small comfort and grounds for optimism seemed to lie in the fact that:

 Our frontier force is large, well-equipped and strongly dug in ... Our commanders, who take the long view, are not despondent. They are convinced that the next time the pendulum swings it will go in our favour, and the swing will be deeper.

Nonetheless, the fall of Tobruk was especially demoralising for the British, particularly when, just a few days previously, it had looked as if Rommel's forces had been close to defeat. Excuses were produced such as that the German tanks were equipped with heavier guns and much thicker armour than the Allied tanks, and the blame was directed firmly at the British commanders for not committing all their tanks to the earlier battles, when the Afrika Korps was close to defeat.

The *Völkischer Beobachter*, for its part, was understandably euphoric:

 Rommel's Glorious Victory: Tobruk
Tobruk represents the fall of the last and most important corner-stone of the British defence system in the desert of North Afrika

Somewhat ironically, the German press was then swift to condemn British propaganda for having tried to mislead its people and the whole world deliberately as to the true course of the desert war, and even mocked the British for having described Tobruk as an 'unconquerable fortress'. By 24 June, the papers were celebrating Axis troops driving the Allies back to the Libya–Egypt border, Hitler's promotion of Rommel to field marshal and Rommel's triumphant radio broadcast to the German people in which he claimed that:

 The Nation's Victory is Assured!

The first German newsreel about Rommel's victory was released on 1 July. Illustrated with excellent maps, a detailed description of Rommel's capture of Tobruk was given, describing how repeated break-out attempts by British tanks had been foiled. With the Allies' surrender of Tobruk on 21 June, the newsreel was able to show dramatic images of endless lines of Allied prisoners and claimed that 1,000 tanks had been either captured or destroyed, along with the seizing of 33,000 prisoners.

THE FIRST BATTLE AT EL ALAMEIN

By 30 June, Rommel was continuing to make rapid progress along the coast and, at one stage, was only 90 miles from Alexandria. The Commonwealth forces had been forced to withdraw to pre-prepared positions behind El Alamein, and General Auchinleck had assumed control of the whole Eighth Army. Early in July, Rommel launched an infantry attack against the positions at El Alamein, but, despite initial success, his troops failed to break through the British lines.

This setback was simply not reported in the German press, and it heralded the start of completely contradictory headlines emerging in Germany and Britain about the course of the conflict. For example, the German press of 3 and 4 July was only too keen to celebrate:

 Breakthrough at El Alamein
Enemy positions penetrated in the North and the South

It was claimed that more than 2,000 British soldiers had been taken prisoner, and that thirty cannons and numerous tanks had been captured or destroyed. There was absolutely no mention of any counter-attacks by the Allies, either at this time or in the following days.

At exactly the same moment, however, while failing to admit the extent of any of their own losses in terms of men or equipment, the British press was claiming proudly that:

 Heavy Attack repelled in Egypt
British Positions intact
Counter-blow at flank of Rommel's forces

Therefore, readers on either side could be excused for believing that their armies were gaining the upper hand. Surely they could not both be telling the truth? In fact, a sort of stalemate had emerged, perhaps best illustrated by the competing media coverage of 13 July.

On the one hand, the German press that day was to claim that the British *in the southern sector* had been forced to retreat with the loss of forty-five aircraft. On the other hand, the British press claimed that the Eighth Army's advance *in the northern sector* had been consolidated with the taking of 2,000 Axis prisoners and the destruction of eighteen enemy tanks. Both sides were telling the truth – they just were not painting the whole picture.

In practice, during July both sides were to make frequent counter-attacks in which substantial prisoners were taken, and many tanks and other vehicles were destroyed.

Each side was keen to say how much damage it had inflicted on the enemy but rarely detailed its own losses. Both armies were exhausted and simply did not possess the necessary strength to dislodge the enemy. The lack of real progress by the Afrika Korps is clearly reflected in the fact that, for much of July, reports on the campaign in North Africa were relegated to a few short paragraphs in the inner pages of such German newspapers as *NVZ*. The front page was reserved for highlighting spectacular German successes on the Eastern Front – such as at Sevastopol – and on the total destruction of one of the Arctic convoys – an incident that is examined elsewhere in this book.

The German newsreel of 22 July did contain images of captured forts at Maria Matruh and a rather amusing board pointing towards El Alamein on which the words 'Wavell's Way' had been scored through and overwritten with 'Rommel Weg' – Rommel's Way.

In truth, by the end of the month, the first Battle of El Alamein had more or less come to a halt, with both sides dug in and consolidating their positions.

THE SECOND BATTLE AT EL ALAMEIN[6]

Little happened in the desert war during much of August 1942. Montgomery took over control of the Eighth Army, and Rommel continued to strengthen his forces for a final, desperate attack on the Allied lines at El Alamein; this was launched on the last day of that month. Ironically, on that very same day the German press was carrying detailed reports of the Allies' disastrous Dieppe Raid, which had taken place earlier in the month.

It took some time for the renewed action in North Africa to reach either the British or German press. At last, on 3 September, *The Times* reported there had been a major tank battle in the left centre of the British lines, but that the Allied defences had not been penetrated. By 7 September, it even went so far as to claim that Rommel's attacks had not only been repelled, but that he was now on the retreat:

 Rommel still withdrawing westward
Severe losses in tanks, men and vehicles

In reality, after two days of fighting, Rommel had, indeed, been forced to withdraw when it was obvious that his troops were not going to overcome the Allied forces at Alam Halfa Ridge. To make matters worse, his retreat was then intercepted by a New Zealand division, whose Maori battalion alone claimed to have killed 500 Axis soldiers in close-quarter fighting. Little wonder that, for once, the British press

---

6   *Some historians will claim there were really only two battles at El Alamein – the battles in July and October – with Rommel's attacks in August not constituting a proper battle.*

was able to mock the German claims that this had only been 'a reconnaissance in force'. It was all too reminiscent of Allied claims following the failure of their raid on Dieppe a few weeks earlier.

Somewhat surprisingly, throughout the whole period from 31 August, when Rommel launched his initial attack, to 4 September, there was little mention of the desert campaign by the German hierarchy, other than accounts of local skirmishes. The main reporting was left to the Italian Army Command, which talked of many prisoners having been captured, fifty-one enemy tanks destroyed and twenty-four enemy aircraft shot down, with only five Axis planes failing to return to base. By 5 September, they even contended that it was only the British who were on the offensive, and that their attacks were being repulsed successfully. Once again, the main press reports concentrated on further success on the Eastern Front, and North Africa hardly merited any mention. It was as if Rommel's failure had never occurred.

THE THIRD BATTLE AT EL ALAMEIN

From early September and through much of October, there was little meaningful action on the desert front. Montgomery was content to build up his supplies as he prepared for a big attack to dislodge the Axis forces, and Rommel, conscious that such an attack was imminent, was content to strengthen the positions he already held.

On 23 October, Montgomery was finally ready, and he launched the largest artillery barrage ever witnessed in that part of the world. It was designed to prepare a way for two corridors to be driven through the enemy lines, as the Allies drove westwards from El Alamein.

You might well have expected that such a major offensive would certainly be headline news in the British press. This was simply not the case. *The Times* of 24 October actually carried a report about the western desert from the previous day, which declared that:

Apart from patrol activity there is nothing to report, except some enemy artillery and machine-gun fire against our forward positions in the Ruweisat area, but the air offensive which opened on 9 October is still in full swing.

The German press of the same day, which was usually quite punctilious in reporting any new development, was scarcely more enlightening. Admittedly, it did talk of 'lively reconnaissance activity on the ground in the northern sector' but, like the British press, more attention was paid to air activity and of twenty enemy planes having been shot down.

Allied tanks waiting to advance at dawn for the final El Alamein battle.

It is hard to say whether this lack of reporting was purely due to the time delay in information being relayed home or a deliberate attempt to play down the significance of increased activity. Most likely, nobody realised the true scale or significance of the bombardments, and it was certainly far too early to ascertain their effectiveness.

By 26 October, *The Times* was at least carrying the report from GHQ Cairo that the Eighth Army, with strong air support, had attacked on the Friday night, and that fierce fighting had developed and was continuing, with counter-attacks by the enemy having failed. There was still no mention of what had been the biggest artillery bombardment in desert war history.

For their part, the German press showed no signs of panic. It was as if North Africa was very much a sideshow and, almost with a stifled yawn, mention was made that the British had finally launched their long-expected attack. But the precise wording used was very carefully chosen:

THE SUCCESSES OF THE AXIS AIR FORCE

After a heavy artillery preparation, the British tried to penetrate both flanks with strong infantry and tank forces. They encountered stubborn resistance from Axis troops. In support of their attack, the British had heavy air support which was engaged by German and Italian fighters […] all in all the British lost 20 planes to the Axis Powers in North Africa on 24 October and numerous tanks.

It is obvious that the German report was being somewhat economical with the truth. Of course, the Axis ground forces were going to offer dogged resistance, but the report fails to say whether or not the British attacks were, in fact, successful. Nor is the number of enemy planes shot down of any significance – unless we are also told how much damage the enemy planes inflicted, or how many planes belonging to the Axis Powers were shot down at the same time. After all, at exactly the same time, the Allies were claiming to enjoy air superiority in the desert.

In the following days, we continue to see the emergence of divergent reports on the progress of this latest battle at El Alamein. For example, on 28 October, the *NVZ* talked proudly of the success of the German Army in North Africa:

 In the continuing battles around El Alamein, the British until now, despite their huge superiority in terms of numbers of troops, tanks and aircraft, have not managed to achieve any of their military objectives and instead the Axis troops have managed to hold their key positions along the whole front.

A similar message was to be repeated on an almost daily basis, reinforced with examples of how short-term breakthroughs by the Allies had been repulsed and dramatic statistics of the ever-increasing numbers of enemy planes and tanks that had been destroyed. Nevertheless, despite the admitted severity of the battle, reports of the fighting were almost invariably kept to the inner pages of the *NVZ*, as if the North African campaign was not of much significance relative to the rest of the war, and even though the front page headlines were often remarkably dull.

Conversely, during exactly the same period, almost every day *The Times* was to carry some fresh triumphant headline:

26 October:
Rommel's Main Position Penetrated – gains held in spite of counter-attacks

27 October:
Eighth Army Holding on to New Positions – 1,450 Axis prisoners taken

28 October:
Allied Progress in Desert Battle – gap in Rommel's defences widened and all gains held

29 October:
Big Tank Battle in the Desert – Axis Forces hurled back

30 October:
Eighth Army beats off counter-attack

2 November:
Eighth Army pressing forward – more German prisoners taken

4 November:
Great tank battle raging – many prisoners taken in infantry attack

5 November:
Rommel's Army in Full Retreat – 9,000 prisoners taken

General Montgomery watching his tanks moving forward in North Africa in November 1942. *NARA 535939*

Allied newsreel coverage thereafter was equally bullish. The *British Pathé News* report of 9 November was entitled 'Rommel on the Run' and was full of very arrogant and dismissive rhetoric:

 The Montgomery mincing machine is chewing the Afrika Korps to shreds [...] Rommel has been out-generalled and out-fought.

By the end of the month, the major newsreel companies were able to release detailed reports of all of the fighting in this last battle at El Alamein and showed countless lines of captured enemy planes and Axis prisoners. Indeed, the surrender of many thousands of Italian soldiers was more reminiscent of the round-up of sheep, albeit with one small tank rather than a sheepdog.

In reality, neither side told its own people the whole truth about this third El Alamein confrontation. Despite the intensity of Montgomery's artillery and aerial bombardment, the advancing Allied forces were initially unable to break through the main German defences. So, the initial successes reported in the Allied press were not

Italian prisoners of war captured in fighting near El Alamein. *LOC LC-USZ62-132809*

quite as conclusive as might have been suggested. In the last few days of October, all the attention turned to the northern section, but Rommel's counter-attacks against the Australian 9th Division and the British 1st Armoured Division were repelled, and the field marshal was forced to divert more of his tanks northwards to counter fresh attempts by the Australian Division to reach the coast. By 1 November, Montgomery had diverted the main focus of his attack further south and, by 3 November, the German defences had started to buckle. By 4 November, the Axis forces were in full retreat towards the Egyptian border, and this final Battle of El Alamein had been won by the Allies.

Quite amazingly, none of this was reported in any of the German media. Instead, there was a continued focus on the tonnage of shipping being sunk by U-boats, and especially on the number of convoys being wiped out. As late as 2 November, the official German reports talked of the enemy, and Australian units in particular, suffering heavy losses in Axis counter-attacks in the north. The Italian agencies even referred to favourable developments in the northern sector and the capture of 100 Australians and forty lorries.

It was not until 4 November that the press included an admission from the Italian High Command that 'our losses are also high – heavy fighting still on going'.

On 6 November, the *NVZ* provided a summary of the whole of the North African campaign from 31 October:

> Bitter fighting in North Africa
> British have suffered heavy tank losses

Even by the end of the report, there was still no recognition that the Axis forces had been defeated. History now records that the Battle of El Alamein had been won by 4 November but all that the German press reported for that day was that:

> To relieve some of the pressure on the Front, some troops from some sectors were withdrawn to pre-prepared secondary positions.

The Italian High Command's report for 5 November was just as reticent about admitting the terrible truth:

> After a particularly bitter resistance, troops of the German/Italian Army with-
> drew to new positions further west. The enemy suffered heavy losses in men
> and material. Our losses are heavy.

But, that was not the end of the story. Not only would the German press fail to admit that the Afrika Korps had suffered any dramatic defeat at El Alamein, but even after British-American troops landed in Morocco and Algeria on 8 November, the emphasis simply shifted to a description of how the Axis forces were stopping the Allied advance from their new positions.

From 22 July, the weekly German newsreels had featured virtually nothing about North Africa. The newsreel of 28 October did include a bombing attack on British positions in the desert and while it might be said that the newsreel of 4 November was preparing its viewers for some bad news, there was still talk of successful counter-attacks and certainly no hint of defeat:

 The units of the German and Italian tank armies stood against an enemy who is much superior in numbers of men and materials, and who is continually throwing more divisions into battle.

There was certainly no mention of the desert campaign in the newsreels throughout the rest of November, although there was a rather curious change in focus – with the bad news being spun from a new propaganda angle. America and Britain were accused of acting as criminals in invading France's colonies and it was claimed that the Axis Powers were simply fighting to defend France's interests. This was to be echoed in German newsreels, where the triumphant movement of German tanks to Marseille and other ports in the south of France was portrayed as if Germany was rushing to protect Vichy France from an enemy invasion from North Africa.

CONCLUSION

The backwards and forwards nature of the desert war in North Africa gave both sides ample opportunity to celebrate victories and advances in their respective media coverage.

The fall of Tobruk to the Germans on 21 June was a major humiliation for the Allies, and the British press found it difficult to play down the significance of that defeat. Likewise, Rommel's undoubted success came as a surprise to most of the German public and, along with the news of fresh triumphs on the Eastern Front and their apparent control of the seas with their U-boats, everything seemed to be going well for the German war machine.

Within a matter of months, and after the three battles at or near to El Alamein, the situation was to become more complicated and, ultimately, to result in a complete change of fortunes.

By the end of the first battle in July 1942, the Allied and Axis Powers were both claiming victory when, in fact, it had ended in a stalemate. But, there is no doubt that the press coverage gave grounds for optimism and celebration to the public on both sides.

Rommel's attempt to break through in the second battle, in September, did end in failure, and the British press, for their part, were able to make the most of this setback to the Afrika Korps. However, it was a setback that was never reported to the German people. Reports of destruction to enemy planes and tanks continued largely unabated, and when the press fell silent about North Africa, it could naïvely be assumed that nothing much was happening in Egypt; anyway, there were always fresh victories for the Germans to celebrate on other fronts.

When it came to the third and final Battle of El Alamein, both sides misled their own people to a certain extent. There is no doubt that for a while the Allies, who had already suffered many setbacks in North Africa, might not have achieved victory in that battle. The Germans did put up very stubborn resistance, but the British press was loathe to produce any negative headlines once the battle was in full swing. Nevertheless, with their ever-increasing superiority in terms of men and materials, it was going to be only a matter of time before the Allies would be successful.

For once, Rommel was outwitted. Nevertheless, the Germans were still not prepared to admit defeat to their own people. The extent of their own losses in terms of men and equipment was hardly ever mentioned. The word 'retreat' was never used. It was always a matter of withdrawing to pre-prepared defences, and of these new defensive lines being defended successfully. When all else failed, it came down to accusing the allegedly criminal Allies of seeking to seize France's colonies in North Africa – whereas all the Axis Powers were doing was to try to protect Vichy France's rightful property.

Not that the landings of further Allied troops in Algeria and Morocco, immediately after the third Battle of El Alamein, did actually end the war in North Africa. Rommel had considerable success in rebuffing the Allied advances both in November 1942, and more notably, against American troops in late February 1943. But the die was cast. The German and Italian troops were gradually being outnumbered and outflanked and were finally forced to surrender on 13 May 1943.

However, much like the British reaction at Dunkirk, in 1940, the German and Italian High Commands were just as skilled at turning the defeat into a victory. The headline in the *NVZ* of 14 May read:

 Honourable End to the Heroic Campaign in Africa

The *Völkischer Beobachter* of 15 May even reported that the Italians were so proud of their forces that they were claiming:

'Today – We have Greater Belief in Victory than ever before!'

There were stirring stories of Axis soldiers fighting to the last bullet and the incredible assertion by Hitler that his African fighters 'had completely fulfilled all their military objectives'. The justification for this claim was that, because of the stubborn resistance of the Axis forces in North Africa for so many months, the Allies had suffered devastating losses in terms of men and equipment. This, in turn, had deprived the Allies of much-needed resources that would otherwise have been diverted to fight on other fronts, and it had also given the Axis forces time to build up their strength elsewhere. It was a stunning manipulation of the truth designed to conceal the true extent of the Axis losses. The fact that no fewer than 275,000 of their soldiers had been forced to surrender was never reported in the German press.

In any event, Rommel had already foreseen the likelihood of failure and had returned to Europe in March 1943, leaving someone else to take responsibility for the final defeat. Wishing to distance Rommel from any blame and foreseeing the imminent disaster, the German High Command had actually released a statement on 11 May reminding the German public how the highly decorated Field Marshal Rommel had been forced to return home to Germany in March for vital medical treatment, but that his health was now improving and once he was fully recovered the Führer would entrust him with a new task.

10

THE BATTLE FOR STALINGRAD

INTRODUCTION

If Allied successes in the Battle of Britain and the Battle of El Alamein were key turning points in the war for the British and their allies then, arguably, the German Army's resounding defeat at Stalingrad, early in 1943, was an even more significant event for the Axis Powers. Notwithstanding the death of more than 147,000 German and Axis soldiers, trapped in the Stalingrad pocket, and the final surrender of 91,000 troops, the true significance of the catastrophe lay in the psychological impact it had on the course of the rest of the war. Despite all their early triumphs, the Axis forces had still failed to conquer the Soviet Union and the German Army was fatally crippled – even though it would struggle on defiantly for more than two years; other than through some miraculous intervention, the ultimate defeat of Germany was assured.[7]

However, just as the British had managed to transform their defeat in France and the retreat from Dunkirk into a national celebration of victory and deliverance, the Nazis were to exploit the example of their heroic forces at Stalingrad to reignite the whole German nation's determination to achieve final victory in what was now declared 'Total War'.

---

[7] In the spring of 1943 Goebbels took the decision to forbid the screening within Germany of the Nazis' own version of the film Titanic, almost as soon as it had been released, and despite the fact it was the most expensive German film produced until that point. It is claimed this decision was driven by his fear that the German population would be demoralised by all the death and destruction in the film and would draw parallels between the sinking of the Titanic and the fall of Germany.

BACKGROUND TO THE WAR IN THE SOVIET UNION

When it was announced in special editions of German newspapers on Sunday 22 June 1941 that Hitler had launched the greatest military attack in world history on the Soviet Union, ordinary German citizens could well be excused for being somewhat confused by this turn of events.

Having previously been told by the Nazis, in the early years of their struggle to come to power, that the evil Bolsheviks were a threat to all civilisation, much of this anti-Soviet rhetoric had subsided with the signing of the Non-Aggression Pact in August 1939. Earlier feature films, such as *Um das Menschenrecht* and *Friesennot*, which had been particularly hostile towards the Soviets, had been immediately withdrawn, and the attitude towards the people of Russia had become far more conciliatory.

How then was Hitler going to justify this apparently new change in direction? As with many of Hitler's pronouncements, it was never going to be a simple explanation. Hitler began by reminding his people that it was only because of the warmongering British – as evidenced in the past through their destruction of Spain and wars against Holland and France – that Germany had been dragged into the First World War in the first place. He also claimed that all recent British actions had been designed to encircle and stifle Germany. Then, he blamed Russia for taking the opportunity to seize Lithuania and for threatening Romania – a country whose safety Germany had guaranteed – and for a continued build-up of their troops on Germany's eastern border. This latter claim was certainly true, and the final lines of Hitler's proclamation were particularly convincing:

> Moscow not only broke our treaty of friendship, but betrayed it! ... Today around 160 Russian divisions stand on our border [...] During the night of 17–18 June, Russian patrols again crossed the German border and could only be repelled after a long battle [...] now the hour has come when it is necessary to respond to this plot by Jewish Anglo-Saxon war-mongers and the Jewish rulers of Moscow's Bolshevist headquarters.
>
> The purpose of this front is no longer the protection of individual nations, but rather the safety of Europe, and therefore, the salvation of everyone.
>
> May God help us in this battle.

In fact, as late as 14 June, the Russian press had been carrying official government statements denying vigorously that the Soviet Union was preparing for a war with Germany and, for his part, even when the Germans did attack, Stalin was not initially prepared to believe that it was anything more than a provocation.

The Russians were simply caught off guard and, for the next six months, the Germans made remarkable progress, advancing more than 800 miles across a 1,000-mile front and causing the Russians more than 4 million casualties. However, while they had captured Kiev by September, subsequent setbacks at Moscow and Kharkov meant that a stalemate started to develop, as the Germans were not well equipped to carry their campaign through the ravages of a Russian winter. By the spring of 1942, the Germans had lost almost 1.7 million men to a combination of death, wounds, capture, illness and frostbite. Ninety per cent of vehicles and pack animals lost had not been replaced.

Consequently, Hitler was obliged to halt his advance across such a wide front and concentrate instead on capturing the valuable oil supplies in the Caucasus region.

THE ATTACK ON STALINGRAD

While the capture of Stalingrad was not an essential requirement for the completion of the mission in the Caucasus, it was still considered a valuable prize, so the Germans launched their all-out attack on the city on 23 August 1942. The actual focus of the German press in much of the final week of August 1942 was an unrestrained mocking of the Allies for continuing to claim that their disastrous Dieppe Raid had been a success. In particular, the *Freiburger Zeitung* of 24 August included a direct quotation from the *Chicago Sun* to the effect that the Allies had recorded a 'decisive victory' and that 'since Dunkirk Western Europe had seen nothing to compare with Dieppe'. The German newspaper readily agreed that this latter comment was certainly justified, since in their assessment:

 Dieppe was in reality the greatest defeat for the British that Western Europe had witnessed since Dunkirk.

How ironic then that, at the very moment the German press was poking such ridicule at this Allied disaster, the Germans themselves were about to launch an attack on Stalingrad that would ultimately turn into their own greatest ever single military defeat – a defeat that would far outweigh the significance of Dieppe – and which undoubtedly hastened the Red Army's march on Berlin and an end to the war.

When it came to its reporting of the war in Eastern Europe, one of the major difficulties confronting the British press was that it frequently had to rely on the respective official announcements and press reports produced by the Russians and the Germans themselves, as the Allied press often did not have their own independent correspondents on the ground to give an objective analysis of what was happening.

Reporting on events of 23 August, the headlines in the German press the following day were:

Tank battle near Stalingrad – June 1942. *RIA Novosti Archive, 129362/Zelma/ CC-BY-SA 3.0*

 Crossing of the River Don forced through northwest of Stalingrad
Break-through of heavily defended enemy positions

The German papers were full of triumphant reports of German troops, supported by the Luftwaffe, carrying all before them and of counter-attacks on the Don Front being repulsed by Italian troops. It was claimed that the Soviets lost 157 planes, with only eight German planes reported missing.

However, the report in *The Times* from the same day painted a far more confusing picture:

 Soviet Counter-blows in Don Bend
Axis mass huge army for assault
Footholds on Eastern Bank

The actual report on which these headlines was based came from an announcement from the Russian High Command, which steadfastly refused to mention that fighting was even taking place close to Stalingrad.

The truth was that since Stalin had changed the city's name from Tsaritsyn to Stalingrad in 1925, the city had simply become too important a symbol of Russia to be allowed to fall. This was reflected in the rather confusing Russian accounts of the battle. Where Russian reports conceded that the Germans had succeeded in advancing, this was always countered by the claim that the Germans had advanced only at the cost of enormous losses. Likewise, where there was mention of Russian advances, then it was claimed that German counter-attacks had been repulsed. In short, it was very difficult to determine from the Russian reports which side was making more progress, and the British press did well to reach a more balanced conclusion.

The following day, the Russian High Command still refused to mention Stalingrad by name. It did report, however, that in one encounter, the enemy had lost eleven tanks, eight anti-tank guns and 300 men. This may well have been true, but what the communiqué completely failed to indicate was whether or not that particular German attack had been successfully rebuffed.

The German reports, at that time, were always far more bullish – and often with good reason. In fact, while the Red Army did manage initially to slow down the German advance and prevent German tanks from entering Stalingrad itself, within just a week of the commencement of their advance, the Germans were 30 miles from the centre of Stalingrad, and intensive Luftwaffe bombing raids had killed up to 40,000 inhabitants of the city in the first two days of fighting alone.

In reality, it was to be the start of a long battle of attrition, where the value to both sides either of taking or holding the city would mean far more in propaganda terms than it would ever mean in strategic terms. By the end of August, both sides were in surprising agreement. The Germans' progress had been checked, and even the High Command in Berlin was forced to concede that the so-called 'decisive assault' it had launched the previous week had not achieved a conclusive result.

On 5 September, the Russians did launch a major assault on the Germans' XIV Panzer Corps, but it was so unsuccessful that, within a few hours, the Red Army had lost more than thirty tanks and was forced to withdraw. Indeed, the attack ultimately achieved so little that it failed to register in either the British or the German press.

Nevertheless, for all the fact that Russian counter-attacks were failing, the harsh truth was that the Germans were making little progress in their own capture of Stalingrad and kept having to play down earlier expectations of a quick victory. Stalingrad was repeatedly described as a 'fortress', which would only be overcome after a long and tedious campaign.

This also helps to explain why, despite all that was happening on the Eastern Front, the *Freiburger Zeitung* of 6 September was still prepared to devote more space on its front page to a report on an attack by the IRA on a police barracks in County Fermanagh than to events around Stalingrad.

At last, on 7 September, the German public was greeted with some more encouraging headlines:

 Heavy counter-attacks at Stalingrad all in vain

It was reported that German and Romanian troops had captured more ground in heavy fighting, that counter-attacks were beaten off and that 108 enemy tanks had been wiped out. Nevertheless, as the headlines in the British press made clear to its readers over the following days, while the Russians around Stalingrad were gradually going backwards, German progress was still very slow. *The Times'* headlines were indicative:

7 September
   Russians Holding Firm at Stalingrad
8 September
   Russian Gains north of Stalingrad
9 September
   Germans press near Stalingrad
10 September
   Slow Axis rate of advance
11 September
   New Stalingrad Threat checked

This gave almost entirely the opposite impression of that which German readers would have gleaned from the headlines in the *Freiburger Zeitung* for the very same days:

7 September
   Heavy (Russian) counter-attacks at Stalingrad all in vain
8 September
   High positions (Russian) around Stalingrad stormed
9 September
   Controlling heights on outskirts of Stalingrad taken
10 September
   Fierce struggle in the fortified territory around Stalingrad
11 September
   Successful progress in the battle for Stalingrad

The often contradictory headlines from those five days alone, even if often simply because of the respective timing of reports, shows just how difficult it was going to be for both sides to agree on the key outcome of any particular day's fighting.

Nevertheless, whatever spin either side might want to place on the actual facts and on a specific, meaningless little triumph here or there, the plain truth was that there was intense fighting around Stalingrad, the Germans were making slow headway at great cost and the Russians were giving up ground very slowly – but again at immense cost.

Hitler was certainly not pleased with the lack of progress, relieving Field Marshal Wilhelm List of command of Army Group A and assuming control himself. The Germans were forced to justify why it was taking so long to conquer Stalingrad. Their excuses ranged from the nature of the territory with its treacherous ravines, clefts and chasms to how the Soviet soldiers were fighting with 'an indescribable ferocity'.

Growing frustration at the delay in taking Stalingrad meant that activity on the Eastern Front soon ceased to make front page news at all. It would actually take the Germans more than two months to move from a position just some 7 miles west of the River Volga to the heavily defended factory district on the very banks of the Volga.

By 8 November, the Germans still held only 90 per cent of the city but, in a speech that day, Hitler declared that he was satisfied that the city was 'as good as taken except for some small pockets of token resistance'. Nonetheless, the commander in charge of the German forces, Friedrich von Paulus, recognising the dangers posed by the onslaught of the Russian winter and with temperatures falling as low as -60°C, asked Hitler for permission to withdraw. This was refused. It was a decision soon to be rued since, only a few days later, on 19 November, the Soviets were to launch their own major offensive, code-named Operation Uranus.

OPERATION URANUS – THE SOVIET COUNTER-ATTACK

Such was the intensity of the two-pronged Soviet attack from north and south that even the German press was forced to concede the following day:

 Soviet attacks in various sectors

This proved to be one of the greatest understatements in military history. While the Germans' Romanian allies fought bravely, they incurred 55,000 casualties on that first day and, within another forty-eight hours, the Russian armies had met up close to Kalach, thereby trapping 290,000 German and Axis troops in a pocket, 36 miles long and 25 miles deep, to the east of the River Don.

Other than short reports on the stout defence of the Axis troops and the losses being suffered by the Soviets on other fronts, there was absolutely no indication in the German press in the following days of the calamity that was developing at Stalingrad.

As late as 23 November, the key German headline was a mocking reference to the great victory Churchill had achieved in removing Sir Stafford Cripps from his war cabinet. While there was passing recognition of further heavy 'defensive battles' south and west of Stalingrad, there was no indication as to who was gaining the upper hand. In reality, the Russians had advanced between 40 and 50 miles towards Stalingrad the previous day, and they were to claim that 24,000 prisoners had been captured in recent fighting. For once, even those members of the British public with no knowledge of tactical warfare could see from the maps printed in their newspapers just how obvious it was that the Russians' pincer movement was almost complete, and that the Axis troops were being detached from their colleagues and supply lines to the west. Paulus believed that there might still be a possibility for the 6th Army to break out to the south-west before the Russians could complete their encirclement, but permission to withdraw was again refused on the night of 23 November, since Hitler was convinced that other German forces could still break through to relieve the 6th Army without it having to suffer the humiliation of retreat.

The first indication to the general German public that everything might not be going to plan appeared in the following announcement from the German High Command on 24 November – and even that appeared only as a subsidiary article:

HEAVY FIGHTING SOUTH-WEST OF STALINGRAD AND ON THE GREAT BEND OF THE DON

In a ruthless commitment of men and material the Soviets broke into the defensive front in the Don area. Counter-measures are being taken. In the tough and ever-shifting battles of the last two days several hundred enemy tanks have been destroyed. In spite of the poor weather conditions, units of the German and Romanian air forces have been constantly intervening in the land battles.

Reports over the following days offered little additional clarification and tried frequently to divert attention by giving greater importance to breakthroughs and victories on other sections of the Eastern Front. There was absolutely no mention of the 'disorderly Axis retreat in the north-west' or of 'the retreat from Stalingrad' – headlines that appeared in the British press on 26 and 27 November.

While the *Wochenschau* newsreel of 26 November did mention Stalingrad, with action shots of Stukas dropping their bombs on apartment blocks and of some Bolshevik soldiers being taken prisoner, there was no indication as to how the battle was proceeding. The closing statement from the reporter was equally unenlightening:

The battle for Stalingrad demands tremendous physical and mental strength from every man.

In fact, far from being on the defensive, the impression given in the German press throughout late November was that it was the Russians who were in disarray:

Soviet snipers in camouflage cloaks entering a destroyed house in Stalingrad – December 1942. *RIA Novosti Archive, 450/Zelma/CC-BY-SA 3.0*

Heavy Soviet attacks in the Don bend region repulsed

Failure of Soviet attacks on all Fronts

247 tanks destroyed/devastating Stuka attacks/Cavalry division wiped out

Successful counter-attacks in the Don bend region

However, a closer analysis of the actual report from the German High Command for 30 November suggests the editor was being somewhat economical with the truth. The fact that fighting was taking place between the Rivers Volga and Don at all implied that the Soviets had made considerable advances, and if the Germans were having to counter-attack this could only mean that they had certainly been on the defensive.

Throughout December, it soon became obvious to the German High Command that Göring's rash promise of being able to fly in 500 tons of supplies daily to the besieged troops would never be fulfilled. In fact, Paulus had originally indicated that they would require 800 tons of supplies per day, but he was lucky if they ever received more than 10 per cent of what was needed.

The situation was deteriorating rapidly, but there was little suspicion of impending doom in German newspapers. In fact, the more the position deteriorated, the less mention there was of Stalingrad by the German High Command. Throughout most of

December, the emphasis was on fighting on other fronts or on vague successes against the Soviets, without detailing exactly where the action was taking place. The success of the Japanese in the war in East Asia also provided a welcome distraction for the German press from having to report the fighting on the Eastern Front.

The first real admission from the German High Command that ground was being lost came on 21 December:

 In the middle of the Don area […] the enemy succeeded in breaking through the German front-line. It was achieved at the expense of huge numbers of Bolshevik losses. To avoid being outflanked, German divisions located there moved according to plan to pre-prepared positions and, thereby, prevented any broadening of the enemy's initial success.

Despite the rather clumsy wording and the impression that the Germans were in full control of what they were doing, there is no doubt that the move to pre-prepared positions did in fact represent a retreat.[8]

'Here is Stalingrad'

On Christmas Eve, the German High Command resorted to one final trick to try to conceal the truth about Stalingrad. The content of a radio broadcast that day consisted of representatives of the German armed forces serving across the world signing in and wishing the troops in Stalingrad well. Eventually, there was a seemingly rather crackly response from the army in Stalingrad and the troops on the Volga front:

 Here is Stalingrad …

It was a complete sham. Broadcasts from Stalingrad had actually ceased the previous week, and this message had been faked in a Berlin studio.

The lies and misinformation were set to continue. By 31 December even the Allied press was starting to say what many in the West, and perhaps even in Germany, had realised for some time, that it was only a question of time before the Axis forces at Stalingrad would be overcome.

On 8 January, the very day Soviet Commander Rokossovsky offered Paulus surprisingly generous surrender terms, the report issued by the German High Command was still completely out of touch with reality:

8   *Even today, eye-witnesses of the time can still recall how the use of the word* Frontbegradigung *(straightening of the front) became an increasingly frequent explanation for what everyone could plainly see was nothing other than a gradual German retreat on the Eastern Front.*

In the areas of the Central Caucuses, the Don and north-west of Stalingrad German troops are engaged in heavy but successful army battles against strong Soviet infantry and tank forces. In counter-attacks the enemy was beaten back in several places and suffered heavy losses. Thirty-two tanks were destroyed.

There was still no mention of comparable Axis losses but, reading between the lines, there was an apparent admission that not all the enemy attacks had been repelled.

However, throughout the second half of January, the careful change in the vocabulary used to describe the conflict gave the first real hint to a German audience that some bad news was imminent:

 Shining Example of German Soldiery
For Weeks Heroic Courage displayed in the Defence of Stalingrad
In Stalingrad the 6th Army has added Great Honour to its Colours in a Heroic and Sacrificial Battle against overwhelming Superior Force.
The Spirit of the Defenders is Unbroken

Conscious that no German field marshal had ever been taken alive, Hitler rather cynically bestowed this status on Paulus on 31 January, in the genuine belief that Paulus would either commit suicide or fight with his men to the very end. It was reported in the *Völkischer Beobachter* of 1 February:

 The Führer honours the band of heroes at Stalingrad

It was a futile gesture. Paulus actually agreed surrender terms on that very day and, on the same day, the British press was carrying definitive reports that the Germans had been defeated:

All Resistance over at Stalingrad
Remaining German Forces Capitulate

Neither comment was actually correct, since we now know that some isolated units did fight on until March, but the Germans were still very slow to release such disheartening facts to their own people. Finally, in a special radio report on 3 February, the announcer simply and solemnly declared:

The Battle of Stalingrad has come to an end.

'They died so that Germany might live' – the dramatic headlines appearing in the Nazi newspaper on 4 February 1943 concealed the fact that the 6th Army had not fought to the last man. *The British Library/Public Domain*

There was still no use of the word 'defeat' and, by the following day, the German press prefaced the moving declaration issued by the German High Command with the following rallying headline:

 ### THEY WERE HEROES – LET US BE WARRIORS!

The Battle for Stalingrad is over – True to their oath to fight to their last breath, the 6th Army under the exemplary leadership of Field Marshal Paulus, has been overcome because of the overwhelming strength of the enemy and unfavourable circumstances.

The sacrifice of the army was not in vain. This army, bulwark of a historical European mission, for several weeks withstood the onslaught of six soviet armies.

[…] Thereby, they gave the German leadership the time and the possibility for counter measures on which the future of the whole Eastern Front depended.

Two enemy demands for surrender were proudly refused. Generals, officers, non-commissioned officers and ordinary soldiers fought shoulder-to-shoulder right to their last bullet. They died so that Germany might live. Their example will last far into the future, in spite of all the untruthful Bolshevik propaganda. New divisions of the 6th Army are already in the process of being formed.

While it was a very emotive piece of prose, what the statement failed to admit was that the German soldiers did not all fight to the last man and that, in fact, Paulus and twenty-four generals had surrendered. For its part, some of the German media declared, firstly, that Paulus had been badly wounded and, later, that he was actually dead. This was quite untrue.

There was no mention that, of the 260,000 German and Romanian soldiers trapped in the Stalingrad pocket from the previous November, close to 147,000 had died either in combat or from a mixture of disease, cold and hunger. While 40,000 of the wounded had been flown to safety, just under 91,000 were taken prisoner – including 2,500 officers. None of this was reported in the German press.

German newsreel, which had been so quick to show images of Stalingrad the previous November, mysteriously now failed to show any images of the fall of Stalingrad. At the very same time, the event was of such propaganda importance for the Soviets that the Russian soldiers actually re-enacted for their newsreel cameras the very moment that they rushed forward to link up with their comrades.

The *British Movietone* newsreel of 1 March 1943 was also keen to set the record straight with action shots of advancing Soviet soldiers and of endless lines of Axis prisoners being marched into captivity. The British reporter could not contain his desire to accord the triumph the highest of superlatives:

A victory that has meant the crushing of an army [...] A great blow to German military prestige [...] An open wound in German morale [...] Stalin's ruined city has itself started an avalanche of ruin which will one day overwhelm the Germany of Hitler.

CONCLUSION

Having grown accustomed to quick victories in France and, initially, achieving rapid progress in the onslaught against Russia, the setback at Stalingrad came as a real surprise to many Germans, especially when the media had conspired with the German High Command to keep silent about the true state of that battle.

For the Germans, it was a catastrophe of epic proportions. Of the 91,000 men who surrendered in February 1943, only 15,000 would still be alive by the end of May. Only 5,000 would make it home to Germany after the war – some as late as 1955. The Battle of Stalingrad became a cause whose psychological significance to both Hitler and Stalin far outweighed its immediate strategic importance.

If the German military losses were high, then the losses on the Soviet side were even greater with probably around 750,000 soldiers killed, wounded or missing. While the German troops at Stalingrad did indeed divert six Russian armies from the fighting elsewhere and did delay the course of the war, it was still regarded as a major turning point, not just by the Germans and the Soviets but by the whole world. Neutral countries, conscious of this turn in fortune, started to be less accommodating towards Germany. Portugal and Turkey ceased to supply Germany with tungsten and chromium respectively. The resultant shortage of these two chemical elements was to have a seriously detrimental impact on German arms production.

A captured German prisoner of war being escorted by a Soviet soldier – Stalingrad 1943.
Rare Historical Photos

Nevertheless, ironically, Goebbels was cynically to exploit the disaster at Stalingrad by appealing to all Germans to honour the sacrifices made by the men of the 6th Army by engaging in 'Total War'. The disaster at Stalingrad probably did have a unifying impact on the whole German nation, with ordinary Germans forced to accept that they would now need to slog it out to the end rather than fall victim to the Bolshevik menace and the awful vengeance Soviet soldiers were likely to inflict on a Germany that had shown so little mercy in its own invasion of the Soviet Union.

The final outcome of the war was probably now inevitable, even if it would take more than two years of hard fighting for the total defeat of Germany to be achieved. Hitler certainly recognised the importance of the defeat at Stalingrad and was already starting to live in a fantasy world far removed from the reality of what was actually taking place on the battle front. When, in the spring of 1943, he was asked what he thought about the men who had surrendered at Stalingrad, Hitler was simply to respond:

 The duty of the men of Stalingrad is to be dead.

In reality, in Nazi eyes, their ignominious surrender was an unwelcome distraction from the 'Total War' creed that was now being promoted and, therefore, the survivors were simply to be ignored and forgotten.

11

D-DAY AND BEYOND – THE INVASION OF MAINLAND EUROPE

INTRODUCTION

In the early hours of the morning of 28 April 1944, a fleet of German fast-attack E-boats, on one of their regular ad hoc raiding missions from Cherbourg, intercepted nine large Allied tank landing ships (LST) full of men, tanks and other vehicles about to deposit their cargoes on shore.

With only one escort for protection, the slow-moving LSTs provided an easy target for the German torpedoes and, within a matter of minutes, two of them had been sunk and another badly damaged. It is officially recorded that 749 American army and naval personnel were killed that morning, although no mention of the event was ever made by the Allied authorities at the time.

This was not D-Day, and these ships had not been about to land in France but rather on Slapton Sands, close to Dartmouth on the south coast of England.

In fact, this was one of a whole series of rehearsals that took place at various locations in the United Kingdom in preparation for D-Day. Nevertheless, such was the extent of the losses in that particular exercise, caused by the unexpected attack by the German patrol vessels, that there was a real danger that the plans for the actual invasion would have to be amended. Indeed, it was only when the bodies of key men involved in the exercise were recovered that this threat was finally lifted.

While the German authorities, at the time, certainly reported the successful sinking of numerous small naval boats and the torpedoing of a destroyer that morning, they seemed blissfully unaware of the true significance of the flotilla of vessels they had intercepted or of the full extent of the carnage they had inflicted in their attack.

Nonetheless, D-Day itself was only a few weeks away. Any Allied report of this disaster would hardly have been good for the morale of those about to participate in Operation Overlord – the code name for the Battle of Normandy. Its failure would have set back the Allied cause by many years and, perhaps, even allowed Hitler time to perfect his own weapons of mass destruction with which he could have won the war. Instead, its eventual success would accelerate the liberation of mainland Europe from the control of the Nazis, and little wonder it was to be described by the media as 'the greatest combined operation in world history'.

OPERATION OVERLORD

Scarcely had the British completed their withdrawal from Dunkirk in June 1940, than Churchill had established the Combined Operations Staff and charged it with producing a plan for Britain and its allies returning to the mainland of Europe.

As early as March 1942, Hitler had ordered the construction of an Atlantic Wall that was to stretch all along the coast from the south-west of France to Norway and whose purpose was to ward off any attempted invasion by the Allies. The so-called 'wall' was never fully completed, and rather than being a purely physical wall, it largely consisted of a line of gun batteries, bunkers, pillboxes, ditches, mines and barbed wire fortifications, aided by the shoreline's natural contours and obstacles. Most major ports en route were also heavily fortified to resist any sea-borne attack and, in November 1943, Field Marshal Rommel was transferred to Normandy with specific responsibility for strengthening the wall along the coast of France.

Several locations along the coast of northern France were considered by the Allies as suitable invasion targets. The Pas-de-Calais area was obviously the most attractive, being the shortest distance from Britain and with good access towards the Allies' final objective of Berlin. For those very same reasons, however, it was also the area most heavily defended by the Germans.

It was also recognised that, post-invasion, major harbour facilities would be required for the supply and reinforcement of the initial landing parties, and that the Allies would have to provide their own floating harbours to satisfy this need. The decision to attempt to capture and use a pre-existing port such as Cherbourg for this purpose had already been discounted, even before the disaster of the Dieppe Raid in 1942, although some vital lessons were learnt from that raid that were put to good use when D-Day did arrive.

After a number of postponements, the date finally chosen for D-Day was 5 June, when there would be a full moon and the tides would be high. As that date approached and the weather forecast for the Channel area for that period was so poor, there was a real danger that the whole invasion would have to be postponed. However, largely due to the advice of the Scottish meteorologist, Group Captain James Stagg, who calculated that there would be a short window of acceptable weather in the midst of the storm, General Dwight Eisenhower, Commander of Supreme Headquarters Allied Expeditionary Force (SHAEF), took the decision that the invasion would proceed on Tuesday 6 June.

Gliders at an English airfield in May 1944 being prepared for D-Day with the addition of black and white invasion stripes.

It was to be the biggest combined operation in world history, involving more than 20,000 airborne troops, 150,000 amphibious forces and 7,000 ships and boats of all sizes. General Montgomery was to be the commander of all the land forces involved in the invasion.

Assisted by British and American airborne landings inland, and by prior aerial and naval bombardments, the sea-borne invasion was to consist of mainly British, Canadian and American troops being landed on five designated 'beach' areas – with the code names Utah, Omaha, Gold, Juno and Sword – stretching along the north coast of Normandy from points located south-east of Cherbourg to the north-east of the city of Caen.

While the landings came as a complete surprise to all the defending forces, the respective landing groups encountered very wide-ranging degrees of resistance. The Americans destined for Utah Beach were fortunate to land virtually unopposed, albeit south of their intended target. By comparison, the 2nd Ranger Battalion, charged with destroying the six-gun battery at Pointe du Hoc east of Utah Beach, encountered heavy resistance. The actual guns from the batteries had been moved inland and, while the Rangers were eventually able to locate and destroy these, they were to suffer a 60 per cent casualty rate in the process.

Through a series of errors and misfortunes, the American troops landing at Omaha Beach, adjacent to Utah Beach, were far less fortunate. First, they started their landing runs far too far out to sea and, given the heavy seas, many of their landing craft were flooded during the 12-mile journey to the shore. Twenty-seven of their thirty-two special floating tanks (DDs) sank before they could even reach the beaches, and many of the engineers responsible for blowing up beach defences were prevented from reaching their objectives. Second, and unbeknown to the Allies, the German 352nd Infantry Division was on exercise in the area at the time, adding battle-hardened veterans to a defending force that had been temporarily doubled in number. The result was that, while the Americans on Omaha Beach eventually did win the day, they were to lose more than 2,500 men in the process.

Meanwhile, because of the poor weather, the British landing at Gold Beach decided to unload their tanks by landing craft directly on to the shore rather than relying on the DD amphibious versions. This was an important decision that ultimately allowed them to overcome some heavy German resistance with relatively few casualties. By midnight, they had established a bridgehead 6 miles wide and deep. This included the capture of the town of Arromanches, where the Allies were to construct one of their two floating Mulberry harbours.

Company E, 16th Infantry, 1st Infantry Division was one of the first waves of American troops to land at Omaha Beach.
US Army Center of Military History/CG 2343

The Canadians and Royal Marines were charged with landing at Juno Beach, further east, at one of the most heavily defended enemy positions. Unfortunately, the bombardments by the Allies were not as successful as had been intended and caused a number of delays. Initial resistance from the Germans was very strong and, while this beach was secured and considerable progress inland achieved in some sectors, not all objectives were achieved. In particular, the German 21st Panzer Division managed to drive a wedge between the Canadian 3rd Division at Juno and the British 3rd Division, which was emerging from its relatively unopposed landings on Sword Beach. Nevertheless, by the end of D-Day, the Allies had established a number of significant bridgeheads along the coast of Normandy.

MEDIA REACTION TO THE NORMANDY LANDINGS

In the days and even weeks leading up to the events of 6 June, there was a marked similarity in the news reports emanating from both sides of the Channel – similar in as much as there was a complete dearth of information about any impending invasion of mainland Europe.

Given that both sides were obviously aware of the seeming build-up of men and equipment in various parts of southern and south-east England, speculation was rife – not just in higher military circles, but also among every man and woman in the street – as to just where and when any invasion would take place.

In the very days immediately preceding the landings, there was still no indication whatsoever in the German press that an imminent attack was expected on the northern coast of France. Instead, the focus was on the fighting on the Eastern Front and in Italy.

Even when the Normandy landings were reported in the German press of 7 June, there was absolutely no sign of panic. The headlines of the inner pages of the *NVZ* stressed that:

 Eisenhower has not caught us Off-guard
Element of Surprise Fails – the Full Force of our Army has immediately taken up the Fight against the Aggressors

An article by the war reporter, Erich Wenzel, claimed that it had been clear to the German leaders for weeks that the enemy had been paying special attention to the area between Le Havre and Cherbourg and that, consequently, the German Army had already concentrated its forces in that area. While further press reports described the battle as a test of strength between two great armies, the continuing emphasis was on how vigilant the German Army on the Atlantic Wall had been in repelling the enemy attacks:

Nowhere has the German army been caught unawares [...] from the very first moment the enemy forces were subjected to the full force of our army causing them to suffer heavy losses.

Official quotations from the German High Command in Berlin talked of whole units of enemy parachutists being captured or blown up by mines, and of German shore batteries destroying many invasion ships and landing boats. The report was dated 6 June, and it is obvious that the battle was still in full swing with additional German forces rushing to the coast.

 Moscow's vassals had to launch an Invasion

The lead article in the *Völkischer Beobachter* went on to claim that such a risky invasion had come about only on the orders of Moscow, and that the enemy had completely underestimated the will of every German man, woman and child to resist and repel all the attacks by the enemy.

All in all, the impression was given that there was absolutely no cause for alarm, and that the Allied forces were being repulsed by brave, well-armed and experienced German soldiers. These latter claims were actually far more credible than some modern historical accounts might sometimes suggest. As we have already seen, and at Omaha Beach in particular, many of the defending forces did consist of battle-hardened veterans. Furthermore, faced with a shortage of hard facts, the German press went as far as to suggest that the delay in the release of any reports by the British and American authorities about the invasion – other than Reuters' publication of the German reports – was indicative of a lack of success by the Allies, who had failed to achieve their key invasion objectives.

In reality, it would always have been difficult for the Allied press to have included any comment in the editions of 6 June, although newspaper reports for that date, such as that in the *Daily Mirror*, did contain rather misleading information:

 French Coast gets it again

The accompanying front page article described how Boulogne and Calais had been the main target of an intensive Allied bombing attack the previous day. While this might have been quite correct we now know that these were deliberate diversionary tactics employed by the Allies to conceal where the actual landings would take place.

The official communiqués issued by SHAEF by 7 June were still lacking in any detail, but this certainly did not prevent the British press from painting a completely positive picture of the invasion:

The Great Assault Going Well
Allies Several Miles Inland

Churchill was reported as having said that the sea passage had been made with far fewer losses than had been predicted and that the operation was proceeding in a totally satisfactory manner. However, deprived of hard facts, *The Times* admitted to being obliged to quote liberally from the German reports, which gave far more details about the exact location of the landings.

Back in the German press, among all their other reports on the landings, there was an almost inevitable, lengthy, pre-prepared propaganda tirade from Goebbels entitled:

 Unbroken desire for victory

The basis of his diatribe was that the enemy was deluded if it thought that, despite all the terror bombings and the prospect of the fighting coming to Germany, the German people would succumb, since the whole war was about the very existence of their people:

 We are ready, if the enemy comes our soldiers will teach him a lesson

Even if the initial German reports remained confident of victory, then it might well have been expected that more concern about the invasion would be raised in the German press in subsequent days. This was simply not the case. By 8 and then 9 June, the headlines read:

 Heavy Enemy Losses
Paratroop Units Wiped Out in Night Battles

***

Second Invasion Wave
Attackers suffer further Heavy Losses on the Normandy Coast – German Bases in the Enemy Bridgehead hold Firm

This later article claimed that, far from being perturbed by this second wave of landings, the Germans had clearly anticipated such an attack since so many Allied soldiers had been thrown back into the sea or forced back to narrow strips of coastal land following the initial landings. Looking back at the events of 6 and 7 June, eyewitness reports told of the first British and American troops landing on French soil being virtually wiped out by German guns. Countless landing boats were destroyed, and many of the British landing forces raised white flags of surrender before being taken prisoner. Allegedly, quotations were included from an American war correspondent who was reported to have said that:

>  The Americans were mowed down. Wave after wave of Americans landed on the coast but few of them survived the hail of bullets. They dug in and returned fire with their rifles. The urgently needed tanks were disembarked in heavy seas. The Germans shelled the attackers. Our losses in men were very high.

The German papers certainly still did not give the slightest indication that the invasion might have been a success. Eisenhower was still saying very little to the Allied press, which the Germans continued to interpret as meaning that the Allies had achieved less than they had desired. As if to stress the point that the Germans were expecting the attack, quite a bit of space was devoted to an item on American Major General Henry Miller, who had been demoted and sent back home for revealing at a cocktail party that the invasion would take place before 13 June.

Photograph taken on 8 June 1944 at Pointe du Hoc – the highest point between the Utah and Omaha Beaches – showing captured German prisoners being escorted by American soldiers. *US Army Center of Military History/SC190240*

To all intents and purposes, life on mainland Europe seemed to be going on as normal. Paris remained unperturbed. Air raids continued over England. Further successes were reported in the fighting in Italy and on the Eastern Front. Hitler was even having a long-arranged meeting with the Hungarian Prime Minister and handing out military awards to German servicemen.

However, if you look more closely at the content of these two later incidents, you will discover that they actually occurred prior to the landings on the night of 6 June. Furthermore, as the German High Command reports themselves told of heavy fighting around Bayeux, then this must at least suggest that, whatever the scale of their losses in terms of manpower and equipment, some Allied soldiers had not only managed to establish some sort of defensible bridgehead but had also penetrated inland. Understandably, there was no negative comment whatsoever about the defending forces and nor was there any indication of German losses in terms of men or materials as a result of these landings.

WHAT WAS THE TRUTH ABOUT THE SUCCESS OR OTHERWISE OF THE INITIAL LANDINGS?

Viewed from their own perspective, both sides actually told a fair amount of truth. Had the Allies landed in northern France? Yes. Did this mean the war had been won? No.

Albeit at considerable cost in some sectors, the Allies had, indeed, managed to establish wide and deep bridgeheads across much of Normandy. Despite their denials, the Germans had been caught largely unawares. The French Resistance had managed to sabotage communication links between the German headquarters and the coastal defences. Given the poor weather, Rommel had even gone home to celebrate his wife's birthday. All in all, it was absolutely reasonable for the Allies to contend that the assault was going at least reasonably well.

Nevertheless, German misgivings as to the success of the landings were also completely justified. At Omaha Beach, the Germans genuinely believed they had driven the invaders back into the sea, being largely unaware of what was happening elsewhere. The Allies certainly did not achieve all of their initial objectives on the first day: towns such as Carentan, Saint-Lô and Bayeux were not taken. In fact, all five bridgeheads were not connected until 12 June. The German defenders had shown stout resistance and wiped out many Allied soldiers in several sectors. Even despite their initial shortage of armour, the Germans had counter-attacked in several places and, while not forcing the Allies back on to the beaches, they had certainly stopped or slowed their advance in many key areas. In terms of losses, around 10,000 Allied soldiers were killed or wounded on the first day, compared with around 1,000 casualties on the German side.

The build-up at Omaha Beach. Reinforcements of men and equipment moving inland. *US Army Center of Military History/SC193082*

Indeed, even by 8 June, and, although it was claimed that Bayeux had already been captured, in sharp contrast to the more upbeat headlines of the previous day, the British press was forced to show a lot more restraint:

 Heavy Fighting in Normandy
Most Difficult Stage Ahead
Handicap of Weather

By 9 June, the British were still reporting fierce fighting in Normandy and grim resistance everywhere. Reading between the lines in this and subsequent reports in the British press over the following couple of weeks, it is obvious that the ultimate success of the landings was still hanging very much in the balance. Prisoners were certainly being taken, and ground gained was being consolidated, but progress was painfully slow and, in many areas, the Allied advances had been brought to a halt by determined German resistance, bolstered by the arrival of more German armour.

This stalemate was also largely reflected in the German media coverage until, by Saturday 10 June, the hitherto positive German headlines certainly did start to belie the content of the items to which they referred:

Fierce Tank Battle south-east of Bayeux
Enemy Cruiser and Destroyer Sunk together with Two Large Ships used for transporting Speed Boats
Also Good Success by our Air-Force with Six Cargo Ships Sunk

Notwithstanding all these encouraging high points, the report from the Führer's head-quarters was remarkably forthright in admitting:

 Despite heavy losses resulting from actions by the German navy and air-force the enemy has succeeded in strengthening its bridgehead on the Normandy coast.

To counter this bad news, the German High Command report continued by listing the tonnage of ships destroyed and asserting that forty-five enemy planes had been shot down. Further German successes were reported in Italy, in the Mediterranean and against the Soviets. Reports in subsequent days continued in this vein – highlighting enemy losses and how enemy advances were being stopped or repelled – but if towns mentioned were to be traced on a map, then it would have been obvious to any reader that the Allies had gained a substantial foothold and that, at best, all the German forces were generally achieving was to delay their progress southwards or eastwards through France.

Nonetheless, the British press could be just as guilty of assigning positive headlines to articles that simply did not match the content of the event to which they referred. For example, the German headline on 14 June was:

 Extension of Bridgehead successfully repulsed

On exactly the same day, the headlines in *The Times* were:

 General Advance in all Sectors
Wide Pincer move against Caen

They could not both be telling the truth, and when you delve into the detail, it is apparent that, whatever progress might have been made by the Allies, the Germans had still counter-attacked at Montebourg and Carentan:

 And at Montebourg especially the position is obscure [...] The fighting between Bayeux and Caen in which heavy armoured forces are engaged is described as most interesting.

The rather vague and unusual language employed suggests that the outcome was still far from certain. However, the Allies were now starting to report that they held 600 to 700 square miles of territory and had taken 10,000 prisoners since the start of the invasion.

For their part, the German High Command immediately felt it needed to respond with its own statistics regarding the alleged huge losses suffered by the enemy. On 15 June, it claimed that, during the first ten days of the invasion, German forces had destroyed 400 enemy tanks, more than 1,000 aircraft, two cruisers, nine destroyers and twenty-three transport ships – not to mention an even greater number of enemy ships that were severely damaged. But there was no indication of German losses nor of the amount of territory lost. Indeed, by 19 June, the emphasis had switched to the reporting of the heavy bombing of England – with any mention of Normandy kept to the inner pages. Not that the Allied press was able to give its readers any more grounds for optimism. *The Times* of 16 June was even forced to talk of:

🇬🇧 Signs of a Real Counter-Blow

It was admitted that increased levels of violence had turned the conflict into a war of attrition. German counter-attacks, while becoming stronger, had been largely unsuccessful although Allied advances had become very restricted. The impact of German V-1 rockets falling on the south-east of England was beginning to become more newsworthy, as was the reporting of the successes of Allied bombers in destroying flying-bomb bases.

As late as 30 June, and despite the Americans' capture of the fortress of Cherbourg a few days earlier – albeit a port that had been completely destroyed – it was obvious that the battle for Normandy was far from won by the Allies:

🇬🇧 Fierce tank clashes south of Caen
British pressing on against bitter resistance
German reinforcements arriving

The equivalent German reports were also fairly accurate, even if they did tend to report events in the most favourable of ways. The official report from the German High Command on 30 June was still talking of the enemy only extending its attacks in Normandy over a twenty-five kilometre front. While there was an admission that the enemy had made some small breakthroughs south-west of Caen, this was countered by the assertion that the enemy had later been forced back by German counter-attacks. It was claimed that one German tank division had wiped out fifty-three enemy tanks, and that the enemy was continuing to suffer heavy losses in men and materials. While the port of Cherbourg had been destroyed, it was reported that several of the German bases were continuing to hold out against the enemy forces.

In short, several weeks after the initial invasion, there was still no clear indication as to whether the landings would ultimately be successful, and ordinary citizens on both sides would have been justified in concluding that, to all intents and purposes, little real progress had been made.

The Allied Newsreel Coverage

If the Allied press was saying little concrete about the actual success of the D-Day landings, then the newsreel coverage was scarcely more enlightening. *British Pathé News* and *Movietone* both issued separate newsreels of the event on 12 June. Both film reports were very patriotic, but the only hard facts that tended to emerge were that 20,000 tons of bombs were dropped in pre-landing raids on railway and road junctions, airfields and river barges, and that 4,000 ships and many smaller craft had been involved in the landings on the Normandy coast. With titles such as 'Greatest Combined Operation in World's History' and action shots of bombing raids and troops and armoured vehicles landing on some of the already secured beaches, the film reports were all designed to seem very exciting and gave the impression that real progress had been made. The viewer could certainly see the Allies had established some sort of bridgehead, and there were scenes of captured German prisoners, but there was far more rhetoric than precise detail.

We are informed in the *Pathé News* report that the troops who were due to be landed on the beaches were told:

 'We want you to raise all the Hell you can on the backs of the Boche' and that, 'they did that and more.'

But what does this equate to in real terms? There were no images of any dead soldiers – only of the care being taken of wounded soldiers being transferred back to Blighty. There was no mention of how many troops were involved in the landings, nor any indication of the numbers killed or wounded in the raids. All the viewer was told was that:

 we expected far greater numbers of injured – but we were mercifully spared heavy casualties.

More ominously, abandoned Allied tanks were clearly shown lost in rough seas and the viewer was informed that:

stiffening of resistance was to be expected.

The *Movietone* reel was more optimistic but again short of detail when it talked of:

 the brilliant success of Allied landings [...] first phase was an Allied victory of the first magnitude.

It was very British-orientated in focus, especially when it enthusiastically mentioned how the British had returned to France four years after Dunkirk. This is why it was perhaps felt necessary to produce a separate *Movietone* reel for the American market on 20 June, where the emphasis was much more on this being a combined operation of British, American and Canadian troops. This reel was prepared to concede that the landings on some beaches had proceeded more smoothly than others, and that much bitter fighting remained to be done. But, this was countered by the positive revelation that the Allies had thrust inland against heavy enemy opposition and that:

 Nazi prisoners had been taken by the thousand.

The German Newsreel Coverage

If mixed messages were being presented to the Allied audience – albeit with a generally positive spin – just how was the same event being 'sold' by the German media to their viewers?

The *Wochenschau*, which was screened on 7 June, made no mention of the landings whatsoever but concentrated on the fighting in Italy and on the Eastern Front. This is perhaps understandable, because they would hardly have had time to react. However, the newsreel produced on 14 June did contain a full account of the landings. Nevertheless, it would have been difficult for any independent observer to guess that both sides were reporting the same event.

The German newsreel certainly recognised 6 June as a date of historical significance for the world, but it stressed that the long-trumpeted invasion – undertaken under pressure from Moscow – had been expected, and that the Germans had been ready for it.

Just as with the German press, the newsreel contained some partial truths. Yes, an invasion had been expected, and there may even have been some strong indications that it might take place in June of that year. However, the Germans certainly did not know exactly where the landings would take place. The Allies had gone to great lengths to give the impression that the invasion might take place in the Calais area. Deception methods included the creation of a mythical army based in eastern England, whose lines of dummy tanks and planes certainly deceived German air reconnaissance. With the possible exception of Hitler, most of the German High Command's officers, including Field Marshal Rundstedt, were convinced that the Pas-de-Calais would be the target. Nor did the Germans know exactly when the invasion would take place. The weather forecast for the period around 5 June was so poor that they had all but discounted the numerous rumours concerning that date. Even when the Germans intercepted radio messages containing lines from the first verse of Paul Verlaine's poem, *Chanson d'automne*, which was believed to herald the start of the invasion, all they did was to put troops in the Pas-de-Calais area on alert. The eventual delay until 6 June served only to heighten their suspicion that the reported landings in Normandy were a diversionary tactic.

As for the German newsreel itself, interspersed with film of boats approaching landing beaches, it mainly consisted of a lot of historic footage of flak batteries shooting into dark skies and of German soldiers running to take up positions when the alarm was sounded.

The overall tone gave the impression that, whatever the size of the attack, the German defenders had been more than a match for the aggressors:

> Shock troops dealt with paratroopers who landed from the night sky [...] the invading forces were immediately engaged by machine guns, tanks and artillery [...] in many places, close-quarter fighting cost the enemy dear.

However, the report was full of conflicting messages. On the one hand, there were close-ups of enemy landing boats stranded on beaches whose occupants were said either to have been wiped out or taken prisoner. On the other hand, there was an admission that there was heavy fighting around Bayeux and Caen, and heavy German armour was shown rushing towards the area to take up the fight.

Panning across lines and lines of gliders strewn across the ground, the commentator gave the impression that these had all been shot down by German flak when, in reality, it is obvious that most of the gliders had successfully split apart to release their occupants.

Mention was made of hundreds of prisoners being captured and especially of Canadian paratroopers and of troops from northern Scotland but, as the shoulder lapel badges of the soldiers in the accompanying footage bear the name North Nova Scotia Highlanders, it is obvious that there had been some confusion on the part of the commentator as to the true identity of the prisoners.

At first, it seems somewhat surprising that the film conceded that ever more waves of bombers had arrived to provide support for the invaders. Nonetheless, the inclusion of this scene made more sense when the editor used this admission as an excuse to show German fighters pursuing the enemy planes and the shooting down of a four-engined bomber. It also provided an opportunity to condemn the Allies for their indiscriminate bombing of French civilian targets, and to make the ironic assertion that the people of France had started to experience what was meant by the 'promised liberation'. It is just as noticeable that Allied newsreel played down the destruction being caused to civilian property and the fact that tens of thousands of French civilians were forced to flee from the coastal areas before the advancing Allied forces.

Supported by images of burning tanks and of even more prisoners, the commentator was able to contend that, on every front, the enemy had come up against such resistance that they were suffering horrible losses. Nevertheless, just as the Allied newsreels were unable to claim outright victory, the German newsreel was ultimately just as ambivalent in its final assessment that:

 The decisive battle for Europe's future has begun!

As if to play down the importance of the landings in Normandy, the subsequent weekly newsreel of 21 June began as if life in Germany was going on as normal, with coverage of the football cup final between Dresden and Hamburg and then talk of successes on the Eastern and Italian Fronts, before switching to the situation in France. Still in denial that the original Allied landings had been at all successful, this newsreel contained positive images that bore an uncanny resemblance to earlier film of the initial landings but taken from a slightly different perspective. The images were reinforced with an upbeat commentary about the Germans having defeated the enemy in the first weeks and of their having prevented further landings. However, the very fact that more German troops and tanks were being rushed forward to prevent a widening of the bridgehead demonstrated that the Allies had at least gained a foothold in France.

By 28 June, the report of the campaign in northern France was again restricted to the closing frames of that newsreel, when the focus was on German tanks having successfully beaten back the invaders near Saint-Lô. But, the emphasis on one particular action, the lack of any indication as to how much ground had been lost or gained overall and the seeming need to highlight the satisfaction felt by the German troops at learning of the damage being inflicted by Germany's new V-1 rockets over southern England were all obviously intended to divert the German viewers' attention away from the fact that the war was gradually being lost.

CONCLUSION

In truth, the D-Day landings themselves did not result in immediate victory for the Allies and, in the subsequent weeks and months, the outcome did, indeed, hang in the balance. This meant that in their media coverage both sides could accentuate the positive and make the most of apparent triumphs while playing down or ignoring the negatives completely.

For the Allies, the negatives included the number of soldiers or other military personnel killed and the failure to achieve all their objectives. Cherbourg was eventually captured but was no longer usable as a port. The Mulberry harbour at Omaha Beach was completely destroyed in a storm that started on 19 June, and the harbour at Arromanches was also considerably damaged, thereby delaying the arrival of much-needed supplies and equipment. Little of this would be reported in the Allied media. The delays allowed the Germans to make some successful counter-attacks when their much-needed armour finally arrived, and it meant that the road to Berlin was going to be far slower and much more costly for the Allies than they might have hoped. The town of Caen itself was not completely captured until 21 July.

The invaluable Mulberry harbours were to be badly damaged by a storm which started on 19 June. *IOC USW33 56556-ZC*

For the Germans, their failings were that their armoured strength was never quite sufficient to drive the Allies back into the sea, and that the Allies had secured a bridgehead in Normandy from which they would eventually break out and head towards Germany.

On 1 July, the Germans did make one final attempt to drive the invaders back off the beaches with the combined force of four armoured divisions, but it was all too late. The Allies had already landed too many men and too much equipment, so the counter-attack was unsuccessful. Von Rundstedt telephoned Field Marshal Keitel to advise that the battle for Normandy had been lost, but it was never an announcement that would appear in any German newsreel.

Even after 1 July, the weekly German newsreel reports continued to play down the importance of the invasion. It was never the first item included in any report and when the fighting in France was mentioned, the German soldiers were always described as being well trained and in good spirits. The continuing implication that the Germans were being successful was perhaps best summarised in this comment in the newsreel of 13 July:

 After more than six weeks of fighting the Allies have hardly advanced beyond the range of the guns of the ships which brought them there in the first place.

Nevertheless, the very fact that scenes of smiling German soldiers still showed them reading newspapers with headlines about Eisenhower not having caught them off-guard – headlines that we know actually appeared in the press more than a month earlier – does raise doubt as to the credibility and timing of the content.

Admittedly, further German counter-attacks would occur, and it would take until mid-August to clear the German formations from Normandy, following the entrapment of 50,000 German troops in the Falaise pocket. In fact, it was to take until the end of August for the Germans to be forced to retreat back across the River Seine and, even then, this was still reported in the *Völkischer Beobachter* as a mini-victory and as if a new front was being established in the West:

 The enemy could not prevent march-off across the Seine

The newsreels throughout August continued to follow the same predictable format. There was always the same map of Normandy, with no indication that the front line was moving south or east. German tanks and reserves were always counter-attacking. There were almost always images of destroyed Allied tanks and ragged, depressed Allied prisoners. Any ground gained by the Allies was always reported as having been achieved at great loss to the enemy.

However, the overall emphasis of those newsreels did begin to change. There was more frequent mention of 'Total War', and images of women, desperately digging ditches or being called up to serve as clippies, policewomen and firewomen all implied that the war was about to reach the very borders of Germany.

By the newsreel of 30 August, it is not what was said but rather what was not said that becomes more significant. The map still did not show the respective location of the front lines. The feature on Invasion Front was very short, and the images of the destruction of Allied tanks could well have been historic footage. There was much more emphasis on the fact that Hitler's infamous terror weapon, the V-1, was bringing death and destruction to London and south-east England by day and night.

In reality, it is doubtful whether the fact that the enemy might have been suffering just as much would have brought any real solace to the German audience. By then, it must have been clear to even the most fanatical of Nazis that defeat was only a matter of time, as the newsreel and press reports simply could not conceal the fact that, regardless of however many small German victories might be recorded here or there, the war in the West was moving inexorably closer to the German border.

12

THE DESTRUCTION OF CONVOY PQ17

INTRODUCTION

This book has already revealed how, during the war, both sides were often able to twist the facts so that when it came to the reporting of key events, they each sought to maximise the importance of their victories while minimising the significance of their setbacks.

Nonetheless, it would be wrong to conclude that the misreporting of any event was the only transgression of which the respective governments and their media were guilty. There were several significant incidents that were hardly reported at all by one side, as to have done so would have been at best extremely embarrassing for that side's government or, at worst, completely demoralising for the citizens of one of the parties concerned.

The following three chapters consider three such incidents: the destruction of Convoy PQ17; the massacre of Polish officers and intellectuals in the Katyn Forest and the downplaying of the existence of the V rockets.

THE END OF CONVOY PQ17

Throughout the early years of the war, and regardless of what other setbacks German forces might have been encountering by late 1942 and early 1943, there was one area of operation where the German media could always report major successes. It was the incessant destruction of merchant shipping by the U-boat fleet and the Luftwaffe, especially as this had an adverse effect on vital supplies being shipped to Britain across the Atlantic from the United States.

With Hitler's tearing up of the Non-Aggression Pact and subsequent attack on the Soviet Union on 22 June 1941, Britain and the other Allies soon found themselves obliged to arrange equally hazardous convoys to assist Stalin, whose army was perilously close to defeat. Within six months, the Russians had lost 20,000 tanks and the Germans were only 15 miles from the centre of Moscow. Churchill promised

Stalin that he would provide supplies of guns, planes, tanks and fuel to Stalin every ten days. This was to be achieved by sending convoys northwards around occupied Norway towards the Russian ports of Murmansk and Archangel. The convoys typically advanced in a square formation with the merchant ships in the middle protected by an escort of cruisers and destroyers. Despite the harsh weather conditions and the ten-day journey, the early convoys were remarkably successful in reaching their destinations. Consequently, given the vast quantities of supplies and equipment the convoys delivered, the Germans soon intensified their efforts to sink as many ships as possible before they could reach their destination.

On 27 June 1942, the largest Arctic convoy ever assembled set sail from Iceland. Code-named PQ17, it consisted of thirty-five British and American merchant ships, packed full of tanks and planes. Bound for Archangel, it was protected by a total of twenty-eight warships and submarines.

The Germans were only too well aware of its departure and indicated in advance that they planned to destroy the convoy down to its very last ship. Rather surprisingly, there was absolutely no mention of the convoy in the Allied press, and nothing more was heard from the German side until 8 July, when the headlines of the *NVZ* read:

Huge convoy of 192,400 tons wiped out in the Arctic Ocean

Merchant ships and escorts assembling at Hvalfjord before Convoy PQ17 set sail.

The accompanying article went on to describe in detail how, since 2 July, German bombers and submarines had managed to sink an American heavy cruiser and twenty-eight merchant ships – and in so doing had rescued and taken prisoner a large number of American sailors. It painted a dark picture of a complete catastrophe for the Allies, with heavily bombed merchant ships being torpedoed by submarines and tons of priceless tanks, planes, munitions and food supplies lost to the bottom of the sea. It gave the impression that the convoy was completely helpless and that any remaining ships were bound to suffer a similar fate. The following day the *Völkischer Beobachter* claimed that U-boats had sunk a further four ships and that the convoy losses now exceeded 217,000 tons. By 10 July, there was a clear frustration in the German media at the Allies' persistent reluctance to admit the extent of the disaster:

 London keeps silent about the Convoy Catastrophe
No information available – 'as is always the case in such circumstances'

The Germans mocked the Allies for using the excuse that, in the interests of security, they would never comment on the fate of a particular convoy until it had reached its destination. By 11 July, the Germans were sufficiently confident as to be able to report that, of the original convoy of thirty-eight ships, only three remained and that it was still uncertain as to whether even these survivors would ever reach their destination. Indeed, the *Völkischer Beobachter* for that day went as far as to claim that the remaining three ships had in fact been sunk by German U-boats and German bombers.

And yet, it is quite remarkable how, throughout this whole period, there was virtually no mention of the convoy in the British press – other than some passing reference on 8 July with the accurate reproduction of a summary of the contents of an article reported in the German press about the losses to the convoy.

Surely, the Germans were exaggerating, and no convoy could ever have been destroyed to such a great extent? Or could it? What was the truth?

The Tragic Fate of Convoy PQ17

So, what really happened to Convoy PQ17? In reality, the convoy that set sail on 27 June consisted of thirty-five merchant ships rather than the thirty-eight or thirty-nine claimed by the Germans, but it was easy to confuse the real number as there was also an oiler and three rescue ships.

For the first seven days of the voyage, there was little to concern the convoy. A report then reached the Admiralty in London that the German battleship *Tirpitz* was on the move, and there was real concern that the convoy might encounter it. Unwilling to risk his naval ships, and yet reluctant to turn the whole convoy around,

Sub-headline of *Freiburger Zeitung* of 8 July 1942 with map reporting that thirty-two ships from Convoy PQ17 had been sunk. *Freiburg University Library/CC BY-SA*

First Sea Lord, Admiral Dudley Pound, took the momentous decision to recall the cruisers accompanying the convoy and ordered the rest of the convoy to scatter. Without clear orders the remaining destroyers also turned for home, leaving the convoy virtually unprotected.

The result was that twelve German U-boats, twelve torpedo aircraft and more than 100 bombers were able to attack the remnants of the convoy relentlessly over the next forty-eight hours. During the first twenty-four hours alone, twelve merchant ships were sunk. The carnage was to continue the following day.

Standing out among all the confusion and turmoil was the coolness and ingenuity shown by Lt Leo Gradwell, commanding the lightly armed trawler HMS *Ayrshire*, which had been adapted for anti-submarine warfare. He guided three of the US merchant ships northwards and, with the use of white paint and sheets, camouflaged them from view as they lay trapped in the snow-covered Arctic pack ice. He eventually managed to guide the three vessels safely to Archangel and was awarded the Distinguished Service Cross for his actions.

Contrary to the German claims, no American heavy cruiser was, in fact, destroyed in the action – but, in total, twenty-four merchant ships were sunk. So, the losses were not quite as severe as the German High Command had reported, but it was still a major catastrophe for the Allies, denying the Soviets 210 planes, 430 tanks and countless other supplies and equipment – together with the loss of 153 sailors. Churchill later declared that the event was one of the most melancholy episodes to occur during the whole of the war.

Despite the fact that this was to be the greatest loss to an Arctic convoy in the whole of the war, there was absolutely no admission by the Allied Powers, at that time, of the disaster that had befallen the convoy. This was somewhat ironic since *The Times* of 30 June 1942 was only too ready to praise the success of the Soviet steamer *Old Bolshevik* for reaching a Soviet port in an earlier convoy despite having been set on fire. Likewise, on the very day that PQ17 was to suffer its greatest losses, namely, 4 July, the Admiralty was prepared to admit that the Allies had lost a cruiser and five destroyers in attacks on their convoys in the Mediterranean.

Such was the significance of the destruction of the convoy to the Germans, however, that they were even able to include a five-minute report in the *Wochenschau* newsreel of 15 July 1942. There was an introductory map showing the course of the convoy through the Arctic Ocean north of Norway and then action shots of the convoy first being spotted by a reconnaissance plane and then being attacked all day by bombers and U-boats so that, in the end, thirty-nine merchant ships were annihilated and prevented from reaching their destination. While there was no mention in this report of a destroyer having been sunk, the commentator still did rather 'egg the pudding' in that, having initially indicated that the convoy was protected by countless battleships, aircraft carriers, cruisers, destroyers and corvettes, he failed to inform the viewer later that, by the time the convoy was attacked, virtually all the defending naval ships had, in fact, disappeared. Nevertheless, the whole event must certainly have left German viewers feeling extremely proud of their armed forces:

 None of the ships in this convoy reached their destination [...] [we know this was not quite true] 260,000 tons of tanks, planes and food supplies destined for the Soviets are lying at the bottom of the sea [...] our planes and submarines have inflicted yet another devastating defeat on the enemy [...] yet Moscow still asserted that the convoy arrived completely unmolested.

By 4 August, some of the Allied press did at least carry still photographs of an attack on PQ17 by German torpedo planes, but the accompanying commentary in the *Daily Herald* still claimed:

In spite of repeated attacks, the convoy, with its badly needed war cargoes, got through.

While conceding that actual Allied losses had not yet been announced, even the American *Life* magazine of 4 August went so far as to claim that Allied losses were 'certainly a great deal smaller than the extravagant claims of the Germans'. This was wishful thinking and, frankly, untrue as only four merchant ships finally managed to reach their destination.

Perhaps it was felt that further bad news would be just too hard for the Allied public to take but, whatever the reason, it is a clear indication of how the Allies were prepared to hide unwelcome truths from the public at large. History has accorded Admiral Pound a fairly poor evaluation, but it is perhaps worth noting that the *Tirpitz* did, indeed, set sail with the intention of intercepting the convoy, but not until around noon on 5 July – some thirty-six hours after Pound had given his fateful order for the convoy to scatter. Hitler was concerned that the Allies might have an aircraft carrier in the vicinity and were perhaps trying to lure his prize ships to a spot where other Allied capital ships would be lying in wait. Consequently, given that the scatter order of 3 July meant that his planes and U-boats were already inflicting such heavy damage on the convoy, Hitler soon ordered the *Tirpitz* to return to port. So, perhaps Pound had been justified in ordering the convoy to scatter. It was just that his order was a little premature and that he had failed to give sufficient recognition to the opportunity that a scattered, unprotected convoy would present to the enemy.

13

THE MASSACRE IN KATYN FOREST

Another clear example of the desire by the Allies to suppress unpalatable and politically sensitive information is to be found in their treatment of German revelations about their gruesome discoveries in Katyn Forest, in western Russia.

As a consequence of Hitler's pact with Stalin, Poland was attacked by both Germany and the Soviet Union, and was formally divided by the Ribbentrop–Molotov Line on 28 September 1939. Many Polish prisoners were subsequently exchanged between the Germans and the Red Army. The Russian Secret Police, the NKVD, eventually took control of these prisoners, who were subjected to a lengthy process of interrogation and indoctrination. Those prisoners unwilling to transfer allegiance to Russia were considered enemies of the Russian State and were often subjected to harsh labour conditions and even death.

More than 15,000 of these prisoners, consisting primarily of Polish officers and intellectuals, were imprisoned in three special camps in Russia at Kozielsk, Starobielsk and Ostashkov. During April and May 1940, the prisoners from the camp at Kozielsk were taken to the Katyn Forest near Smolensk where they were shot and buried in mass graves. The prisoners from the other camps were killed at other sites across Russia.

In 1943, the Germans occupied the area around Katyn and, having been made aware of rumours of a vast massacre, the German High Command eventually announced its gruesome discoveries to the world on 13 April. Sarcastically pointing out that the Soviets were Roosevelt's and Churchill's allies, the headlines of the *NVZ* of the following day dramatically read:

 GPU – Murder of 12,000 Polish Officers
Huge mass graves of victims found in the Katyn Forest near Smolensk

The GPU was what we would have called the NKVD at that time. The discovery of the graves allowed the German press to condemn, in the most emotive manner, the murderous activities of what they would describe as the Jewish/Bolshevik secret police:

The discovery represents the most horrific happening in the history of mankind. The dreadful nature of fearful crime far exceeds any of the shameful acts already perpetrated by the Bolshevik beasts in the course of their reign of terror.

By 15 April, the *Völkischer Beobachter* was claiming that there were eye-witnesses who would swear that the victims had been slaughtered by Jewish commandos. The Germans realised immediately that they were going to require physical proof both of their discovery and of the perpetrators. They claimed that the identity of the victims was evident from the uniforms the dead soldiers were wearing and the documentation found with the bodies, albeit that all watches and jewellery had been removed by the 'Bolshevik thieves'. Several experts, under the direction of a professor from the University of Breslau, also confirmed the timing of the murders as being during the spring of 1940. This was highly important, as it was said to prove that the murders had been committed while the land was under Russian control and long before Germany had declared war on the Soviet Union.

The article claimed that until that point, two huge graves had been discovered – one with 4,000 and the other with between 5,000 and 6,000 executed prisoners. Other graves had also been discovered. In fact, the figure of 12,000 bodies mentioned in the headline was a complete fabrication. At that point, the Germans had no idea how many bodies they were going to find, but they did know that the 15,000 Polish prisoners who had been held at the camps at Kozielsk, Starobielsk and Ostashkov had gone missing, and they wrongly assumed that they might all have been murdered at the same spot. In reality, only around 4,500 bodies were found in the Katyn Forest.

The German press continued to make political capital out of the event in subsequent days, as they sought to cause Britain and the United States maximum embarrassment for refusing to comment on the grim discoveries.

 How long will England remain silent about the mass murders at Katyn?

It gave the Germans an opportunity not only to cast further blame on their greatest enemies but also to portray the war against Russia as almost being a justifiable crusade of good versus evil:

 All of Europe is united in its disgust at the appalling murder of 12,000 Polish officers by Jews and Bolsheviks [...] in the strongest possible way the media of all countries, except for those dependent on plutocracy or Bolshevism, have denounced this crime, and the lesson drawn from it is that it is essential to wage a relentless war against these creatures from hell.

Furthermore, to give added credibility to their claims, the German authorities even allowed a special eight-minute film documentary to be produced that adopted even more emotive language than was found in the press coverage. The film began by showing modern accommodation buildings close to the Katyn Forest, where it was claimed the GPU held wild orgies with the women they brought there. To the accompaniment of suitably mournful music, the camera then panned across rows and rows of corpses with gruesome close-ups of the dead piled twelve high in deep graves. There was even a suggestion that some victims had been buried alive, because of sand found in their windpipes. It was claimed that scientists and European Red Cross representatives from Bulgaria, Denmark, Italy, Switzerland and Hungary had all been brought in to witness and testify to this 'slaughter of defenceless men' by the Bolsheviks.

Notably, this dramatic film was certainly never shown in Britain at the time, and the Germans were quite accurate in their assertion that the British Government failed to make any comment whatsoever about the discovery. Indeed, any reporting in the British quality press was restricted to official statements from representatives of the Polish Government.

The Times of 17 April carried a detailed announcement from the Polish Minister of National Defence explaining that, since December 1941, a number of approaches had been made to Stalin regarding long lists of missing Polish prisoners, but that Stalin had claimed that all Polish officers had been released. Nevertheless, the Poles had never received any satisfactory answer from the Russians as to the fate of the missing prisoners and, given the detailed information being reported by the Germans:

the necessity has arisen that the mass graves which have been discovered should be investigated and the facts verified by a proper international body, such as the authorities of the International Red Cross.

Admittedly, the Poles did find themselves faced with something of a dilemma as in seeking to establish what had happened to their missing citizens, they did not want to be seen to be condoning the actions of the Germans in the war. Thus, two days later, *The Times* of 19 April carried a further statement from the Polish cabinet stressing that they:

deny to the Germans the right to draw from a crime which they ascribe to others arguments in their own defence. The profoundly hypocritical indignation of the German propaganda will not succeed in concealing from the world the many cruel, repeated, and still-lasting crimes committed on the Polish people.

The same edition of *The Times* even went on to report a radio announcement from the Russians claiming that it was all a 'hideous frame-up' and that the bodies were actually Polish prisoners murdered by the Gestapo in 1941, which is why the bodies had not yet had time to decompose.

Notwithstanding, there was still a deafening silence from the British Government throughout this whole period.

So, what was the truth? Was it all a fabrication by the Germans or had the Soviets really committed such a heinous crime?

The Truth about the Katyn Forest Massacres

The sad fact is that, while the Russians vigorously denied their involvement at the time, Stalin had, indeed, ordered these influential prisoners to be executed because, looking to the future and the end of the war, it is likely that he wanted to deprive Poland of key men who might raise any objection to the Soviets' continued occupation of parts of eastern Poland.

To their eternal shame, not only did the Western Allies keep silent, but Churchill went so far as to support Stalin in his refusal to allow an independent International Red Cross investigation, which had also been called for by the Germans. Anthony Eden, in his capacity as Foreign Secretary, even sought to persuade the Poles that this was all German propaganda, and that they should let the matter drop. The Poles, however, refused to keep silent, and Stalin was so angry with them for bringing up the issue that he formally cut off diplomatic relations on 25 April 1943. By 10 May, Churchill even apologised to Stalin for the Polish statements and he promised that better control would be kept over the Polish press in future.

Quite obviously, the Germans did want to make political capital out of the discovery and to drive a wedge between the Allies. Indeed, they may well have discovered the bodies as early as 1942 and decided to release the information only when they thought it might be of most benefit. Regardless of the politics, there was absolutely no doubt that the victims were all executed by pistol shots to the back of the neck. They were buried in their uniforms and there was copious documentation, including photographs and official documents, confirming their identity.

The retreating Germans were able to hold this territory only until September 1943 and, as Goebbels feared, once the ground was retaken by the Russians, they went to great lengths to produce their own experts who would subsequently claim that the executions dated back only to the summer of 1941, when the land was under German control, rather than to the spring of 1940.

At the Nuremberg war trials in 1946, the Russians even tried to add the Katyn massacres to the list of indictments levelled against the Nazis, but the British and American judges quickly dismissed the charges.

Front cover of report about the Katyn Forest massacres produced by an American Congress Select Committee in 1952. *NARA 6851171*

After the war, an American Congress Select Committee investigated the whole matter in depth in 1952 and concluded that there was absolutely no doubt that the murders had been committed by the Soviet Secret Police.

It was not until 1990 that the Soviets finally admitted NKVD responsibility for the massacres, which eventually led to a formal declaration in 2010, blaming Stalin and other members of the Politburo for having personally authorised the deaths. No Russian citizen was ever charged with having participated in this war crime.

14

THE 'V' ROCKETS AND THE BOMBING OF PEENEMÜNDE

Much of Germany's early successes in the Second World War arose not only from their *blitzkrieg* tactics but from their superiority in terms of modern weaponry such as Messerschmitt 109 fighters, Stuka bombers and Panzer tanks. Nevertheless, following subsequent setbacks in Normandy and on the Eastern and Southern Fronts, the Nazis were to become increasingly dependent on new 'wonder' weapons, and especially those that could be launched from a distance and were unmanned – such as the V-1 and V-2 rockets. At different times, both the British and the Germans were to restrict the media's reporting of the existence and effectiveness of these weapons, and even of the bombing of rocket launch sites.

As early as July 1927, a number of German enthusiasts had founded the Association for Space Travel and initiated research into rocket technology. In 1930, the German Army provided two of these enthusiasts, Rudolf Nebel and Werner von Braun, with access to restricted areas north of Berlin where they could test their rockets. Such was the importance of this work that, in 1933, Hitler decreed that the Army Weapons Agency (AWA) should maintain overall control over rocketry development, and the AWA was key in providing finance and facilities for projects it thought could be of military significance. As the research developed, work on a new much larger site at Peenemünde on Germany's Baltic coast began in 1936. This site was jointly occupied by the Luftwaffe and the German Army. The Luftwaffe was responsible for work on the pilotless V-1 rockets and, although much of the research and development work was undertaken elsewhere in Germany, the first glide testflight of the weapon was to take place at Peenemünde on 28 October 1942, with the rocket being released from the underside of a Focke-Wulf Fw 200 bomber.

Rather surprisingly, work by the German Army on the much more ambitious A4 rocket – later known as the V-2 – had actually started much earlier. As early as 1940, it had determined that the A4 rocket was the first long-distance rocket that it considered to be 'usable in war'. Werner von Braun and his colleagues had already produced plans for a rocket that could deliver 1,600lb of explosives to a precise target up to a distance of almost 200 miles away.

By the summer of 1941, and after the failure of the Luftwaffe in the Battle of Britain, Hitler placed much faith in this new retaliatory weapon that would be able to continue to terrorise London and other British cities. After a number of initial failures, it was still very much a theoretical weapon until, at last, on 3 October 1942, one of these new guided rockets was launched successfully and flew for over five minutes before crashing into the Baltic 120 miles east of Peenemünde.

The Reporting of the Attack on Peenemünde

As early as December 1942, the British were provided with information from an agent who had overheard a conversation about trials of a long-range rocket being held near Swinemünde on the Baltic coast. By the spring of 1943, reports were received from other sources that specifically pinpointed Peenemünde, with aerial photography revealing 40ft-long rockets either standing upright or lying horizontally on lorries. Churchill was not prepared to take any chances and, following a meeting on 29 June, he ordered that the plant had to be attacked on the heaviest possible scale.

And so it was that, during the night of 17 August 1943, some 600 aircraft from Bomber Command made the 1,000-mile round trip to bomb Peenemünde. In fact, that attack on the Peenemünde Army Research Centre heralded the start of a whole series of strategic bombing operations by the Allies that aimed to destroy all aspects of Germany's long-range weapons programme.

The bombing mission to Peenemünde was divided into three waves, with the initial intention being to attack from the north and destroy, in turn, the experimentation buildings, then the V-2 factory works and, finally, the sleeping and living quarters of the German workers and their families. The aim was to kill as many scientific and technical personnel as possible. In practice, because of a change in the wind direction, the order of attack had to be reversed and several of the initial bombs and incendiaries landed on the Trassenheide Foreign Labour Camp that lay to the south of the German living quarters and barracks.

While the British authorities were only too aware of the potential significance of the research centre, the full importance of the raid was somewhat underplayed by the British press. The headlines of *The Times* of 19 August 1943 read:

 New Air Blow to Reich
Biggest Research Works Smashed
Baltic Target Hit

While the accompanying article certainly admitted it was the heaviest moonlight attack made on a German target that year, and that forty-one Allied bombers had been lost in the mission, there was absolutely no mention that Peenemünde was a base for producing long-distance rockets:

This establishment, the largest and most important of its kind in the Reich, specialized in aircraft, radio-location, and armament development and experiment.

Of course, one has to remember that even the first so-called 'doodlebugs' did not actually fall on London until June 1943, so there was little point in alarming the British population with details of a hideous enemy weapon that might never be fired in anger or, indeed, in alerting the Germans to the fact that the Allies were aware of the research the Germans were undertaking. However, a later report on 23 August did claim:

Shattering Attack on Peenemünde 'outstanding success'

All the other comments in that report suggested that the mission was a complete success, and that the facilities there had been completely annihilated. Was this true? Was this really the end of Peenemünde? What did the press coverage fail to reveal? In reality, although subsequent reconnaissance missions suggested the raids had been entirely effective, this was simply not the case.

Admittedly, much of the accommodation for the German scientists and their families had been destroyed but, as many of the inhabitants had taken refuge in air raid shelters, only around 178 out of the 4,000 or so Germans living in that area were killed. Only two significant German scientists were killed – including Dr Walter Thiel, who was responsible for the V-2 rocket propulsion department.

While some of the research facilities and production works were also badly damaged, the destruction was not as severe as it appeared from the air. Indeed, the Germans blew up some huts themselves to make the damage look far worse than it was and painted black lines on the roofs so they might resemble from a distance the exposed beams of a building.

Above all, the wind tunnel and the telemetry block, where radio signals measured what happened to rockets during flight, were untouched – as was the workshop that produced trial parts for rockets.

While none of this was reported or perhaps even known by the British, what the British press also failed to report, however, was that out of a total of 733 people killed in the raid, 500 of these victims were mainly Polish forced labour workers held in the Trassenheide Camp. The bombs that had fallen short of the German housing estate had set fire to the wooden huts in the camp, and sixteen out of a total of thirty were destroyed within a matter of minutes – long before the inmates were able to flee to safety. These tragic details would certainly have been known to the British authorities within a few days or weeks of the raid.

In reality, the attacks caused a delay of only around a couple of months to the rocket programme, with test launches of the V-2 – albeit thereafter, only at night and in fog – resuming on 6 October.

Nevertheless, the raids did force the Nazis to abandon plans to assemble rockets at Peenemünde, with all subsequent production being transferred to assembly lines deep underground in the Harz Mountains near Nordhausen. Most trial launches were also relocated to Blizna in Poland.

While these were certainly substantial setbacks for the Nazis at that time, there was absolutely no official mention by the Germans themselves of the flying bomb and rocket programmes or, indeed, of the significance of the raid on Peenemünde. All we find in the *NVZ* of 20 August is a passing reference on an inside page to a report from the German High Command admitting that during the night of 17 August:

the enemy had dropped a large quantity of high explosive bombs and incendiaries on coastal locations in the north of Germany. Lives were lost. Night fighters and ground artillery shot down at least 37 planes of the British bomber units.

Remarkably, this gave no hint of the destruction of the works at Peenemünde. Indeed, it was not until the end of September 1943 that Albert Speer indicated publicly that a secret reprisal weapon was even being produced that would allow the Germans to retaliate against the Allies' blanket bombing of German cities.

Grainy photograph of V-1 rocket in flight over London in 1944. *NARA 541919*

The Reporting of the Use of V-1 and V-2 Rockets

The first V-1 rocket to be directed against Britain was not to be launched until the morning of 13 June 1944, a week after the Allies had landed in Normandy. It was to crash into the ground at Swanscombe, a village lying between Dartford and Gravesend. While nobody was killed in that particular explosion, six people were killed by a subsequent flying bomb that landed in Bethnal Green.

There is no doubt that the British did initially play down the arrival of, and damage caused by, these new flying bombs. While *The Times* of 14 June mentioned there had been some bombing attacks on London the previous night, there was no indication this emanated from a new type of pilotless aircraft:

 A few bombs which fell in the night caused some damage and a small number of casualties.

Somewhat surprisingly, because you might have thought that it would have been good for civilian morale, the German media were also rather slow to report the damage being inflicted by this new weapon. This was partly because the German High Command did not want to reveal too much to the British about these new pilotless aircraft, but also because they could not be certain just how much damage their flying bombs were inflicting. In reality, because of a combination of sabotage and ever improving countermeasures, only 4,200 out of 10,000 V-1 flying bombs aimed at London actually hit their target.

Annoyed and surprised by the lack of response to the attacks in the British press and, even more so, after a much heavier launch of 244 flying bombs on 15 June, the German Army issued its own rather short and mysterious statement on 16 June:

 Last night and this morning Southern England and the area around the city of London were hit by strange, high-calibre explosives.

The accompanying article explained how the German people were taking great comfort from the sorrows being inflicted on the British by these new bombs after the months and months of indiscriminate terror bombing by Allied aircraft of the homes of innocent German women and children. The headlines of the *NVZ* of 19 June were:

 Strips of flame in the London sky
English Army completely baffled

The article claimed that the British press was being forbidden from talking about this new weapon, and that the British were simply at a loss as to how to deal with it. This was partly true. Despite the first V-1s appearing over Britain on 13 June and no fewer than 144 of the V-1s launched on 15 June actually hitting London and the surrounding area, there would be no British press comment about this new weapon until 17 June.

Nevertheless, the British knew they could not keep quiet about the flying bombs forever, even if they could prevent the press from reporting in any detail the amount of damage being caused. So, on 16 June, Herbert Morrison, Home Secretary, speaking in Parliament, sought to reassure the British public by claiming that:

 The damage these pilotless aircraft has caused has been relatively small, and the new weapon will not interfere with our war effort and our sure and steady march to victory.

Somewhat similar to German claims about the Allied landings in Normandy, other headlines were keen to stress that:

 New weapon is not a surprise

By 19 June, more negative details about the actual damage caused and the number of lives lost were countered by positive claims that a combination of the bombing of launch sites and attacks by RAF fighter and anti-aircraft guns was having great success in destroying these pilotless aircraft before they could reach their destination.

Nonetheless, the press certainly did not provide full details either about the number of V-1s arriving over London or the damage which was being caused. For example, the *Daily Express* of 19 June was to report that the previous day:

 ### FLYING BOMBS HIT CONGREGATION

Morning service had just begun in a south of England church yesterday when suddenly a flying bomb crashed through the roof [...] A number of worshippers were killed but the clergyman who was to have preached was unhurt.

This report gave the impression that very few of the congregation had been killed, but, in reality, no fewer than 189 people were killed or wounded that day, during the church service in the Guard's Chapel at Wellington Barracks. Given the lack of reporting by the British media, it was still not until 26 June that the Germans' *Sprauer Tageblatt* felt sufficiently confident to talk of:

 Retaliation weapon 'V 1' thunders against England
The uncertainty is leading the English to panic

The latter headline was certainly justified. Whether or not the new weapon was a surprise, the reality was that 500 V-1s had been fired by 18 June, and 2,500 people had been killed by 5 July. Consequently, it was of little surprise that, within ten weeks of the first rocket being fired, as many as 1.25 million people were to forsake London for the countryside.

An even greater reticence to report was to be found on the part of the British when it came to the arrival of the V-2 rocket later that year. The first V-2 fell on Chiswick in west London on 8 September 1944, killing three people. It was a far more fearful weapon than the V-1, as it simply fell out of the sky with no time for any air raid warning. It is quite obvious why the British would have wanted to conceal the existence of this new weapon when they had few means of countering it – other than to locate and destroy the missile sites from which the rockets were being launched. Consequently, the authorities were quite happy for the damage and deaths arising from this and other attacks during the following weeks to be attributed to gas main explosions.

It is far more difficult to understand why the Nazis would have wished to conceal the use of the weapon from their own people and, indeed, from the rest of the world. Its very existence might have persuaded other countries to negotiate a better peace deal with Germany.

Nevertheless, neither side was to mention the V-2 rockets for two months and, even then, it was left first to German radio on 8 November 1944 and then the *Völkischer Beobachter* the following day, to report that London was under fire from the V-2 retaliation weapon:

 ## V2 AGAINST LONDON

Attacks on London from V1s since 15 June [...] have been intensified for some weeks by the deployment of far more powerful explosives in the form of the V2.

This revelation forced Churchill to admit in Parliament that Britain had been under attack from these rockets for some time, although he claimed that the launch sites were gradually being overrun by Allied forces as they moved eastwards towards Germany. Even *The Times* of 2 January 1945, in its review of 1944, was to continue to try to underplay the significance of the V-2s by declaring that, although they were causing considerable destruction of civilian life and property, they were having negligible effect on the war effort. In reality, the V-2s were to account for almost 10,000 dead or wounded in London alone, before the last rocket landed in England on 27 March 1945.

CONCLUSION

In each of the events described in the last three chapters, we find clear evidence of the efforts taken by both sides to suppress completely undesirable information about the course of the war. The consequence was that the propaganda boost that one side might have hoped to gain from such revelations did not necessarily materialise, especially if the enemy's public was kept ignorant of disheartening news. Nevertheless, the revelation that the enemy had suffered some setback or been placed in an embarrassing position probably did still have some positive impact on morale on the home front.

A captured V-2 rocket being tested by the Allies in October 1945. More than 3,000 V-2 rockets were launched from Peenemünde between 1942 and 1945.

15

OPERATION MARKET GARDEN

INTRODUCTION

In Holland, on 17 September 1944, the Allies launched one of their most ambitious operations during the whole of the Second World War. Planning for the attack had started only seven days previously but, if successful, Operation Market Garden would accelerate the Allies' route to the Ruhr – the focal point of the German arms industry – and, hopefully, bring a swift end to the war.

Despite the superhuman efforts made by the Allies to achieve their objectives and the astounding bravery and unwavering determination displayed by the airborne troops charged with capturing the road bridge at Arnhem, the mission would end in failure.

It was a staggering blow for the Allies and yet, for many days, the Allied media would paint a rather misleading picture of what was happening and were very slow to admit the truth, albeit that several British newspapers were receiving regular reports from their own journalists attached to the Allied forces.

How could some of the British press continue to claim – as late as 25 September – that the British garrison at the Arnhem Bridge was still fighting on bravely, when it was well known that the airborne forces there had been overrun four days earlier? Why did the Allies allow the release of a newsreel that still offered the prospect of the success of the mission on the very same day that their own press was admitting the airborne troops on the north bank of the Lower Rhine had been forced to retreat?

Eventually, the Allies were to try to salvage some morale-boosting propaganda out of the mission by concentrating on the fighting spirit of the troops at Arnhem and their daring withdrawal, while the Germans very effectively exploited the ultimate failure of the operation for their own propaganda purposes, carefully omitting to mention the significant losses they had also sustained during the last two weeks of September 1944.

THE RACE FOR ARNHEM

Following the Allies' successful landings in Normandy, in June 1944, they advanced rapidly eastward across a wide front. By late August, the Second British Army was advancing by as much as 50 miles a day, and this was causing massive logistical problems. Short of key supplies, they were eventually forced to halt their advance near Antwerp on 4 September.

Some new initiative would be required for the Allies to press home their advantage. Field Marshal Montgomery believed the Germans were so demoralised and debilitated by the way the war was progressing that a concentrated offensive through Holland would give the Allies an opportunity to gain access to and control over the River Rhine. From there, the Allies would be in a position to attack Germany's industrial infrastructure in the Ruhr basin and reduce significantly the supply of munitions and heavy equipment that fuelled the Nazi war effort.

General Eisenhower, the Supreme Allied Commander, was far more cautious and eventually agreed a scaled-down version of what Montgomery had proposed. The revised plan involved dropping three airborne divisions behind enemy lines to seize and hold a series of key bridges in Holland, across which units of the Second British Army, under General Dempsey, would advance. The mission would involve a total road journey of some 64 miles.

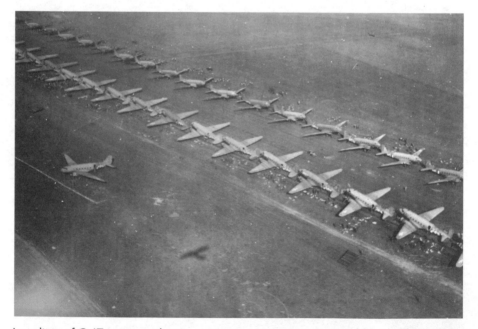

Long lines of C-47 transport planes preparing to carry paratroopers of the 1st Allied Airborne Army from Britain to Holland on 17 September 1944. *NARA 535551*

The American 101st Airborne Division was to secure the most southerly bridge at Eindhoven, the American 82nd Airborne Division was to take the bridge at Nijmegen and the British 1st Airborne Division and the 1st Polish Independent Parachute Brigade were to seize the final and most northerly bridge at Arnhem. Reconnaissance reports led the Allies to believe that the German forces around Arnhem consisted of only 6,000 soldiers and around a dozen tanks. To take advantage of the favourable circumstances then pertaining, it was realised that the operation had to proceed as quickly as possible. So, although formal planning started only on 10 September, the operation itself was launched a mere seven days later.

The scale of the whole undertaking was quite breathtaking. The airborne operation alone was the largest in military history, with eventually close to 40,000 men being landed by parachute or glider along the whole route – not to mention the initial delivery of close to 2,000 vehicles and artillery pieces by a similar number of transporters and gliders.

The first news reports of this new Allied advance were to appear in the British press on 18 September. The press had obviously been well briefed regarding the aim of the mission, with most newspapers featuring maps of north-west Germany and Holland, pinpointing exactly where the action was taking place:

 Allies invade Holland by air – 'over Rhine'

The *Daily Express* was pleased to reveal that, as a result of the paratrooper landings, German troops had already been dislodged from several Dutch towns. The numerous sub-headlines were nevertheless rather contradictory. On the one hand, the reader was informed:

 Paratroops from 1,000 plane-armada strike at German flank ... The blow achieved surprise and succeeded 'beyond all expectations'

On the other hand, just a few lines later, the reader was informed that:

 Airborne army meets stiff resistance

Concentrating particularly on the advances made by the tanks of the Second British Army in order to link up near Eindhoven with American airborne forces, the renewed emphasis on more optimistic headlines continued on 19 September:

 16-Mile Dash links Tanks to Air Army
A vast process of disintegration has begun all the way up to the Rhine

On the same day, news of the operation appeared in the German press for the first time and, concentrating on the German response to the airborne landings, the headlines and accompanying commentary gave their readers a completely different assessment of what was happening:

 Airborne Troops sealed off
Concentrated assaults on enemy paratrooper units

The official report from Berlin and the accompanying articles gave the clear impression that the paratrooper landings had certainly not been successful, since not only had the German forces shot down many gliders, but they had also prevented the widely scattered groups of paratroopers from assembling into larger fighting units and from linking up with the Allied forces heading north from Eindhoven.

Deliberately or otherwise, the British press did, unquestionably, paint a rather misleading picture of what was happening on the ground. When *The Times* of 19 September reported that British armour had reached the airborne troops, the reader might well have assumed that only one set of airborne troops had been

Paratroopers dropping in waves over Holland during Operation Market Garden. *NARA 531392*

landed, and that all was going well. Good progress continued to be reported over the next couple of days and, by 21 September, the *Daily Express* was able to give the exciting news that the first British soldiers had actually managed to enter Hitler's Reich:

 We're in: British cross German Frontier

There was certainly no such acknowledgement in the German press which, while admitting that the enemy had been able to widen its attack to the north-west and south-west of Aachen, highlighted the fact that the Allies had suffered heavy losses of men and equipment in the Arnhem area, and that 1,700 prisoners had been captured:

 Airborne troops hemmed in even further

Cromwell tanks of 2nd Welsh Guards crossing the bridge at Nijmegen on 21 September in the rush towards Arnhem.

It was only from 22 September onwards that the British press made any specific reference to a separate, hard-pressed airborne force at Arnhem and, even then, the headlines in most of the British newspapers were still fairly positive:

22 September – *The Times*
British Tanks Driving on to Arnhem

22 September – *Daily Express*
Arnhem sky army sight first Dempsey men – Germans moving out

23 September – *Daily Express*
Sky Men will keep going
Dempsey only 5 miles from them now

Indeed, it was left to the *Daily Mirror* to present a more downbeat assessment of the situation with its headlines:

Airborne in Arnhem Hell
Fighting for their lives as British Second Army struggle to reach them

In fact, the German press for that very same day, while accepting that the Allies had advanced north of Nijmegen, was, in fact, declaring that the German forces had been victorious, and that the battle for Arnhem was already more or less over:

 In the area of Arnhem some fighting continued to wipe out what remained of the 1st British Airborne Division which was trapped there.

DECIPHERING THE TRUTH

Given the apparent contradictory accounts, not just between the German and British press but even between some of the British newspapers, just what was the truth?

First, the German forces were not nearly as weak, either in terms of strength or experience, as the Allies had anticipated. The Dutch resistance had actually warned the Allies that some German panzer units were refitting in the Market Garden area, but this information was not included in the Allies' final intelligence summaries – partly due to the fact that the British had lost confidence in all Dutch resistance reports because of earlier infiltration by Nazi agents. In fact, the Allied soldiers at Arnhem and Nijmegen would come under attack from the 9th and 10th SS Divisions of the II Panzers Corps, which were recuperating in that very area at the time. Furthermore, by 17 September, the Germans' 59th and 245th Infantry Divisions found themselves in just the right position to attack the American Airborne Divisions and the advancing tanks and vehicles of the XXX Corps of the Second British Army. Initial good progress by the Allies was soon cancelled out. The Germans' successful detonation of the bridge at Son forced the British to build a pontoon bridge across the Wilhelmina Canal – thus delaying the arrival of the Allies in Eindhoven until 18 September. Likewise, counter-attacks by the Germans delayed the final capture of the vital bridge at Nijmegen by another three days.

Second, at Arnhem, the Germans were quick to deduce what the Allies had in mind and reacted quickly to the developing situation. The closest unit to the British landing zones was the 16th SS Panzer-Grenadier Depot and Reserve Battalion, which just happened to be training in the woods some 7 miles from the main bridge at Arnhem. They managed to inflict considerable casualties on two of the British parachute battalions, before another, the 2nd Battalion, under Colonel Frost, could finally reach the bridge on the evening of 17 September. Although the Germans managed to retain control of the southern end of the bridge, their initial attempts to dislodge the British from the northern end failed completely. Nevertheless, in the days that followed, the Germans did manage to prevent the Allies from reinforcing the Second Battalion. Indeed, the Allies were to suffer significant losses in futile attempts to reach Colonel Frost.

By 19 September, and although desperately short of munitions and other supplies, Colonel Frost and his men still refused to surrender, with the result that the Germans changed their tactics and started to blast out the British, street by street and house by house. By 11 a.m. on 21 September, the remnants of the exhausted Second Battalion were finally overrun, signing off with a final radio message 'Out of ammunition. God save the King!'

This news would not appear in any British newspaper at the time and, indeed, the reporting of what was actually happening at Arnhem became rather confused and misleading over the following days.

So, given that we know that British forces at the northern end of the bridge at Arnhem had been overcome on 21 September, although even the German press waited until 23 September to claim that all resistance at Arnhem was more or less over, just how could the British press in the days following 21 September continue to claim that the battle for Arnhem was still under way?

Admittedly, even *The Times* of 23 September had felt it necessary to talk of the 'crisis on the Rhine' and mentioned the Germans were now claiming that some 4,000 men of the 1st Airborne Division had already been captured. Nevertheless, hope was rekindled with the revelation that the forces at Arnhem had been reinforced by a Polish airborne regiment.

This confidence was reinforced in the *Sunday Express* of 24 September with the disclosure that on the previous day:

 Strong new airborne landing to aid the heroes of Arnhem

The initial headlines and reports in its sister newspaper the following day were even more encouraging:

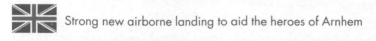 ARNHEM BRIDGE GARRISON STILL HOLDING ON

Relief came just in time for the airborne men, who for a whole week have been holding on by sheer guts.

Indeed, this front page article even carried a small map clearly showing that the 1st Airborne Division had secured bridgeheads both at the Arnhem Bridge and at Oosterbeek, to the west of Arnhem. These headlines certainly gave the misleading impression that the whole operation was going to be a success, and it was only in a subsidiary paragraph that it was finally admitted:

Those holding the northern end of the main road bridge in Arnhem itself [...] are still out of touch and there is some anxiety for them.

However, given that the *Daily Express* was only one of several newspapers that had its own reporters located in the very midst of the airborne forces, it is hard to believe that it would have been unaware that the British forces at the Arnhem Bridge had already been defeated on 21 September. Therefore, the headlines and maps in the *Daily Express* were not only misleading but simply untrue.

In fact, throughout the whole operation, the headlines and reports in the *Daily Mirror* were generally far more accurate. For example, the *Daily Mirror* indicated on 25 September that, although General Dempsey's infantry were well consolidated on the south bank of the Lower Rhine, they had not actually crossed it:

 Great bid to aid Skytroops

This contrasted sharply with the rather disingenuous headline in the *Daily Express*:

 RELIEF ARMY CROSSES THE RHINE IN DUCKS

The accompanying article did not quite live up to the claim of the headline:

British infantry, carried in Ducks, have burst through to the Lower Rhine west of Arnhem. All night and all morning they have been ferrying food and other supplies to the heroic airborne troops on the northern bank.

So, in reality, it transpired that only some food and supplies were reaching the airborne troops on the northern shore – rather than more men, and there was no acknowledgement that even these supplies were reaching only the airborne troops fighting west of Arnhem.

Indeed, the primary reason for all the apparent inconsistency in reporting – even between British newspapers – was that neither the Germans nor the Allies made it particularly clear that a distinction needed to be drawn between the fate of the airborne troops fighting in Arnhem for control of the main bridge over the Lower Rhine and those troops fighting further west at Oosterbeek.

Troops of the 1st Airlanding Light Regiment defending their positions at the Oosterbeek perimeter west of Arnhem on 20 September.

The point was that although Colonel Frost and his men holding the northern end of the bridge had been forced to surrender on 21 September, thus forfeiting any realistic ambition by the Allies of capturing the bridge, the rest of the 1st Airborne Division, although trapped in an increasingly small pocket west of the bridge centred on Oosterbeek, continued to resist.

This discrepancy would never be made public in the British press; therefore, British readers could well be forgiven for believing that, several days later, the British forces at Arnhem were still holding the bridge.

Likewise, for some odd reason, the Germans also failed to make this vital distinction, and it is possible to sense an increasing frustration in the likes of the *Völkischer Beobachter* when, having already reported on 23 September that the resistance at Arnhem had been more or less wiped out, it was obliged to continue to give repeated updates in the days that followed. On 24 September, it talked of how the British and Americans had not made as much progress as they would have liked:

 Only weak remnants of the British 1st Airborne Division are left.

26 September:

MORE HEAVY ENEMY LOSSES IN HOLLAND

Another 800 wounded from the fighting remnants of the Airborne Division brought in.

27 September:

HEAVY LOSSES OF THE 1ST AIRBORNE DIVISION
THE HARD STRUGGLE AT ARNHEM

The hard-pressed remnants of the 1st British Airborne Division at Arnhem suffered heavy losses from concentrated artillery fire – yet continued to display desperate resistance.

There were numerous photographs of captured British paratroopers and, rather surprisingly, the German reports were often remarkably forthright, albeit with any bad news always balanced with some good news:

 Heavy fighting continues in central Holland and especially in the Eindhoven area. While enemy attacks south-west of Vechel failed, east and south-east of Helmond the enemy was able to advance a few kilometres eastwards.

Attacks to the west of Arnhem to relieve what remained of the trapped 1st English Airborne Division were beaten back in counter-attacks. Our adversary suffered heavy losses. North of Nijmegen, supported by tanks, the English continued their strong attacks but could only make small territorial gains.

Enemy lost 23 planes in air battles.

28 September:
British Crack Division completely wiped out
Successful conclusion to the fighting in Arnhem

At last, the German High Command was able to report how the last resistance of
the 1st Airborne Division around Arnhem had been broken on 26 September:

In ten days of heavy fighting [...] and despite tough resistance and reinforcement from
the air, German army units [...] have managed to wipe out a whole division of English
crack troops.

All attempts by the enemy to relieve the trapped division from the south failed with
heavy, bloody losses. All together 6,450 prisoners were taken and thousands were
killed. 30 tanks and 250 vehicles were captured. In addition, 1,000 gliders were
destroyed or captured and over 100 planes shot down.

Were any of these dramatic statistics accurate? Even today, it is difficult to ascertain
the precise losses suffered by either side. Best estimates suggest that, of approxi
mately 10,500 airborne troops that landed in the vicinity of Arnhem, only 2,500
managed to escape, almost 1,500 were killed and the remainder, many of whom
were badly wounded, were captured. In total, the Allied losses were around
16,000 killed, wounded or captured. While the number of gliders lost was far
fewer than 1,000, the figure was somewhat irrelevant as they were never going
to be able to fly home. Throughout the whole operation, including sorties flown in
support of Market Garden and the eventual withdrawal of survivors from the northern
bank, close to 300 Allied aircraft were lost.

So, on the one hand, the German statistical reports were fairly accurate and,
indeed, in some cases underestimated the extent of the Allied losses. On the other
hand, the German media generally omitted to make any mention of their own
losses, which it is now reckoned ranged from somewhere between 7,000 and
10,000 men.

What the failure of the operation did mean was that the Germans were able
to make some much-needed capital out of the Allied defeat. The headlines of the
Völkischer Beobachter of 29 September read:

THE GROWING STRENGTH OF THE WESTERN FRONT
ENEMY ADMITS: EISENHOWER'S ENCIRCLEMENT PLAN WRECKED

Not only the destruction of the 1st British Airborne Division at Arnhem, which was
described by the English and American press as a German success which quite frankly
'ought not to be scoffed at' but also and above all the growing stability of the German

Western Front is forcing the general public in the western enemy countries to bury any hope of a swift end to the war.

For its part, by 26 September, even the *Daily Express* had been starting to prepare its readers for some unwelcome news:

ARNHEM POCKET NARROWS DOWN
GERMANS AGAIN HURLED FROM THE CORRIDOR
AIR ARMY IS FIGHTING HEROICALLY AGAINST ATTACKS BY PICK OF GERMAN TROOPS

The position at the top of the corridor is that west of Arnhem further small units of British infantry have crossed the river to reinforce the 'red devils'.

Much of the harsh truth was actually there. It is just that it was often wrapped up in so much colourful language or interspersed with more positive reports of fighting elsewhere that it could often be overlooked. The fact that all was not going well was certainly evident in the newspaper's report the following day, which began:

 While Supreme headquarters drew a strict news black-out over the fate of the heroic few of Britain's First Airborne Division west of Arnhem [...]

All that the news blackout achieved was to oblige the British press to report what the Germans were claiming instead – an outcome that was presumably never intended, given the triumphant nature of the German reports.

By 28 September, the focus of the British press changed again with yet another attempt by the British, just as at Dunkirk, to claim victory from defeat:

 The Story of the Retreat is a bluff that succeeded magnificently
Men of Arnhem walked out through the German Lines
Password was 'John Bull'

However, the *Daily Mirror* was still prepared to go a step further and detail the actual Allied losses:

 ## 1 IN 4 RESCUED FROM HELL OF ARNHEM

About 2,000 of the 8,000 British airborne troops who made the epic eight-day stand [...] have been evacuated [...] had to leave behind 1,200 wounded – reports indicate the Germans are treating them well.

Such an admission had to be countered with a more upbeat conclusion, and it certainly was:

 Victory cost the enemy dear. Between 12,000 and 15,000 Germans were killed, according to an official Allied estimate [...] The red devils' sacrifice was not in vain. Without it the British Second Army could not have hoped to capture the even more vital Nijmegen Bridge.

Ultimately, the inability to complete the mission would be blamed on the delay and inability of the Second Army relief column to cross the north bank of the Lower Rhine and on the bad weather that prevented the dropping of adequate supplies in the right place to the airborne troops fighting at Arnhem. In reality, fewer than 8 per cent of stores destined for the British 1st Airborne Division reached their intended recipients, but such an appalling statistic would never be reported at the time.

NEWSREEL COVERAGE

Not surprisingly, the first newsreel that featured Operation Market Garden was the *British Movietone* film released on 28 September. The emphasis of the report was that the arrival of Allied troops was returning freedom to those citizens in Holland whose towns had been liberated. It contrasted images of downcast, wounded German prisoners with the cheering and dancing of ordinary people in the streets of Eindhoven.

Nevertheless, there was an admission that the battle for the Rhine crossings was still ongoing, and that help was on its way for 'that very gallant force battling at Arnhem'.

The simple truth is that, at the very moment this film was released, even the British press was reporting the retreat of airborne forces from Arnhem in a daring escape across the Rhine. Those who made the newsreel would certainly have been aware of the actual situation, but it was simply too late to pull the film – and it did allow some positive comments to be made about Allied successes before revealing the whole truth in a later newsreel. However, it is difficult to know what the typical cinema-goer at the time would have made of this mismatch between what the press and newsreels were claiming. In fact, the next Allied newsreel was released only four days later with the headline:

 Battle of the Rhine crossings – men of Arnhem

With more of the facts then known by all, the commentator was determined to leave the viewer in no doubt as to the heroism displayed by the Allied forces:

No greater gallantry has been displayed in any action in any war than by airborne forces during the battle for the Rhine crossings in Holland!

Even though there was an admission that relieving forces had been unable to alter the situation at Arnhem, that only 2,000 men had been able to be withdrawn across the river and a similar number of wounded had been left in German hands, there was no real attempt to acknowledge that the overall mission had been a failure:

 By their invincible spirit and their sacrifice they gave incalculable aid to the successes won at the other two crossings [...] Aim was to take three crossings. Two out of three were secured. Although the whole operation falls short of complete success these are very solid gains.

The first mention of the Allied operation in German newsreel was in *Wochenschau* No. 735, which was screened on 4 October 1944, several days after the struggle for Arnhem had passed. Amazingly, given the extent of the Allied failure, it was not even the first item featured on that particular newsreel. Nevertheless, against a background map that featured the three major Dutch cities where the fighting had been most intensive, the five-minute report did begin with a quite astonishing claim:

The end of the 1st British Air Division at Arnhem. At the end of the 10-day battle of Arnhem, the British had to concede a German victory of such a scale as has not been seen since the beginning of the invasion in the west.

It was explained how, on 17 September, the British and Americans dropped more than three paratrooper divisions into the region near Eindhoven, Nijmegen and Arnhem:

Within a short time the Germans were able to surround the British 1st Airborne Division which landed near Arnhem and to destroy it within ten days of the start of the operation.

There was great celebration over the Germans' success, with action footage showing gliders and planes being shot down, and the claim that hundreds of British paratroopers were killed before they even reached the ground.

Against images of Germans smoking captured British cigarettes and lines and lines of miserable looking British prisoners, the commentator concluded with this rather upbeat assessment:

For them, 'Operation Berlin', as Eisenhower designated this fiasco, is over. They have personally learnt that the day of German capitulation as stipulated by Churchill, has not only been postponed, but that it does not even come into question!

There was obviously some misunderstanding here, since Operation Berlin was the code name reserved for the final withdrawal – an operation that was actually very successful.

Indeed, the report gave the clear impression that the Allies had not made any gains, which was simply not true, and nor was there any attempt to detail comparative German losses in terms of men and machines over that ten-day period.

CONCLUSION

History has determined that Operation Market Garden was ultimately a failure, in that the inability of the Allies to seize the final bridge at Arnhem meant that the war would not be shortened, and that it would take a further four months for the Allies to cross the Rhine and attack Germany's industrial basin. In fact, the Allies were left defending a 50-mile long salient that led to nowhere, and the retention of which during the remainder of 1944 was very costly in terms of Allied casualties. Furthermore, as a result of the severe reprisals inflicted on the Dutch for holding a transport strike that coincided with the launch of Market Garden, more than 18,000 Dutch civilians would die during the winter that followed. Many houses in the Arnhem area were also looted and destroyed by the Germans in retaliation for the assistance many Dutch civilians had provided to the British and Polish soldiers trapped in the Arnhem enclaves.

Montgomery always claimed that the operation was 90 per cent successful – a view not shared by the then Prince of the Netherlands, who simply said: 'My country can never again afford the luxury of another Montgomery success.'

At the time, in terms of media coverage, both sides tried to make some propaganda capital out of the operation and, in so doing, failed to tell their own people the whole story.

We find that neither the German nor the British press sufficiently differentiated between the two groups of airborne soldiers fighting near Arnhem. This caused some embarrassment for the Germans who, having rather prematurely declared on 23 September that the battle for Arnhem was already over, found themselves repeatedly having to report further fighting in the days ahead. It also explained how comparative headlines for the same day in Britain and Germany could be contradictory. However, overall, the Germans were able to make far more capital out of the Allies' failure to achieve their ultimate goal, and they drew a convenient veil over their own losses and the Dutch territory recaptured by the Allies.

For the Allies, we find that even the British press was divided as to how it would report the success or otherwise of the mission. Long after the brave force at the Arnhem Bridge had been overrun, the impression was given that the battle for Arnhem and its bridge was still being fought. This was certainly misleading, and the *Daily Express*, in particular, was certainly always far more confident about the likelihood of final success than some of the other British newspapers. Allied newsreel for the period was also slow to report the truth about Arnhem, even after the full story had been reported in the British press. By concentrating on the numbers of prisoners taken and enemy gliders and planes destroyed, the German newsreel could afford to sound a triumphant note. It gave the Germans hope that they could still sue for an honourable peace – a hope that would be raised even further with the launch of their own counter-offensive in the Ardennes just a couple of months later.

16

THE BATTLE OF THE BULGE

INTRODUCTION

Following the success of the D-Day landings and the relentless drive of the Allies eastwards, there was an expectation among the British public, at least, that the defeat of Germany would be only a question of time. After all, the German Army was already fighting a losing battle against the Soviets in the east and against the Americans, British and Canadians in the south of Italy.

Nonetheless, by mid-November, 1944, not all was going smoothly for the Allies and the optimism for a swift end to the war had been tempered somewhat. Following the failure of Operation Market Garden in Holland, in September, rain and driving snow had forced the Allies to call a halt to their winter campaign in Italy. The British found themselves engaged in trying to keep the peace in a Greek civil war, and the Allies were even starting to fall out over the future of Poland.

By December, while the Allies, bolstered by the arrival of the American 3rd Army, were certainly preparing for a fresh offensive from the west into Germany, they had allowed a perilous gap to develop between Patton's forces in the south and the British and Americans to the north. A mere six US divisions were employed to defend the 60 mile long front in the Ardennes region. The German High Command was all too aware of this weakness in the Allied lines so, just at the very moment when the thoughts of Allied soldiers were turning towards Christmas and the prospect of a pause in heavy fighting until the following year, Hitler launched one of his most daring counter-attacks in the whole war. If the Germans could break through in the Ardennes and sweep northwards to recapture the port of Antwerp, then it would change the whole course of the conflict. For a number of weeks, the fate of the world undoubtedly did hang in the balance.

Just how was this unexpected development reported by the media in Germany and Britain? Less than a fortnight earlier, a final parade by the British Home Guard had been held in London. So, given that the British public had certainly been led to believe that the war with Germany was all but over, would the Allies now be prepared to admit to their own people that the war was far from won? For their part, would the Nazis dare to raise the hopes of their long-suffering citizens yet again by reporting this major counter-offensive if there was a danger that this final gamble would end in yet more failure?

THE LAST ROLL OF THE DICE

In the early hours of the morning of 16 December 1944, the German Army launched Operation Wacht am Rhein with the unleashing of a massive artillery bombardment on the American forces stationed in the snow-covered hills of the Ardennes. After an hour, the barrage stopped, and the silence was replaced by the rumbling of tanks, as the first of twenty German divisions emerged out of the woods and the freezing fog. The Allies were caught completely by surprise.

The Times had actually carried an article the previous day explaining how Rundstedt and his men, using a new kind of tank, had seized an important vantage point 25 miles south-west of Mulhouse, far to the south of the Ardennes. This had obviously been a deliberate diversionary tactic by the Germans, and in the panic ensuing from their unexpected attack further north, they made rapid progress towards the Belgian town of Bastogne. On paper, at least, it was an unequal struggle. Six US divisions of scarcely more than 80,000 soldiers and 400 tanks found themselves confronted by 250,000 men and 950 tanks. To make matters worse, persistent fog denied the Allies the use of their superior air power, and English-speaking German soldiers in US uniforms wreaked havoc behind the American lines.

Given the confusion that existed in this remote area, it is somewhat surprising that by as early as Monday 18 December the British press was already able to carry detailed reports acknowledging the extent and significance of the German offensive. The *Daily Mirror* headlines read:

 Major German Attack: American Line Holed
Don't Underrate this Punch

The whole world clearly recognised just what was at stake. The press reported the astonishing efforts being made by the Germans to achieve victory, including the use of black-coloured parachutes to drop scores of paratroopers at night behind Allied lines, with orders to disrupt communications and to hold key roads and bridges for the advancing German forces. However, the *Daily Express* was keen to highlight how exposed lines of German vehicles had fallen easy prey to hundreds of American Mustangs, Lightnings and Thunderbolts. The impression that German advances were being achieved only at tremendous cost was promoted further in the British press in the following days:

20 Miles into Belgium
Cost to Germans: 121 tanks and armoured cars knocked out
Luftwaffe lose 97 Aircraft in all-day Battles
Allies Hitting Back

As for the Germans, it is obvious that they were unwilling to report this new offensive at all, until they were absolutely certain that it, at least, stood some chance of success.

Hence, it was only on 19 December that the likes of the *Völkischer Beobachter* carried an official announcement from the Führer's headquarters, dated 18 December, about what had occurred on 16 December, but even this contained very little factual information:

 German Offensive in the West
Enemy taken completely by surprise

In their initial attack [...] powerful German forces [...] after heavy artillery bombardment [...] had overrun the forward American positions between the High Venn and the northern part of Luxembourg.

The report continued by claiming that their fighters and anti-aircraft guns had shot down a total of sixty nine enemy planes. There was no mention of their own losses either in the air or on the ground. Undeniably, the news of this unexpected counter-attack certainly did boost German morale. Even though the extent, purpose and outcome of the offensive remained unknown, it gave German journalists an opportunity to stress the undaunted determination of the German forces to defend the Fatherland right to the end, with all their might:

 Fight for the Liberation of our Homeland

Over the next couple of days, the confidence of the German High Command continued to grow and the reports appearing in the German press became increasingly optimistic as to the success of this counter-offensive:

 Offensive in the West proceeding 'according to plan'

However, it was obviously felt that such comments would carry more credibility if they were supported by confirmation in the Allied press, so they were keen to report how even the American press was talking of, 'Germany striking back and of the US Army falling back in the face of German tank and infantry divisions.'

Captured film of a heavily armed German soldier advancing into territory seized during the Nazi counter-offensive in the Ardennes. *NARA 111-SC-197561*

Increasingly positive reports emerged over the next few days as key Allied strong points were overrun, and it emerged that experienced German soldiers were engaged in battles against hastily assembled American reserve troops.

Thursday 21 December:
10,000 prisoners captured, 200 tanks captured or destroyed and 124 planes shot down.

Friday 22 December:
Number of prisoners now exceeds 20,000 – a further 43 tanks and 50 artillery pieces captured and 136 tanks destroyed.

However, what was missing from all these reports was the scale of comparable German losses, and whether any real progress was being made on the ground. Another feature missing from the German reports was any comment on the repeated claims in the Allied press of the indescribable savagery being perpetrated by the German forces in their drive westwards:

 Huns Slay Unarmed Prisoners

The *Daily Mirror* of 21 December had already reported how German soldiers had slaughtered 125 American artillerymen and medical personnel who had surrendered in the area of Monschau. Even worse were later reports of the deliberate massacre of civilians – including two small children in the village of Stavelot. Many of these reports were subsequently proved to be completely accurate and led to retaliation by American troops, who had reportedly been ordered not to take any prisoners.

Nevertheless, there is no doubt that over the first five or six days of the offensive, the position on the ground was very fluid, and there was certainly a degree of confusion in the British press as to who was actually winning the battle. The *Daily Express* of 22 December was excited that:

 the German northern drive through Belgium is still pinned down.

Nevertheless, at the very same time, the *Daily Mirror* was far less optimistic and reported how even the Allied Supreme H.Q. had:

 confirmed Rundstedt's claim to have thrust thirty-six miles into Belgium and cut a vital north-south highway.

By 23 December, while the Germans were still able to claim that they had pushed further west and established several bridgeheads over the River Ourthe, much of the focus had shifted to the more general assertion that all attempts by the Allies to halt their progress had failed. There was even a claim that the Americans were putting up far stiffer resistance in Saarlauter further south.

Fighting continued over Christmas and by 26 December the German High Command was reporting how the German ring around Bastogne was tightening. However, the fact that the report was restricted to claiming that 700 enemy tanks and armoured cars had been destroyed during the *whole* of the offensive – rather than simply reporting the number of enemy vehicles destroyed the *previous day* – perhaps best illustrates that the Germans' earlier successes were gradually grinding to a halt.

Troops from the 101st Airborne Division watch supplies being dropped over Bastogne from C-47s on 26 December 1944. *US Army Center of Military History/SC415376*

The *Daily Express* of 24 December had already decided that the pendulum had started to swing in the opposite direction, and it continued to accentuate the positive:

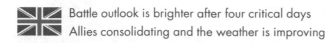

Battle outlook is brighter after four critical days
Allies consolidating and the weather is improving

It was a view not shared by the *Daily Mirror* of 27 December, which was still talking rather worryingly of how Rundstedt had merged his twin drive into a single bulge 40 miles deep and 35 miles wide and was thrusting ever northwards and closer to the River Meuse.

Irrespective of the uncertainty of the British press, the tide was unquestionably turning as the weather improved. On 28 December, the *Daily Express* was finally able to report that the garrison at Bastogne had been relieved:

Bastogne Relieved
Tanks cut through German ring

Over the next couple of days, the good news continued with reports of more towns being recaptured by the Allies and of how the Germans were having to retreat rapidly in some areas.

However, just as the German High Command had been relatively slow to report the launch of the offensive in the Ardennes a fortnight earlier, it was even slower to report that this offensive had ultimately failed, and that the German Army was once again in retreat.

Indeed, the focus of the German headlines completely changed on 3 January with the quite astonishing claim that in daring attacks on airfields in Belgium and Holland, on the morning of New Year's Day, the Luftwaffe had managed to destroy no fewer than 400 enemy planes on the ground and had shot down a further seventy-nine in the air:

579 Enemy Planes Destroyed
They dived on the Allied airfields!

For its part, and in complete contradiction, the *Daily Express* claimed that New Year's Day had resulted in:

Luftwaffe's worst day
UP – then 221 down

The relief of the American troops at Bastogne had started on 26 December, and this photograph from 29 December clearly shows members of the 101st Airborne Division moving out of Bastogne to attack German positions in a neighbouring town. *NARA 12010172*

Closer examination of the article revealed that, in fact, only 125 German aircraft had been downed in the German raids over the Belgium and Dutch airfields, but it was still a remarkable figure and especially when contrasted with the closing aside:

 We on our side have lost some aircraft on the ground, but only four pilots were shot down.

How could this possibly stack up against the Germans' exuberant claims that 600 Allied planes had been destroyed that day? What was the truth?

Best estimates now suggest that, in fact, 156 Allied aircraft were destroyed in the raids. It was nowhere near 600 but still a very sizeable number – and a figure that would never be reported in the British press. Nevertheless, the Luftwaffe losses of 277 aircraft were even more significant – accounting for more than a quarter of the fighters and bombers they had managed to assemble for the raids. Similarly, this was a loss statistic that would never appear in the German press.

Indeed, throughout the final days of December and well into the first week of January there was still no German admission that Bastogne itself had been relieved:

 Heavy fighting at Bastogne

The repeated claim that the enemy was still failing to break through the German lines was, of course, an indirect admission that German advances had more or less stopped, but it would not have appeared this way to a German reader especially when – as late as 4 January – it was still being reported there was heavy fighting south and south-west of Bastogne.

In fact, the bulk of the emphasis lay entirely on the fact that the American 3rd Army was still suffering heavy losses, and that the total number of enemy tanks destroyed in the period since 16 December had now exceeded 1,000. It was as if the repetition of impressive statistics about the scale of enemy losses would compensate for the lack of any meaningful progress on the ground in the Ardennes.

Only on 5 January was there an acknowledgement that the enemy had launched a major counter-offensive to relieve Bastogne and, even then, the impression was given that the enemy had been beaten back having suffered great losses:

 Large-scale attack by enemy was expected to try to bring relief to its hard-pressed units in Bastogne [...] our Divisions cost the enemy huge losses [...] the Americans lost 34 tanks.

In fact, as indicated earlier, we now know that Bastogne had started to be relieved late on 26 December, and this was certainly known to German Army Command West at the time. By 10 January, there was, at last, a recognition from Berlin:

 On Monday, in the south of the West Front and in Hungary, our troops stopped their advance with their heads held high.

But even this rather negative admission was immediately countered by far more positive headlines and details of enemy losses:

 HEAVY ENEMY LOSSES IN THE WEST AND THE EAST
SUCCESSFUL CONTINUATION OF THE GERMAN ATTACKS

In the 20 days of the Ardennes campaign, 90,000 of the enemy were killed or wounded, close to 25,000 were taken prisoner, 1,350 tanks and 350 guns were destroyed and 248 planes were shot down by anti-aircraft fire.

Captured German photograph shows a lanky GI leading a file of American prisoners following the Germans' surprise attack through the Ardennes. *NARA 111-SC-198240*

Actually, some of those human statistics were remarkably accurate. Even today, the estimates of Allied casualties vary from 89,000 to 108,000, including as many as 27,000 men captured or missing. American tank losses were around 730. However, what, of course, the article failed to report was that as many as 98,000 German soldiers were killed, wounded or captured in the onslaught and that the German Army lost more than 600 tanks and assault guns – which was equivalent to some 45 per cent of the total armour at their disposal at the commencement of the campaign.

As late as 17 January, German reporters were still trying to conjure up some positive statements about the whole Ardennes campaign. After all, as far as Germany was concerned, Eisenhower had been prompted into action only because of the embarrassing defeat of one of his armies. This was another clear attempt to seize victory from the ashes of defeat:

 What Germany has won in the West

It was claimed that the German actions on the Western Front had thwarted the Allies' plans by preventing a simultaneous large-scale attack on Germany from both the west and the east.

Whether such a minor victory would really have given much comfort to the German public is hard to believe. With its Luftwaffe decimated and the ordinary German soldier fed up to the back teeth with the war, there is no doubt that morale plummeted significantly after the defeat. The truth was that any delay to the Allies' advance from the west simply allowed the Soviets to make even greater inroads into Germany from the east. Indeed, even the British press was able to report, only two days later, that never before had the Red Army advanced at such a pace and that it was now inside Germany. The fall of Germany to the Soviets rather than the British, French or Americans was an outcome most of the German public would rather have avoided at any cost and would, of course, ultimately lead to the post-war break-up of the country into the German Democratic Republic and the Federal Republic of Germany.

NEWSREEL COVERAGE

Given that it was the Germans who initiated the Ardennes offensive, it was hardly surprising that they were in the best position to provide newsreel coverage of the event. Nevertheless, the first *Wochenschau* newsreel about the new onslaught was not screened until 4 January. The late release of this film may, in part, have been because, as we will see later, the Allies had managed to capture earlier German newsreel and made use of this for their own purposes.

Panning across endless lines of captured American soldiers who had raised the white flag of surrender, the 4 January film was keen to distinguish between these dazed and demoralised troops and Germany's own high-spirited soldiers:

 That's the behaviour and mood of the German foot soldier in the sixth year of war!

By then, the German High Command, at least, would certainly have known that the offensive had actually failed, and that is perhaps why the conclusion of the report rather downplayed what was really at stake and the real objectives of the attack:

 One thing is certain […] the drive of the enemy for the Ruhr and the Rhein has been stopped by the German soldier […] a strong people who will not be broken made sure he had the best available weapons.

Even in the newsreel of 11 January, there was still no hint of defeat in the Ardennes:

 As our tanks and men moved through Luxembourg and southern Belgium, a battle developed which cost the enemy a huge number of men and material.

However, just as with the press coverage, there was a subtle switch of focus to more positive news elsewhere and, in particular to the success of their air raids on Allied airfields on 1 January. They rejoiced in the fact that an entire squadron of enemy bombers had been wiped out in just a few seconds and in how eighty planes had been shot down – both, in themselves, quite significant claims – but which quite frankly fade into insignificance when compared with the press reports of 3 January that had claimed nearly 600 planes had been destroyed in the raids. Perhaps it was hoped that the German viewers of the newsreel would have already forgotten what had appeared in the press the previous week.

Likewise, by 18 January, and with scarcely any mention of the Ardennes at all, the emphasis shifted to showing the first images of V-2 rocket attacks on England and Belgium. Indeed, the largest loss of life in a single attack came on 16 December 1944 when the roof of a crowded cinema in Antwerp was struck, leaving 567 dead and 291 injured.

It was as if bad news in one area always needed to be balanced by more morale-raising events elsewhere. The reporting of the terrible destruction caused by the V-2 rockets raised the German public's optimism that there could still be a satisfactory outcome to the war.

British newsreel of the Battle of the Bulge was certainly in short supply in the early days, and newsreel reporters displayed remarkable ingenuity in not only using captured German newsreel to show what was happening on the ground, but also adding their own propaganda spin to the rather negative images.

Still unsure of the outcome, and mocking the triumphant images in the German film, the reporter of the *Movietone* reel of 1 January gave his own rather bullish prediction:

> What we can say is that these Germans – with their powerful new tanks and any so-called V weapons they may be using – will eventually be smashed by the Allies [...] The Hun has won a success – how big remains to be seen – but the Americans, the British, the French and all the Allies will write the end of the story in German blood.

These were certainly bold words, and especially when the certainty of final victory was anything but guaranteed.

As late as 15 January, the *Movietone* newsreel was acknowledging that the results of the battle could still not be assessed and showed British troops, under Field Marshal Montgomery, arriving to assist their American comrades. In fact, the Germans had deliberately tried to stir up tension between the British and Americans by giving the impression that Montgomery had downplayed the role of the Americans and taken all the glory for himself. While Montgomery may have been rather tactless in some of his comments, the overall accusation was certainly not true. Nevertheless, even in this newsreel, the listener of today can detect a distinct feeling that the British commentator was annoyed by America's somewhat patronising assessment of the contribution to the battle by Montgomery and the British and Dominion troops.

Nevertheless, aside from this internal bickering, it was only with the release of the Allied newsreels of 18 January that a far more triumphant impression emerged, as they were finally able to demonstrate visibly how Rundstedt's troops were being forced back – at the very same moment that the German newsreels had virtually stopped reporting the fighting in the Ardennes altogether.

CONCLUSION

The Battle of the Bulge was clearly a major turning point in the war. While the Americans were to suffer more casualties in this battle than in any other single operation in the war, the ultimate failure of the German Army to achieve its key objectives was even more decisive.

Although the Allies would fail to prevent the remnants of Rundstedt's forces retreating to positions it had held prior to the commencement of the onslaught, the loss by the Germans of so much valuable and irreplaceable armour and munitions would shorten the war.

The British public was certainly kept fairly well informed about the fact the Germans had launched a major offensive but, for the period leading up to Christmas and arguably extending even into the first few days of 1945, there was still some uncertainty as to which side was gaining the upper hand. It was really only with the lifting of the fog after 22 December that the Allies were able to use their aerial superiority to the full and annihilate Rundstedt's exposed tanks. The British press was divided in its coverage during this period of uncertainty. While the *Daily Express* was remarkably upbeat throughout, concentrating on the more positive Allied successes, the *Daily Mirror* was more balanced and continued to voice its concerns about the westerly and northerly progress of the German forces into Allied territory.

The Allies certainly did not keep their public informed as to the true extent of their own casualties or tank and aircraft losses, but then neither did the Germans. In fact, the Germans took far longer to admit they had failed to capture Bastogne. Not only did they never admit the whole operation had been a failure, but they even went as far as to declare a minor victory in that they had defeated one of America's armies and caused great embarrassment to the Allied leadership, who had been forced to rethink their strategy towards the defeat of Germany. In reality, the Germans had far more to lose from failing to achieve their full objectives and this is exactly what happened. They simply could not replace vital fighting equipment in anything like the timescales available to the Allies, and this was the last offensive action by the German Army in the Second World War.

The final Allied newsreel of 18 January provided a fairly accurate summary of the operation:

 The Battle of the Bulge may have delayed but will not prevent the Allied defeat of Germany in the west as well as in the east.

It was a conclusion that could never have been uttered by the German media, nor indeed could the revelation that by 28 January all the territory seized by the Germans in their Ardennes' campaign had been retaken by the Allies.

17

CONCLUSION

The truth Is rarely pure and never simple

(The Importance of Being Earnest, Oscar Wilde)

In his classic tome, *The Rise and Fall of the Third Reich,* William L. Shirer recalls his experience of working in Nazi Germany and his surprise at just how easily the most educated and intelligent of people could be:

taken in by a lying and censored press and radio in a totalitarian state and [...] how they would parrot some piece of nonsense they had heard on the radio or read in the newspapers.

While his comments about wartime Germany were undoubtedly correct, the question his observations raise is whether the British, living in a democracy that supposedly supported press freedom, really had any more reason to trust what they read in a newspaper or witnessed on a newsreel in a cinema.

Events in the more recent past, such as the Iraq War, have undeniably made the British public today far more sceptical about what they are told, but there is no doubt that during the Second World War, the British Government benefited greatly from the fact that, rightly or wrongly, the public generally had far more faith in their media. Given that the BBC and newsreels were supposedly free from state control, it was felt that these could be relied upon to give an accurate account of how the war was progressing. In contrast, and by implication, it was believed that everything emerging out of a totalitarian Germany and a Nazi-controlled media must have been a lie.

The research for this book has shown that much of this confidence may have been misplaced. Not only did the Allied media frequently provide misleading information, but it is also a mistake to believe that absolutely everything the Nazis reported about the course of the war was a lie.

LIES, DAMNED LIES AND STATISTICS

At the time of its creation, the News Division of the British Ministry of Information aspired to: tell the truth, nothing but the truth and as near as possible the whole truth.

The German Propaganda Ministry (RMVP) had no such remit, and control of the media by the RMVP was simply one of the methods of delivering propaganda to the public in line with its overall responsibility for ensuring the spiritual direction of the nation. The provision of truth was always going to be subordinate to this ultimate goal.

Nevertheless, whatever their respective aims and regardless of how their organisations for censorship were structured, we actually find remarkable parallels in the way that both sides reported key events of the war, even if the content and conclusions of such reports were often quite at variance.

There was one overriding technique used by both sides to dupe the public, and it was the deliberate omission of key information about any demoralising incident, operation or battle, such as facts about their own or even the enemy's losses. The few facts that were provided often gave a totally false impression of the overall success or failure not only of a single operation but even of a whole campaign.

This approach can probably be best described as 'being economical with the truth' – a phrase whose literal meaning has rather been lost over the years, as it has rather erroneously come to signify telling outright lies.

This book has revealed there were a myriad different ways in which this technique was employed for propaganda purposes and the maintenance of public morale. In terms of mendacity, these could range from the most subtle and mild to the most vile and misleading, although categorising the significance of each is a rather subjective exercise.

Distorting the Ultimate Interpretation of an Event While Still Telling the Truth

Without a doubt, the most frequent use of this style of reporting was in the art of creating 'victory out of defeat' – an art in which both sides were to become proficient as the war developed.

Rather than concentrate on the BEF's rather ignominious retreat from the advancing German Army, the British media concentrated on the victory that was achieved at Dunkirk in rescuing hundreds of thousands of soldiers from the grip of the enemy – albeit having to discard much of their equipment and munitions in the process.

Similarly, the Nazis employed exactly the same device when it came to the reporting of their own setbacks. The ultimate defeat of their army in North Africa was presented as a victory in that the soldiers stationed there had achieved all that was asked of them and, by diverting Allied forces to North Africa, had allowed Germany to strengthen its hold on mainland Europe and to gain more time to develop other weapons of destruction. No mention was ever made of the 275,000 soldiers forced to surrender.

Creating a Misleading Impression by Telling Only Some of the Truth

The celebrated French writer, Gustave Flaubert, once wrote: 'There is no truth. There is only perception.' We have certainly seen how it was often possible to give a totally misleading impression of an event without even telling a lie, and this was often down to the persuasive power of perception.

The best example of the use of this sort of misinformation by the British in this book is the Dieppe Raid.

By concentrating on the 'fact' that the Allies had seemingly given the Germans a bloody nose at Dieppe and by not mentioning the scale of the Allied losses, the distinct impression created in the British media was that the mission had been a success. Indeed, one newspaper even carried an article with the triumphant heading 'Britain can invade'. The actual article admitted in some detail the considerable challenges that would face the Allies in such an event, but this practice of misleading the reader by giving an eye-catching headline that totally belied the content of the accompanying article was quite a common device.

Likewise, the newsreel comment, on showing a tank landing craft returning empty, 'and if some of them came home light – well you'd hardly expect to evacuate all the tanks,' created the distinct impression that most of the tanks *were* brought home. We now know that not a single tank was recovered. This is only one such example, but this technique was used time and again by both sides, as necessity demanded, throughout the war.

Concentrating on Military Successes while Downplaying Failures or Other Unwelcome News

When one side was losing – especially when a battle was being fought over a large area of ground and over a long period of time – then, if there was a poor outcome in one area or on one front, there was a tendency to accentuate the positive elsewhere. This is exactly what happened with the reporting of the battle for Stalingrad where, if the Nazis had lost ground in the south but had made gains in the north, then the press would concentrate on what was happening in the north or, if need be, on a totally different front altogether. This helps to explain how the media on both sides were often to issue positive headlines on the same day about the same battleground by concentrating on a different perspective of the battle. Similar trends were found in the respective reporting of much of the fighting in North Africa.

Nevertheless, when it came to the British press, it should be acknowledged that rival newspapers from the same country could even be at odds as to how the facts were reported. When it came to Operation Market Garden or the Battle of the Bulge, the *Daily Mirror* was invariably more pessimistic and the *Daily Express* more optimistic in their respective reporting of those events. This was quite different from the German press, which would always sing from the same song sheet.

Another version of this technique was adopted by both sides in their newsreel coverage. Any negative news would be placed early in a report, and the newsreel would invariably end on a more upbeat note. So, for example, the loss of the port of Cherbourg by the Germans after D-Day was countered by the more positive news that German defenders were continuing to offer stout resistance in other key bases in the area and that other successes were being reported on the Eastern and Italian Fronts.

If a particular battle or attack were a success for one side, then you might at least have expected that the reporting of that event by the victors would be more accurate and honest, but this was certainly not always the case. Take the Dambusters Raid. The breaching of two of the German dams was a great Allied achievement and was rightly reported as such. However, it is probably fair to say that the Allies had not appreciated at the time that the long-term impact on the German war machine would be very limited. What most of the initial press reports clearly failed to admit was that eight planes were destroyed and fifty-three airmen were killed in the raid and, while this was reported later, there was certainly never any mention of the 1,000 or so POWs and the hundreds of civilians who were killed in the flooding that followed.

Ironically, the actual accounts of civilian and POW losses were not only far more openly reported in the German press but were also often far lower than the true figures.

Timing of Release of Information or Delayed Reporting of an Event for Purely Propaganda Purposes

Once again, we find that both sides were prepared to manipulate the timing of the release of information about a particular subject or event for their own purposes.

In the case of the Nazis, the most obvious example was Hitler's refusal to allow any reporting of the grievances voiced by Germans who suddenly found themselves redesignated as citizens of Poland or Danzig under the Treaty of Versailles. It was only when he was ready for war that the German press was actively encouraged to raise any acts of aggression being reported by these former German subjects.

In a similar way, but on a totally different scale, the Allies were just as guilty when it came to delaying the reporting of bad news. While evacuating Allied troops from the west coast of France, the *Lancastria*, a commandeered Cunard liner, was torpedoed by a German submarine on 17 June 1940 with the loss of close to

4,000 men. The first news of this sinking did not appear in *The Times* until 26 July and only then as a result of a rumour circulating from an American source. Lives lost were estimated to be around 2,500, far fewer than the true number. We know that Churchill would have preferred to conceal the information completely.

Failure by Both Sides to Reveal the Same Unpalatable Facts About the Same Event but for Different Reasons

Of course, we also had incidents where *neither* side wanted to tell the whole truth about the same incident. The bombing of cities is an obvious example. The massive bombing raids on major German cities often created fire-storms that would cause the deaths of many tens of thousands of civilians in a single night. Neither the British nor the German press was to report just how many innocent civilians were being killed. Presumably there was a genuine fear on the part of the British that the public might be repulsed by such butchery, and the concern for the Germans was that their people would become so demoralised as to raise demands for an immediate peace settlement.

Failure by One Side to Report in Any Way Extremely Embarrassing or Upsetting Events

We find that the British were particularly prone not to report events that were just too embarrassing or depressing to admit. This often caused much frustration for the Nazis who, while they might find the reporting of the event would be good for raising the morale of their own citizens, were equally disappointed that it would not have a similarly devastating effect on enemy morale – simply because the British and American public would never hear about it.

For the British, it was the fate of Arctic convoys such as PQ17 that fell into this category. The pretext given for remaining silent about PQ17 was that the Admiralty never reported on the fate of a convoy until it had reached its destination. Likewise, not only did the British remain silent about the discovery by the Germans of the massacre of thousands of Polish officers by the Soviets in the Katyn Forest, but Churchill, conscious of the need to avoid a rift with his Soviet allies, even apologised to Stalin and assured him that the Polish press would be disciplined about such reporting in the future.

Exaggerating Enemy Losses While Under-reporting Own Losses

During the Battle of Britain, both sides tended to exaggerate the damage inflicted on the enemy and under-reported their own losses, but the British were never quite as inaccurate as the Germans. The Germans were guilty of the same misinformation in their reporting of loss statistics on the Eastern Front and of the Allied advances eastwards after D-Day.

Perpetuating a Lie Even After the Truth is Known

There is little doubt that the Nazis were masters of making the most out of a lie. We have seen that there were several occasions when probably, either through ignorance or a genuine mistake, a false report of an event was originally published in the German press in good faith. However, even when the true facts became known, the Nazi leaders were not only prepared to allow the lie to stand uncorrected but even employed it for their own propaganda purposes.

When it came to the Saint-Nazaire raid, for example, the Germans clearly declared in their early press reports that the attack on the dry-dock gates had been a failure because the ship that rammed the gates had caused them only superficial damage. We know that the explosives hidden in the bow of the ship *did* detonate several hours later and completely destroyed the gates. Even if we give the Germans the benefit of the doubt that their press was simply reporting what was believed to be the case at the time of publication, no such excuse can be given for the German newsreel that appeared much later and perpetuated the same myth, and nor would any correction ever appear in the German press to put the record straight.

Here, indeed, is one of the main differences between British and German reporting of the war. The Nazis were only too willing to use a piece of genuine misinformation for their own purposes and never to correct the original report. Another obvious example was the bombing of Freiburg at the very beginning of the war. This was blamed on the Allies, but we now know that German planes dropped their bombs over Freiburg by mistake – wrongly believing that they were still over France. Once again, the original German reports of the attack might have been a genuine blunder but, once the error was discovered, no apology or correction was issued. Indeed, Hitler and Goebbels were to continue to make frequent references to this incident as an example of the terrorist-type behaviour of the Allies in bombing innocent civilians, and they used this as a pretext for reprisal bombings.

Outright Lies

When it comes to telling out-and-out lies, Nazi leaders were unquestionably far more guilty of using their media to convey absolutely false information. This was perhaps most evident in their constant attacks on Jews and Bolsheviks, but it also extended to the reporting of the war, especially when the tide of war was turning against them.

There is no greater example of this than in the portrayal of the fighting on the Eastern Front and, in particular, the Battle of Stalingrad. First, there was the contrived Christmas message – supposedly from the German forces trapped in Stalingrad – which was, in fact, broadcast from a radio station in Berlin. Next, in the reporting of the final defeat and surrender at Stalingrad, much was made of the heroism of the German forces who had resisted to the last bullet. Indeed, at one point, the

Nazi-orchestrated poster in French mocking the cigar-smoking, whisky-drinking Churchill for claiming victories at Saint-Nazaire, Narvik and Dieppe. The poster perpetuated the myth that the raid at Saint-Nazaire had been a failure. The footprint on Churchill's posterior is presumably intended to be a rebuke from Stalin. *Le Grand Blockhaus Museum*

rather misleading impression was given that Paulus had been killed and that the German soldiers had fought to the very last man. It was a conclusion for which Hitler might have wished and even have expected, but it was simply not the case. No mention was ever made of the nearly 100,000 soldiers who surrendered – nor of the total German losses in terms of men and equipment during the whole campaign. This is a more obvious example of how the German media went far beyond simply concealing unpalatable facts in that they reported incidents that were known to be completely untrue.

Of course, this was not always the fault of the individual newspapers, who were simply printing what they were told to report. Indeed, by deliberately falsifying such incidents as the attack on the Gleiwitz radio station at the beginning of the war, the Nazis cynically used not only their own press but also the world's media to promote some of the greatest falsehoods of the war.

This is not to say that the British did not tell outright lies as well. There was the bombing of the town of Penicuik on the night of 6 August 1940, when the official news bulletin the following morning claimed there had been no air attack on British territory the previous night. And yes, there was certainly the deliberate, initial concealment of the damage caused by V-1 and V-2 rockets, which was reported as being due to traditional bombs and gas main explosions, respectively.

INSIGHTFUL GENERALISATIONS

What is extremely revealing from all the research for this book was the willingness of all governments to dupe their citizens during the Second World War. So, what is possibly of most importance for us today is whether we can learn any lessons from the way that events during the Second World War were reported to help us determine whether we are being told the truth about any new conflict or national emergency. I believe there are a number of pointers that are well worth remembering when any similar event is being reported in the future:

- If one side reports a certain event in detail and the other says very little or fails to mention the incident at all, then it is highly likely that the other side has something to hide.
- If a war report gives the impression that something is the case but does not actually say so, then the reader is probably being misled.
- It is right to be suspicious of initial reports where obvious facts are omitted or actual losses in terms of men or equipment are not given. It is likely that actual losses have been high and that bad news is being concealed.
- If there is a huge difference in the loss statistics being presented by two opposing sides, then it is worth remembering that in the Second World War,

both sides tended to under-report their own losses and exaggerate those of the enemy.

- Reports that start listing enemy losses over a long period of time are probably concealing recent failures by their own side.
- As soon as a report uses the word 'hero', then this should serve as a warning to the reader or viewer that there is probably sad news to come. It is the sort of term that is often used only when all hope seems lost or great sacrifices have been made.
- Unreasonably long delays in the reporting of particular events may well indicate something is being concealed.

In general, it is advisable to seek clarification from as many sources as possible. Look at what the enemy and other foreign media are reporting. If anything sounds dubious, then listen to what your intuition is telling you as it is often correct.

WHICH SIDE WAS MORE TRUTHFUL?

In the introduction to this book, I indicated that one of the key objectives of my research was to discover which side was more truthful in their press and newsreel coverage of the war.

However, given that it transpires that both sides manipulated the truth for their own purposes, I have to ask whether it is really feasible to determine which side was more truthful? In fact, perhaps a better question would be which side's misinformation or lies were the more significant or the more harmful?

On the one hand, both sides tended to exaggerate enemy losses and minimise their own losses but, if anything, German reports of enemy losses were often further from the mark than those reported by the British. This was especially true for the Battle of Britain, but we have to remember that it was often difficult for either side to provide accurate loss statistics at short notice as it often took several days for the true picture to emerge.

On the other hand, when it came to the amount of detail provided in German reports – specifically when reporting setbacks to the Allies or when wishing to undermine Allied victories – there was usually far more 'hard' information than in the British reports of such incidents, and much of it was surprisingly accurate.

As we have seen, the big difference between the two sides lay in their attitude towards either the complete concealment of unwelcome information or the telling of outright lies. The Allies simply refused to report at all any incident that they found particularly depressing or embarrassing. On the contrary, the Nazis were more prepared to issue downright lies.

Which is the greater crime – to conceal an event altogether or to tell a lie about that event? Which is worse – to keep silent about the murders at Katyn or to lie about the fate of the German Army at Stalingrad?

There is no definitive answer to these questions, so I have to leave it to you, the reader, to reach your own conclusion as to which side was more truthful or more devious from all the evidence I have presented.

Armed with a clearer understanding of the techniques employed to deceive the public in the reporting of the Second World War, my lasting hope is that we will be less likely to allow ourselves to accept anything that is stated by our media or politicians at face value in the future and, in particular, at a time of national peril, without first thoroughly questioning the accuracy of everything we are being told. Fortunately, modern means of communication and the power and scope of the internet now make it far easier for the ordinary public to check the veracity of any claim across international borders and against multiple information sites.

My parents, like many other families, never had any doubt that Britain would be victorious in the Second World War, regardless of how long this would take. Such touching faith was as much due to the influence of wartime media reporting as to the morale-boosting speeches of their political leaders.

All of this raises the question as to whether, during wartime, it is justifiable to manipulate the truth to maintain public morale and, indeed, whether all lies can be justified when the fate of your country hangs in the balance. Indeed, would the general public have wanted to be told the whole truth or were they content to be kept in the dark?

Happily, however, such philosophical debate is not for the likes of this book, whose sole purpose was to examine the facts objectively and to 'tell the truth, nothing but the truth and as near as possible the whole truth'.

SELECT BIBLIOGRAPHY

BOOKS IN ENGLISH

Addison, P. and Crang, J. *Firestorm: The Bombing of Dresden 1945*. (Pimlico, 2006)

Arnold, J. *Ardennes, 1944: Hitler's Last Gamble in the West*. (Osprey, 1990)

Balfour, M. *Propaganda in War. 1939–1945*. (Faber Finds, 2010)

Battistelle, P. *El Alamein 1942*. (History Press, 2011)

Beckies, G. *Dunkirk and After*. (London, 1940)

Bishop, P. *Battle of Britain*. (Quercus, 2009)

Bowman, M. *The Dam Busters*. (Amberley, 2013)

Burleigh, M. *Germany Turns Eastwards*. (Pan, 2002)

Calder, A. *The People's War*. (Pimlico, 2008)

Chant-Sempill, S. *St. Nazaire Commando Stuart Chant-Sempill*. (Murray, 1985)

Collier, B. *The Battle of the V Weapons 1944–45*. (Elmfield Press, 1976)

Cooper, A. *The Dam Buster Raid: A Reappraisal 70 Years On*. (Pen & Sword 2013)

Cross, R. *The Battle of the Bulge 1944*. (Spellmount, 2002)

Dildy, D. *Dunkirk 1940: Operation Dynamo*. (Osprey, 2010)

Dimbleby, J. *Destiny in the Desert. The Road to El Alamein*. (Profile, 2012)

Dorrian, J. *Saint-Nazaire*. (Pen & Sword, 2006)

Fitzgibbon, L. *The Katyn Cover-up*. (Tom Stacey Ltd, 1972)

Ford, K. *D-Day 1944 – Sword Beach*. (Osprey, 2002)

Ford, K. *D-Day 1944 – Gold & Juno Beaches*. (Osprey, 2002)

Ford, K. *Dieppe 1942 – Prelude to D Day*. (Osprey, 2008)

Ford, K. *El Alamein 1942: The Turning of the Tide*. (Osprey, 2005)

Ford, K. *St Nazaire 1942 – The Great Commando Raid*. (Osprey 2008)

Forty, G. *The Desert War*. (Sutton, 2002)

Friedrich, J. *The Fire: The Bombing of Germany, 1940–1945*. (Columbia University Press, 2006)

Gerlach, H. *The Forsaken Army*. (Cassell Military, 2002)

Grenville, J. *Nazi Germany.* (Macmillan for the Historical Association, 1976)

Grimshaw, A. *D-Day.* (Dryad, 1988)

Harding, D. *Destroyer 2: Operation Chariot.* (Futura 1977)

Harman, N. *Dunkirk: The Necessary Myth.* (Hodder and Stoughton, 1980)

Hart, L. *History of the Second World War.* (Pan, 2011)

Hitler, A. *Mein Kampf.* (Translation – Jaico Publishing, 2009)

Holland, J. *Dam Busters: The Race to Smash the Dams, 1943.* (Bantam Press, 2012)

Hoyt, E. *199 Days: The Battle for Stalingrad.* (Robson, 2001)

Irving, D. *The Destruction of Convoy PQ-17.* (Panther, 1985)

Jones, B. *D-Day & Beyond.* (Pyjama Press, 2011)

Latawski, P. *Falaise Pocket.* (History Press, 2012)

Lewis, T. *Moonlight Sonata: The Coventry Blitz, 14/15 November 1940.* (T. Lewis and Coventry City Council, 1990)

Lund, P. *PQ17 – Convoy to Hell: The Survivors' Story.* (New English Library, 1969)

Macdonald, C. *The Battle of the Bulge.* (Phoenix Giant, 1998)

Mackay, R. *Half the Battle: Civilian Morale in Britain during the Second World War.* (MUP, 2002)

Maresch, E. *Katyn 1940.* (Spellmount, 2010)

Mason, J. *The Danzig Dilemma: A Study in Peacemaking by Compromise.* (Palo Alto, 1946)

McGlade, F. *The History of the British Army Film & Photographic Unit in the Second World War.* (Helion, 2010)

McKernan, L. *Yesterday's News: The British Cinema Newsreel Reader.* (British Universities Film and Video Council, 2002)

McLaine, I. *Ministry of Morale: Home Front Morale and the Ministry of Information in World War II.* (Allen and Unwin, 1979)

Middlebrook, M. *The Peenemünde Raid.* (Penguin, 1988)

Milano, V. *Normandiefront.* (Spellmount, 2012)

Neillands, R. *Dieppe Raid: The Story of the Disastrous 1942 Expedition.* (Aurum, 2005)

Nicholas, S. *The Echo of War: Home Front Propaganda and the Wartime BBC.* (MUP, 1996)

Nossack, H. *The End: Hamburg 1943.* (University of Chicago Press, 2006)

Paine, L. *D-Day.* (Hale, 1981)

Primoratz, I. *Terror from the Sky.* (Berghahn Books, 2010)

Pronay, N. and Spring, D. *Propaganda, Politics and Film, 1918–45.* (Macmillan, 1982)

Rawson, A. *Battle of the Bulge 1944–45.* (History Press, 2011)

Reeves, N. *The Power of Film Propaganda.* (Continuum, 2003)

Richards, J. and Sheridan, D. *Mass Observation at the Movies.* (Routledge, 1987)

Sanford, G. *Katyn and the Soviet Massacre of 1940.* (Routledge, 2005)

Shirer, W. *The Rise and Fall of the Third Reich.* (Book Club Associates, 1983)

Speer, A. *Inside the Third Reich.* (Phoenix, 1995)

Sweetman, J. *Operation Chastise. The Dams Raid: Epic or Myth.* (Jane's, 1982)

Swettenham, J. *D-Day.* (Canadian War Museum, 1970)

Tampke, J. *Czech–German Relations and the Politics of Central Europe: From Bohemia to the EU.* (Palgrave Macmillan, 2003)

Taylor, A. *The Origins of the Second World War.* (Penguin, 2001)

Thomson, G. *Blue Pencil Admiral.* (Sampson, Low, Marston and Co., 1947)

Tsouras, B. *Disaster at Stalingrad.* (Frontline Books, 2013)

Turnbull, P. *Dunkirk Anatomy of Disaster.* (Batsford, 1978)

Turner, J. *Stalingrad: Day by Day.* (Pen & Sword, 2012)

Vorwald, P. *Battle of the Bulge.* (Battle of Britain International, 2001)

Zaloga, S. *Battle of the Bulge 1944.* (Osprey, 2004)

OTHER BOOKS IN ENGLISH

Battlefront: Operation Market Garden: The Bridges at Eindhoven, Nijmegen and Arnhem. (Public Record Office, 2000)

The Danzig Crisis: The Truth about Danzig before and during the Nazi Regime. (Union of Democratic Control, 1936)

Operation Market Garden. Netherlands 17–25 September 1944. (Ministry of Defence, 2004)

World War II: Day by Day. (Dorling Kindersley, 2004)

BOOKS IN GERMAN

Bode, V. *Raketenspuren.* (Links, 2004)

Diedrich, I. *Paulus: Das Trauma von Stalingrad.* (Schöningh, 2008)

Kehrig, M. *Stalingrad Analyse und Dokumentation einer Schlacht.* (DVA, 1974)

Schmid, A. *Frankfurt im Feuersturm.* (Societäts, 1984)

Wildt, M. *Geschichte des Nationalsozialismus.* (Vandenhoeck & Ruprecht, 2008)

BOOKS IN FRENCH

Braeuer, L. & Petitjean, B. *Raid sur Saint-Nazaire.* (Liv Editions, 2012)

Wołoszański, B. *Le Choc des tyrans.* (Jourdan, 2009)

NEWSPAPERS

The Times Digital Archive.
The Scotsman Digital Archive.
The Digital Archives of the *Daily* and *Sunday Express* and *Daily* and *Sunday Mirror* accessed via the website of UKPressOnline.
Neue Vetschauer Zeitung (1942–1944) accessed via the website of the Staatsbibliothek, Berlin.
Freiburger Zeitung (1939–1943) accessed via the website of the University of Freiburg.
Völkischer Beobachter (1939–1945) accessed via the British Library, London.
Frankfurter Allgemeine Zeitung accessed via the British Library, London.

OTHER WRITTEN SOURCES

Archive material about the Ministry of Information held at the National Archives, Kew.
The Public Opinion Quarterly, 5 (autumn, 1941) – 'The British Ministry of Information'.

SELECT FILMOGRAPHY

Newsreel
Die Deutsche Wochenschau 1939–1945.
British Pathé Digital Archive.
British Movietone Digital Archive.

INDEX

Also by Ian Garden

987 0 7509 6817 1

'A good book that covers a wide range of Nazi film, from blatant propaganda films like *The Eternal Jew* to films of no overt political content that are still popular in Germany today … There is no other book available with such an excellent collection of images … If someone asks me about the best way to get a sense of Nazi cinema, this is the book I will recommend.'
– Professor L. Randall Bytwerk